With best wishes,

THE ROSS AND CROMARTY BOOK

Publications edited by Donald Omand:

THE CAITHNESS BOOK, 1972

THE MORAY BOOK, 1976

RED DEER MANAGEMENT, 1981

THE SUTHERLAND BOOK, 1982

Other publications:

THE CAITHNESS FLAGSTONE INDUSTRY (with J. Porter), 1981

A KAITNESS KIST (with J. P. Campbell), 1984

THE ROSS AND CROMARTY BOOK

Edited by
DONALD OMAND

ESTABLISHED
1899

THE NORTHERN TIMES LIMITED

Published and printed by
The Northern Times Limited,
Golspie, Sutherland, Scotland

ISBN 0 9501718 7 5

Acknowledgements

For permission to reproduce illustrations the authors are grateful to the following institutions and persons: Tain Museum and Mrs Rosemary MacKenzie (Fig. 23); Scottish Development Department (Historic Buildings Branch) (Figs. 25 and 26, Crown Copyright); and the Royal Commission on the Ancient and Historical Monuments of Scotland (Figs. 22, 27, 28 and 31, Crown Copyright).

We would like to acknowledge, with gratitude, the help given by the Earl of Cromartie, Mrs Monica Clough, Mrs Rosemary MacKenzie, Mr Geoffrey Stell, and Liet. Col. (rct'd) A. A. Fairie, Queen's Own Highlanders.

To all those teachers in Ross and Cromarty who supplied data on settlements, our sincere thanks.

All the figures were drawn by Dr. Con Gillen and the index was compiled by Mr Stewart Angus.

To Ms. Susan Davison, Aberdeen, and Mrs Janet Mowat, Halkirk, we are indebted for their invaluable secretarial assistance.

The Authors

Editor:
DONALD OMAND   Tutor-Organiser, Department of
                         Adult Education and Extra Mural
                         Studies, University of Aberdeen.

Dr. C. GILLEN   Tutor-Organiser, Department of
                         Adult Education and Extra Mural
                         Studies, University of Aberdeen.

Dr. A. MACLENNAN   Nature Conservancy Council.

Mr L. MacNALLY   Warden/Naturalist, National Trust
                         for Scotland.

Mr R. DENNIS   Highland Officer, R.S.P.B.

Mr F. MACRAE   District Officer, Forestry Commission.

Mr R. GOURLAY   Archaeologist, Highland Region.

Dr. J. MUNRO   Historian and Writer.

Rev. A. MacALPINE   Church of Scotland Minister.

Prof. E. RICHARDS   Professor of History, The Flinders
                         University of South Australia.

Dr. J. S. SMITH   Senior Lecturer, Dept. of
                         Geography, University of Aberdeen.

Mr G. STELL   Royal Commission on Ancient and
                         Historical Monuments.

Mrs E. BEATON   Scottish Development Department,
                         Historic Buildings Branch.

Mr I. FRASER   School of Scottish Studies, University of Edinburgh.

Mrs J. DURHAM   Commissioner on the Board of the
                         Royal Commission for Recording
                         the Ancient and Historical
                         Monuments of Scotland.

ELIZABETH SUTHERLAND Writer.
(Mrs Marshall)

Contents

List of Tables

List of Figures

List of Plates

Preface

The text is concerned primarily with the District of Ross and Cromarty that was created under the reorganisation of local government boundaries in 1975. In the historical chapters, however, discussions of some areas that lay within the former County and are now outside it have been included.

Foreword

Castle Leod
June 1984

Donald Omand has asked me to write a short Foreword to the Ross and Cromarty Book. This work covers a very long period of Pre-history and History as well as including every aspect of our much loved and beautiful County, with its outstanding environmental treasures.

I am very happy to do this and look forward to the day when I can read this work especially as, although there have been some excellent accounts of certain areas of Ross and Cromarty, this publication will include the whole area which, not only is very large, but has the advantage of great variation of scenery, natural history and way of life. There is, of course, another reason, or reasons, why I am grateful to the Editor for asking me to write this foreword. For many centuries my family has been part of this County, and I myself was brought up here at Castle Leod, at Coigach and at Tarbat House in Easter Ross, except for such times as I was exiled to England for part of my schooling. Also, soon after the First War I was serving, mostly in India, with the Seaforth Highlanders. There I had the honour of being close to so many who came from all parts of Ross and Cromarty, and this was repeated with added emphasis during the Second War. It would not have been possible to serve with a finer and braver people.

When I left the Regular Army in 1933 I went into Local Government representing Coigach; then came the War and after that I returned to the County Council this time for Fodderty, and eventually became Convener. Yes, I love Ross and Cromarty and am honoured to be one of its sons . . . Gilean Caber Feidh Gu Brath.

**Cromartie . . . Caber Feidh Chief of Clan MacKenzie
Earl of Cromartie MC, TD, DL, JP, FSA Scot.**

Part one

THE
ENVIRONMENT

Chapter one

THE PHYSICAL BACKGROUND

Cornelius Gillen

ROCKS

Ross and Cromarty is fortunate in possessing an enormous range of rock types and ages as well as stark scenic contrasts from west to east. The oldest rocks in Europe occur on the rocky, highly indented west coast, while the rolling coastal plains of the firthlands on the east have remnants of the youngest rocks in the country. These same young rocks continue out into the Moray Firth where they contain oil and gas deposits. The ancient rocks of the west coast have been the object of intense study for over a century and the publication in 1907 of the Geological Survey Memoir of the Northwest Highlands was a landmark in the geology of Scotland and quickly became a classic of its time.

GEOLOGICAL DEVELOPMENT

South from Lochinver to Lochcarron (Fig 1) are the oldest rocks in the District, the Lewisian Gneiss, which form a basement beneath the Northern Highlands and extend north to Cape Wrath and west to the Outer Hebrides. The basement rocks were formed by the intense deformation and metamorphism of existing sedimentary and igneous rocks at around 2,800 million years and 1,800 million years ago, deep within the ancient crust.

The early continental crust was later broken by a series of NNE-trending rifts that may have marked the initiation of an ocean. About 1,000 million years ago thick accumulations of continental deposits formed in fault-bounded troughs on the continental margin. These are the Torridon sandstones which form the dominant features of the landscape on the west coast.

The modern view of the structure and evolution of the Earth envisages that the Earth's crust is made up of a number of rigid plates,

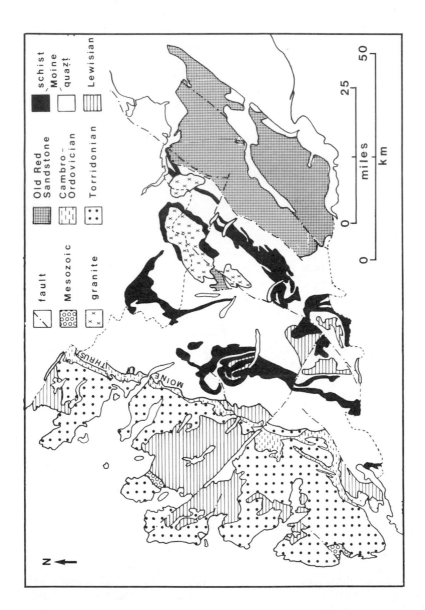

Figure 1 — Simplified geological map of Ross and Cromarty.

the margins of which are marked by earthquake zones. Crustal plates are in a state of motion, with new oceanic crust forming along submerged volcanic mountain chains and spreading outwards. Continental crust is riding on top of thin, denser, oceanic crust rather like rafts, with the result that the positions of the continents change with time. New oceans appear as the oceanic crust is split asunder. Such activity has gone on for at least the last 1,000 million years, and a plate tectonic model of the Earth's crustal structure serves to explain the present configuration of the continents and the structure and development of the Scottish Highlands. The Highlands are considered to have formed when two continental masses carried on moving plates collided with each other. Sediments in the intervening ocean basin were strongly folded and overthrust to produce a mountain range.

Prior to 600 million years ago Scotland lay at the south-eastern edge of a large continent that included Canada and Greenland, facing a 4,000-6,000 km (2,490-3,730 miles) wide ocean, known as Iapetus. When the Iapetus ocean was at its greatest width 600 million years ago, limestones and sandstones were deposited in a shallow shelf sea at the margin, while the ocean basin filled up with sandstones and shales which were later compressed, folded and metamorphosed as the ocean closed, producing the Moine schists that now form the largest outcrop of rocks in the District. These events, collectively known as the Caledonian mountain building period, occurred between 500 and 400 million years ago. By 425 million years ago the Iapetus ocean had closed completely and the European plate had collided with the Greenland-North American plate on which north Scotland was situated.

Rapid erosion of the young high mountain range produced the Old Red sandstone deposits, so characteristic of the land around the east coast firths. A considerable time gap of around 100 million years separates these rocks from the New Red Sandstone and Jurassic sediments of the Moray Firth and Minch margins. Large volumes of sediment were deposited in the subsiding basins of the Minch and the North Sea, while the main mass of the Highlands stood up as positive relief and suffered powerful erosion.

The present Atlantic Ocean did not begin to open until around 150 million years ago. As the Atlantic gradually opened up, rifts around Britain deepened and filled with sediment. The final separation of Scotland from Greenland 55 million years ago was preceded by intense volcanic activity in the Inner Hebrides.

LEWISIAN GNEISS

The oldest rocks in Europe are preserved in a belt on the west coast of Ross-shire, from Enard Bay in the north to Loch Carron in the south with the largest outcrop occurring north and west of Loch Maree (Fig 2). They form the Lewisian Gneiss, a complex of intensely metamorphosed crystalline rocks, which take their name from their occurrence on Lewis. The Lewisian complex may be subdivided into three:

1. The *Scourian* complex, produced by folding and metamorphism of rocks 35 km (20 miles) deep in the crust at temperatures of around 800-900° C, some 2,900-2,300 million years ago.
2. The *Laxfordian* complex, made up of Scourian and younger rocks deformed and metamorphosed at temperatures of 700° C around 2,300-1,700 million years ago.
3. Lewisian in the basement of the Caledonian fold mountain belt.

The Scourian complex, named after the village of Scourie in Sutherland, forms the central belt of the mainland outcrop of Lewisian rocks, from Scourie to just south of Gruinard Bay (Plate 6). The main rock types are grey-coloured banded granulites and gneisses, which amount to 80% of the total, the remaining 20% being composed of metamorphosed basic and ultrabasic igneous rocks (lavas and layered intrusive sheets, which are well exposed at Achiltibuie) and sediments. Despite several decades of intensive research, it is true to say that the ultimate origin of the gneisses in the Scourian complex is still not known, due mainly to the very high grade of metamorphism and to the fact that the rocks were deformed, refolded and brought near to melting point several times over. The consensus view is that the rocks were originally volcanic lavas, tuffs and ash mixed with sandy sediments that formed at the surface of an ancient chain of volcanic islands, with extensive thick sheets of layered basic and ultrabasic igneous rocks intruded at depth, together with enormous volumes of granitic-type magma. These rocks were rapidly buried and after a relatively short time interval were metamorphosed under extremely high-temperature conditions which caused the expulsion of water and potash, together with several radioactive elements such as uranium, thorium and rubidium (Watson 1983).

The *Loch Maree series* occupies a 150 km² (58 miles²) belt at Loch Maree (Plate 3) and Gairloch (Fig 2), and consists of metamorphosed sediments, mainly schists and marbles, with sheets of hornblende schist that were derived from lavas or intrusive sills of basic igneous rock. At Loch Maree these rocks occur between gneisses of the Scourian complex, and are separated from the gneisses by narrow zones of fault rock. The age of the Loch Maree series has posed a problem for many years, but it is now considered that the rocks were deposited at the surface after the main events that produced the Scourian complex. Field excursions to the Loch Maree series are described in Barber et al (1978).

Around 2,200 million years ago the Scourian complex was intruded by a massive swarm of basic dykes — nearly vertical walls of igneous rock trending WNW or NW. Many of the dykes appear to have been injected along steep north-westerly shear zones (narrow belts of high deformation) which continue to move during dyke injection and afterwards. This family of dykes, usually referred to as the *Scourie dyke swarm*, was intruded at a depth of 10-20 km (6.2-12.4 miles) into crust that was being stretched apart under tension.

Evidence for the Laxfordian complex is seen throughout the District, but especially south of Gruinard Bay and more particularly around Shieldaig (Fig 2), where veining by pegmatite and granite is widespread. Upright NW-SE folds are common and the basic dykes and Loch Maree schists were affected by metamorphism during the Laxfordian cycle, 2,200-1,700 million years ago, the granite and pegmatite injection having occurred towards the end of the cycle. The intensity of this metamorphism was less than that of the Scourian cycle, though great enough to cause recrystallisation and the alteration of basic dykes to hornblende schist. The field guide referred to above (Barber et al 1978) contains excursions to the Lewisian rocks around Loch Torridon.

Lewisian rocks occur as inliers of basement material surrounded by younger Moine rocks in the Caledonian mountain chain. In Ross and Cromarty the largest outcrops of this type of Lewisian Gneiss are near Loch Carron, in the zone of the Moine Thrust, in the Monar Forest, at Scardroy and in the Fannich Mountains (Fig 2). Smaller outcrops appear at Loch Luichart and along the Great Glen Fault zone at Rosemarkie on the Black Isle. These inliers have been strongly altered by Caledonian folding and metamorphism in the period 1,000-500 million years ago. Geophysical studies in the Highlands and geochemical research into the origin of the granites of Scotland suggest that much of Northern Scotland is underlain by a basement of Lewisian-type rock.

'TORRIDONIAN' ROCKS

By about 1,000 million years ago, the Lewisian rocks had been uplifted by 30-40 km (18.6-24.9 miles) and eroded to their present level. Thick continental clastic sediments were then deposited on this ancient platform, an older Stoer Group which occurs around Enard Bay, Achiltibuie and Gruinard Bay at around 1,000 million years ago, and a younger (800 million years old), thicker Torridon Group which is widespread along the west coast and gives rise to such impressive mountains as Ben More Coigach, An Teallach (Plate 6), Slioch (Plate 3) and all

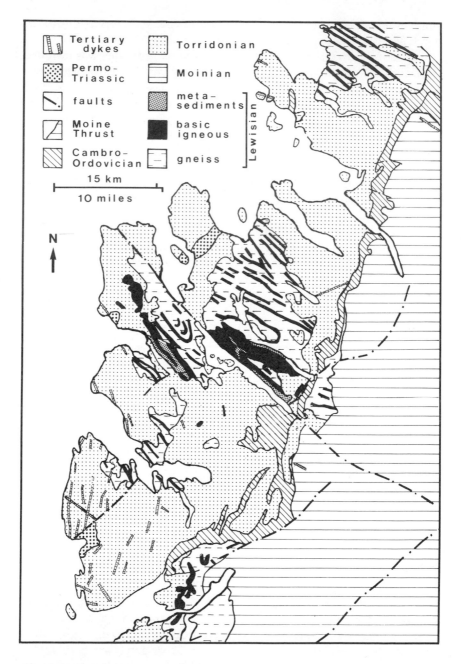

Figure 2 — Geological map of Wester Ross, showing Lewisian Gneiss,
Torridon sandstone and Moine Thrust zone.

the hills of Torridon (Plates 1 and 2) and Applecross (Fig 2). The Stoer and Torridon Groups together are referred to as the 'Torridonian sandstone'. The Stoer Group consists of 2 km (1.2 miles) of red beds — water-lain sandstones, siltstones and mudstones which often show ripple marks, cross-bedding, graded bedding and mudcracks. An important band of water-deposited volcanic ash also occurs, but there is no trace in the vicinity of any volcano of this age. Fossils are present as 1-2 m (3.3-6.6 ft) sized rounded hummocks of hard red limestone, built by algal stromatolites, a type of primitive seaweed which grew in colonies and constructed mounds on the sea floor.

The Stoer Group was tilted by 30° to the NW before the Torridon Group was unconformably deposited on top about 200 million years later. Rocks of the 7 km (4.3 miles) thick Torridon Group are mostly red or chocolate-brown coarse feldspathic sandstones (arkoses), with coarse conglomerates at the base, containing boulders of Lewisian Gneiss. Such conglomerates are well exposed by the roadside on the south shore of Gruinard Bay. These rocks were carried from the west and north by great rivers that were eroding a landmass west of the Hebrides (possibly Greenland which may have been closer to Scotland then) and deposited over an irregular land surface of Lewisian Gneiss. The upland area to the west was probably fault-bounded and the Torridon rocks were deposited in a trough that sank to accommodate the sediments being transported. Certain features of the Torridonian sandstone indicate that the rocks were laid down when Scotland lay very much farther south, in a semi-desert environment which prevailed in the lee of mountain massifs. The junction between Torridonian and Lewisian rocks is strikingly seen at Loch Maree, where the Torridonian on Slioch covers hills and valleys in the Lewisian basement.

CAMBRIAN AND ORDOVICIAN

Cambrian and Lower Ordovician sedimentary rocks (570-500 million years old) occupy a narrow belt in the North-west Highlands from Durness in Sutherland to Skye, 200 km (124 miles) to the south. In Ross and Cromarty these rocks occur west of the Moine Thrust zone, from the district boundary south of Elphin to Ullapool, Kinlochewe, Beinn Eighe and south-west to Loch Kishorn (Fig 2). Most of the Cambrian and Ordovician rocks were laid down in a shallow, warm, tropical shelf sea, on top of tilted Torridonian sandstone. The main rock types are quartzite and 'Pipe Rock' (sandstone with vertical worm tubes) at the base, followed by limestones and dolomites, including the Durness Limestone. Many of these beds are highly fossiliferous, containing trilobites, gastropods, cephalopods, brachiopods, worms, sponges and algae, the genera and species of which are characteristic of a North American fauna, implying that Scotland lay on the opposite side of the Iapetus ocean from England and Wales. At Knockan Cliff, just south of the border with Sutherland, the nature trail demonstrates the relationships between the Cambrian and Ordovician rocks and the Moine Thrust plane (Johnson and Parsons 1979). The enormous grey-white mass of Beinn Eighe is Cambrian quartzite lying unconformably on brown Torridonian sandstone which can be seen on the lower slopes of the mountain.

MOINE ROCKS

At least half the area of Ross and Cromarty is occupied by the Moine schists — an enormously thick series of metamorphosed, shallow-water sandy sediments. Intensely complicated fold structures in the Moine rocks have made it difficult to determine their age and evolution. Even with modern radiometric age-dating techniques, the results are often conflicting and confusing. What is certain is that Moine sediments were deposited on a basement of Lewisian Gneiss, probably around 1,200-800 million years ago and folded and metamorphosed in the Caledonian mountain building, 520-440 million years ago. Some parts of the Moine schists show evidence of an older metamorphism, dated at around 1,000 million years ago, and in places the older Moine rocks have been complexly interfolded with large-scale thrust slices of the under-lying Lewisian rocks, especially in central Ross-shire (Fig 2). Granite pegmatites dated at 750 million years old have intruded some parts of the Moine rocks. Complications in the structure of the Moine rocks arose in the early stages of the Caledonian orogeny (a mountain building phase) when deep-seated low-angled thrust faults became established, with dif-ferent segments of Moine rocks being transported over one another by great distances (50-100 km) (31-62 miles) to the north-west, causing the rocks to be interleaved. The thrust planes were subsequently folded in later stages of the mountain building events.

Moine rocks are rather uniform over large areas, the dominant types being granular quartzites that break into flagstone slabs, and silvery-grey mica-schists which may contain small red garnet crystals.

MOINE THRUST ZONE

One of the most important geological features on the west coast is the Moine Thrust Zone, which marks the North-west edge of the Caledo-nian mountain belt in Scotland. Towards the end of the mountain building events the folded Moine rocks were transported North-westwards by some 50 km (31 miles) (possibly much more than this) on top of the unmoved rocks on the basement.

The zone is about 200 km (124 miles) long, from Loch Eriboll in North-west Sutherland, through Wester Ross to South-east Skye. The Moine Thrust is the main fracture of a set of four major low-angled thrusts; it is also the highest and probably the oldest, although not certainly (see Harris 1983 and McClay and Coward 1981). Movements on the thrust faults caused the underlying rocks to be intensely folded and fractured. At the Knockan Cliff trail it is possible to put a finger on the Moine Thrust plane. Above the thrust the older Moine schists form high ground, while immediately below the plane the (younger) yellow Durness limestone is deformed and fractured. It is quite likely that the Durness limestone was the horizon along which thrusting was initiated, since it is a relatively soft, 'lubricating' rock, compared to the hard Moine schist above, or the equally hard Cambrian quartzite below. For several metres above the thrust plane, the Moine schists have been ground into a powder by movement along the thrust, and recrystallised by the heat generated, aided by water, to give a hard, finely-banded flinty rock called mylonite (= 'milled rock'). The existence of mylonite would seem to suggest that the Moine Thrust was initiated at a fairly deep level in the crust, i.e. that there was a considerable thickness of Moine schist above the fault plane. The thrust dips gently eastward and in places it has been folded or domed upwards, notably in Assynt and in South-west Ross-shire, near Loch Kishorn, where the structures in the thrust zone are highly complex, partly owing to the presence of igneous intrusions.

At the south-western extremity of the Moine Thrust Zone, in the area around Skye, Lochalsh and Lochcarron, mylonites have developed preferentially in Lewisian and Torridonian rocks. Late movements on the thrust plane resulted in zones of brecciation, due to higher level brittle thrusting (in contrast to the earlier deep-seated movements that produced the mylonites). The Moine mylonites have been dated at around 480 million years and the high level brittle thrusting at 430 million years. The later brittle movements affected mainly the rocks of the unmoved foreland (Mendum 1979). A useful summary of the geology of the Moine Thrust Zone and of the Moine rocks and foreland rocks is to be found in McClay and Coward (1981).

IGNEOUS ROCKS

In the north of the District, on the boundary with Sutherland is the large intrusive mass of the Carn Chuinneag granite (Fig 3), a pluton which occupies an area of over 80 km^2 (43 miles^2). This granite is one of the earliest Caledonian intrusions and was emplaced into the Moine

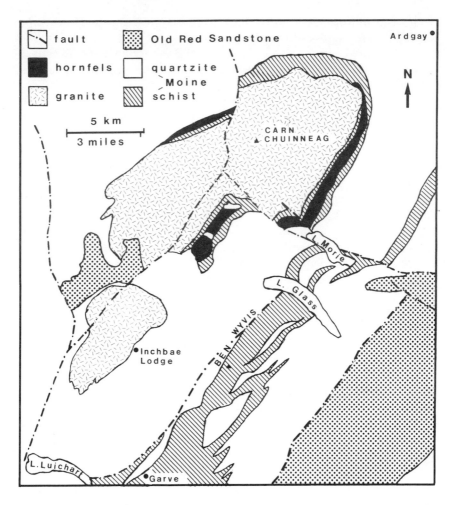

Figure 3 — Geological map of Carn Chuinneag, Inchbae and Ben Wyvis.

schists 560 million years ago and folded together with the schists during the main deformation phase, but after an initial early phase of folding. Heat from the intrusion altered the surrounding Moine rocks into hard, splintery hornfels in a metamorphic aureole (or heat-affected zone). Delicate structures and minerals in the Moine rocks were preserved in this aureole despite subsequent higher temperature metamorphism and more intense deformation (Brown 1983).

Associated with the Carn Chuinneag granite is the smaller but probably better known Inchbae 'augen gneiss', a coarse biotite-granite or granite-gneiss in which the 'augen' or 'eyes' are large crystals of pink potash feldspar often 2-3 cm (over 1 in) across. The feldspar 'eyes' are aligned in parallel orientation due to the fact that the granite was deformed and flattened after it was intruded so that now the long axes of the feldspars are parallel to the NNE-trending foliation in the surrounding Moine schists. The rock is well exposed near the road and in the river banks near Inchbae Lodge. This intrusion has supplied numerous fragments to the glacial deposits of the east coast and boulders of it are widespread around the shores of the Black Isle.

The Fearn granite between Bonar Bridge and Edderton (Fig 4) is one of a number of younger Caledonian granites which were intruded at around 410 million years ago into the Moine schists. Many boulders of the Fearn granite are to be found in the basal beds of the overlying Old Red Sandstone conglomerates.

OLD RED SANDSTONE

Rocks of Old Red Sandstone age (Devonian in SW England; 350-400 million years old) occupy a major NE-SW-trending fold, the Black Isle Syncline (Armstrong 1977) in the east of the District. These sedimentary rocks achieved international fame upon the discovery at Cromarty and Ethie of fossil fish by Hugh Miller, the Cromarty stonemason, whose collected papers were published in 1841 as *The Old Red Sandstone*. The total thickness of the Old Red Sandstone succession in Easter Ross and the Black Isle is around 6,500 m (20,000 ft) of conglomerates, sandstones, shales and mudstones. The fish beds at Edderton, Cromarty and Balintore are Middle Old Red Sandstone calcareous shales, containing hard limey nodules with occasional fragments of primitive armour-plated fishes.

The Old Red Sandstones are terrestrial in origin, having been laid down in the alluvial fans and on the floodplains of large meandering rivers which were eroding the newly-formed Caledonian high mountain range. Siltstones, shales and mudstones represent the deposits of short-lived shallow lakes which periodically formed at the base of the mountain slopes. Some of these land-locked lakes became silted up and decaying animal and plant matter accumulated in the stagnant waters. At this time Scotland lay much farther south and drifted from 20° S during the Lower Devonian to 10° S by the end of the Devonian, about 350 million years ago (Mykura 1983). NE Scotland was situated in the lee of high mountains, far from the ocean and had a hot, dry climate, punctuated by torrential rainstorms which led to flash floods and the transport by intermittent rivers of enormous quantities of coarse sediment from mountain scree slopes down onto extensive flat plains at the foot of the mountain range. The lack of land plants, which had not evolved at that time, meant that there was a high run-off rate, with none of the rainwater being absorbed by plant roots. One other consequence of the desert conditions was the red haematite (iron ore) staining of sand grains, giving the Old Red Sandstone its distinctive and characteristic colour. It is a well-known fact that this rock was widely used as an important building stone around the firthlands, from Elgin to Inverness, Strathpeffer and Dornoch. Old Red Sandstone rocks were deposited unconformably on top of the older folded and metamorphosed Moine schists.

North of the firthlands lay the great land-locked lake or shallow inland sea known as 'Lake Orcadie' which stretched from Caithness to Orkney and possibly Shetland and west Norway.

THE GREAT GLEN FAULT

The Great Glen Fault is one of the most important structural features in Northern Scotland. The fault occupies a zone about 1 km (0.6 miles) wide along which considerable movement has taken place on several occasions during a long span of geological time, starting around 400 million years ago. Even today minor earthquakes are experienced in Inverness and other towns along the 90 km (56 miles) of the Great Glen. During the last two centuries at least sixty earthquakes have been recorded along the fault (Wood 1978).

The Great Glen Fault is one of a set of near-parallel faults which cut the rocks of the Highlands north and south of Glen More (Fig 4). It was initiated during the Caledonian mountain building event, before the deposition of the Old Red Sandstone, and it remained a plane of weakness in the Earth's crust along which movement occurred in several different directions (Smith 1977; Mykura 1982, 1983). Crushing, fracturing and milling-down of rocks in the fault zone produced material that weathered more rapidly than the surrounding hard rocks, so that an early river valley was utilised by glaciers during the last ice age to produce a long, narrow, deep valley, occupied by lochs with rocky floors.

Although there are conflicting views concerning movement on the

Great Glen Fault, it is now accepted that the fault was initiated as a deep and fundamental structure before the deposition of Old Red Sandstone sediments. Basement rocks along the Great Glen display extensive shearing, cataclasis and recrystallization, that leads to the development of thick bands of mylonite (finely-banded fault rock, recrystallized from rock powder), indicating that the fault originated at deep levels within the crust (Smith 1977; Mykura 1983). Original attempts to determine the amount of movement on the fault were based on postulating a match between the Strontian granite at the SW end and the Foyers granite at the NE end of the fault. Other evidence includes matching structures, rock types and metamorphic grades in the Moine schists, and when all this is taken into account we are left with the postulate that the Great Glen Fault is a sinistral (left-hand) transcurrent fault with a horizontal displacement of around 100 km (62 miles). It should be emphasised, however, that the Great Glen follows not merely a simple transcurrent fault line, but a wide complex zone of thrusts and faults which were active at various times in the geological past.

Mykura (1982), in a recent study of the Old Red Sandstone rocks east of Loch Ness has drawn attention to repeated differential vertical movements in the fault zone and along associated NE-trending faults during the deposition of the sediments, and to the existence of several compressive thrust faults and folds in the Foyers section. The conclusion is that there was a complex interplay of normal faulting, folding, thrusting and transcurrent movement in the Great Glen Fault zone in Devonian times. The Old Red Sandstone on Struie Hill has been thrust over the underlying basement of Moine schists, and from the 'Queen's View', the thrust plane can be clearly seen as a distinct near-horizontal break in slope.

When the geography of Middle Old Red Sandstone times in the Moray Firth area is taken into account, the conclusion is that there was an overall dextral (right-hand) displacement along the Great Glen Fault of about 25-30 km (16-19 miles) (Donovan et al. 1976; Smith 1977; Mykura 1982, 1983). Evidence for movement along the Great Glen Fault zone in post-Devonian times is conflicting (Smith 1977). The consensus view, based on off-shore geophysical studies in the Moray Firth, is that during Mesozoic and early Tertiary times (190-55 million years ago), the Great Glen Fault behaved as one of a set of NE-SW fractures which partly controlled the location of sedimentary basins. The Jurassic sediments of the area have been affected by normal faults with downthrow to the SE (Bacon and Chesher 1975).

Some reconstructions of the Great Glen Fault show it as continuing through the Walls Fault in central Shetland and north-eastwards to

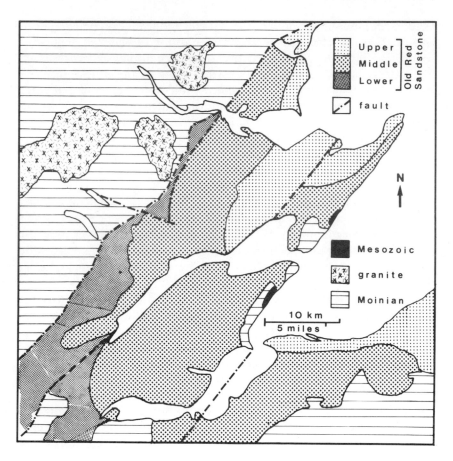

Figure 4 — Old Red Sandstone distribution in Easter Ross.

Spitzbergen, more than 1000 km (620 miles) distant, but this correlation is uncertain and is disputed (Wood 1978; Mykura 1982).

MESOZOIC ROCKS

Younger sedimentary rocks occur on the west coast at Applecross, Gairloch, Aultbea-Laide (Plate 42) and offshore in the Inner Sound and the Minch. On the east coast these rocks appear at Rosemarkie and Balintore and very extensively in the Moray Firth basin (Fig 4).

Patches of unfossiliferous breccia, conglomerate and sandstone of Triassic age rest unconformably on Torridon Sandstone along the coast of Wester Ross (Phemister 1960; Chesher et al. 1983). The largest outlier is at Aultbea where the sediments amount to 300 m (1000 ft) thick comprising coarse fragmental rocks at the base that pass upwards into clays, marls and thin sandstones. At Applecross the marls (lime mudstones) contain nodules of concretionary limestone. Overlying these marls are limestones, sandstones and shales of Jurassic age, similar to rocks found near Broadford on Skye. Fossils include corals and oyster shells.

Jurassic sediments on the east coast are thinner and less well exposed than at Applecross. The rocks are mostly shales, sandstones and thin limestones. Farther north, at Brora in Sutherland, thin coal seams occur. In the Cromarty area and at Port an Righ clays and shales with bands of broken shells and flattened ammonites overlie a thick white sandstone. The Brora Coal is represented by a 10-20 cm (4-8 in) carbonaceous layer above the clays. Many of the beds at Port an Righ and Ethie are highly fossiliferous, containing abundant lamellibranchs, ammonites, belemnites and plants. The rocks were laid down in a delta environment in sub-tropical climatic conditions. Later in time the delta was flooded and Upper Jurassic sediments accumulated in a deeper water offshore basin (Chesher and Lawson 1983).

Upper Jurassic bituminous shales are now known to be very widely distributed in the North Sea and are generally considered to be the source rock of North Sea oil (Hallam 1983). Most of the oil deposits have been found in and around down-faulted graben structures containing thick sedimentary accumulations (Duff 1983). A notable exception is the Beatrice Field in the Moray Firth Basin. One of the thickest successions of Jurassic sediments occurs in the middle of the North Sea, where it amounts to 2300 m (7000 ft).

THE MORAY FIRTH

The Mesozoic sedimentary basin of the Moray Firth practically coincides with the older Orcadian basin in which the Old Red Sandstone was deposited. The present coastline marks the limit of the Mesozoic basin, as thin strips of Mesozoic sediments occur along the shore. Faults define the margins of the basin, with Mesozoic rocks downfaulted against the Old Red Sandstone. Sediments within the basin were affected by normal faults which were active during the deposition of Jurassic rocks, resulting in the formation of fault-bounded rift valleys (grabens) and upstanding blocks (horsts). A major synclinal fold occurs along the line of the Great Glen Fault, which was active as a normal fault during Mesozoic times, when sediments of this age piled up thickly in the Moray Firth basin to the south of the fault, on its downthrow side.

LANDSCAPE DEVELOPMENT

The origin of the present-day landscape dates back to the Tertiary Period, which began about 70 million years ago, at a time when a humid tropical climate prevailed, resulting in deep and extensive erosion of the land surface. The drainage system of Scotland became established during the Tertiary, when major rivers flowed eastwards across the easterly-dipping tilted land surface of the Highlands to the North Sea. During Tertiary and Quaternary times the North Sea area was subjected to deep and rapid subsidence (Anderton et al. 1979). Tertiary sediments are absent from the land area of Ross and Cromarty whereas enormous volumes of mud, shale, silt and sand were carried from the eroding land surface into the subsiding trough of the North Sea by rivers which formed large deltas and submarine fans. Off the west coast, in the Hebrides, was an area of volcanic activity in Tertiary times. A great volcanic province stretched from Greenland through Faroe and St Kilda to Skye, Rhum, Ardnamurchan, Mull, Arran, Antrim and Slieve Gullion in the form of a nearly N-S orientated line of central intrusive complexes with associated swarms of dolerite dykes and extensive floods of plateau basalt lavas. A number of N-S dykes cross the Applecross peninsula from the Cuillins centre on Skye. The dykes average about 2 m (6.6 ft) wide, are of dolerite ('whinstone') and are 60 million years old. A few other dykes of this swarm are found around the north shore of Loch Torridon, at Redpoint and north to Loch Gairloch. The line of the Loch Ewe negative magnetic anomaly that runs NNW from Loch Ewe to NE of Ness, Lewis and beyond may be a very large 500 m (1640 ft) wide Tertiary dyke at depth (Chesher et al. 1983). The anomaly stops against the Loch Maree fault and the top of the dyke is calculated to be 1 km (0.6 miles) below the surface.

The long easterly-flowing rivers of the District cut discordantly across major structures and rock types of the Moine schists, implying that the initial drainage pattern is superimposed on the geology due to rapid uplift and the removal of a once-extensive sedimentary cover

(Sissons 1967). Dissection of the surface by rivers and later by ice sheets during the Pleistocene glaciation resulted in the isolation of high residual hills such as Ben Wyvis in the east and the mountains of Wester Ross from the main massif of the Scottish Highlands. In the central part of the District the mountains are eroded into a dissected plateau, with erosion surfaces at different heights.

ROCK TYPE AND SCENERY

The striking contrasts in scenery between the west coast and east coast of the District result from the nature of the solid geology and the ways in which rocks weather and erode at the surface. Lewisian Gneiss on the west coast forms a landscape of bare rounded knobs and loch-filled hollows and generally low relief. The landscape formed by the overlying Torridon Sandstone is markedly different. This rock has gently-dipping bedding planes and vertical joints and fissures which have been weathered out to produce terraced escarpments and near-vertical cliffs flanked by steep, loose scree slopes. Isolated mountains such as Ben More Coigach, An Teallach and Slioch form spectacular points on the west coast landscape. The Torridon and Applecross hills form a more complete remnant of a once extensive mountain range.

The great grey mass of Beinn Eighe has been carved out by glaciers of Cambrian quartzite which lies above the Torridon Sandstone. Quartzite is an exceptionally hard and durable rock, consisting of sand grains which have become welded together to produce a strong framework. Moreover, quartz is quite an inert mineral that withstands chemical and biological decay very well. The slopes of Beinn Eighe are clothed in a mantle of white and grey angular fragments, the products of frost shattering of the rock mass that have fallen under gravity and accumulated on the lower slopes as sheets of scree.

In the interior of the District, east of the Moine Thrust and west of the Old Red Sandstone coastal lowlands in the east, lies a dissected plateau of rounded isolated mountains around 900 m (2,950 ft) high, wide gravel-filled straths, irregular hummocky moraines and featureless tracts of peat bog. Ben Wyvis (Plate 38), the Fannich mountains and the hills of Strathconon Forest are made of Moine schist with interleaved slices of Lewisian Gneiss, while much of the lower ground is made of Moine quartzite. Carn Chuinneag and Beinn Tharsuinn are granite, which tends to form rounded hills.

Near the east coast of the District the scenery is quite different. Here we see the gentle rolling hills of Old Red Sandstone behind a narrow coastal plain. Much of the area is covered in glacial drift. The Old Red

Sandstone outcrop begins at Strathpeffer, where the local landmark of Knock Farril is a ridge of conglomerate, which is harder than the sandstone. Millbuie Ridge on the Black Isle is one of a series of NE-SW-trending folds in the Old Red Sandstone which have weathered out into a number of parallel ridges and valleys.

THE EFFECTS OF GLACIATION

Ice-sheets over 1,000 m (3,280 ft) thick covered most of Britain during the extensive early glaciations of the Quaternary period, some 2-2½ million years ago. It was not until about 10,000 years ago (recent in geological terms) that the last ice-sheet melted from the Scottish Highlands.

Most of the characteristic landform features of the Highland areas in the District were produced by the work of glaciers. As ice-sheets moved over the surface and down existing valleys, loose scree and river gravel were picked up and became embedded in the base of the advancing ice, causing the bedrock to be scraped and polished. Glaciated valleys are wider and straighter than the original river valleys and tend to have steep sides and wide U-shaped profiles, in contrast to the more typical V-shaped valleys of upland streams. The ice-sheets covered all but the highest peaks and produced a smoother and more rounded landscape. It is not certain if Ben Wyvis was completely under the ice, but there are a number of steep-walled semi-circular corries near the top. These mark the birthplaces of glaciers, which gradually outgrew their corries in successive winters and flowed down pre-existing river valleys. Glacial striae are not often preserved on gneiss or sandstone, but examples can be found on the quartzite bedding planes of Beinn Eighe and on harder sandstones in the Black Isle, such as at Culbokie village.

As the ice moved eastwards, large fragments of loose material were transported and carried considerable distances before being dumped once the ice melted. Erratic boulders of the highly distinctive Inchbae augen gneiss were carried thus, and are now widely distributed around the Black Isle and Easter Ross, but not on the summit of Ben Wyvis.

The Beauly, Cromarty and Dornoch Firths are glacially over-deepened and drowned river valleys dating originally from pre-glacial Tertiary times. The presence of hard crystalline Moine schist and granite at the Sutors of Cromarty caused the ice to excavate more deeply into the softer Old Red Sandstone in the inner Cromarty Firth, which was considerably widened; eventually the ice broke through the Moine rocks and created a narrow entrance to the Firth.

GLACIAL DEPOSITION

Towards the end of the last glacial period, the low land of the District was covered by extensive sheets of glacial and fluvio-glacial drift deposited beneath and at the edges of the moving ice or left behind after the ice had melted completely.

Large channels at Struie record meltwater flow from the Dornoch Firth into Strath Rory, then into the Pitmaduthy esker system near Nigg Bay (Smith 1977). Eskers are long, sinuous mounds of fluvio-glacial sands and gravels which formed in meltwater tunnels beneath the ice. Deep gorges illustrate the powerful erosive effects of meltwater streams. The famous Black Rock gorge of Novar, near Evanton, is an extremely narrow, deep cleft in Old Red Sandstone conglomerate which formed in post-glacial times during a period of rapid uplift. Sediment-laden torrential meltwater cut swiftly through the rock like a saw. Just outside the District boundary the gorge of the River Beauly at the Falls of Kilmorack has been cut into the basal conglomerates of the Old Red Sandstone and all the way down to the Moine schist.

Boulder clay, deposited directly by the ice, consists of boulders and cobbles of mixed size, shape and rock type, held together by a matrix of often sticky grey, red or yellow clay. Clay particles form when rocks such as schist, gneiss and granite weather and the feldspar and mica minerals constituting these rocks break down. The widespread cover of boulder clay throughout most of the Black Isle gives rise to smooth, undulating topography. The red to yellowish colour of much of the glacial and fluvio-glacial sediment indicates a local origin from the underlying Old Red Sandstone.

In the interior of the District, glacial deposits are found in all the valleys, in the form of irregular or conical low mounds and hummocks of boulder clay and loose sand and gravel. The well-named Corrie of the Hundred Hills (Coire a' Cheud-chnoic) at the head of Glen Torridon consists of a large number of hummocky terminal moraines, deposited at the front of the glacier as it melted and retreated up the glen (but note that ice does not move uphill — it melts and the front retreats).

A most impressive example of fluvio-glacial landforms can be seen near Achnasheen (Plate 8), where there are a number of high-level gravel terraces occupying much of the valley floor. Six terraces in all are present, the topmost one forming a wide peat-covered plateau west of the road. The lowest terraces are of finely-laminated clays, deposited in a meltwater lake and subsequently covered by coarser material in the upper terraces, where coarse subangular and rounded gravel predominate. The surface of the plateau on top of the highest terrace shows a number of deep circular depressions, known as kettle-holes, which represent local areas where large blocks of stagnant ice remained buried beneath glacial debris and melted slowly.

Another excellent example of gravel terraces occurs in Strath Rory, on the Struie road to Bonar Bridge. The terraces are the result of the redistribution and sorting of glacial debris by post-glacial rivers developing channels for themselves and meandering from side to side on flat valley floors.

RAISED BEACHES

Well-marked terraces standing at heights up to about 30 m (100 ft) above sea level form a conspicuous feature along the shores of the Dornoch, Beauly and Cromarty firths. They are generally believed to mark the various levels of the sea immediately after the end of the ice age when the land began to rise to its former pre-glacial level as the mass of ice which had depressed the surface melted. Another possibility is that the "raised beaches" are outwash terraces. When the glaciers had finally melted, the sea level rose for a time and drowned much of the east coast lowlands, but as the surface began to rise again, the temporary high post-glacial seas retreated. Raised beaches with low cliffs, old caves and beach deposits are well-preserved around the Beauly Firth, on the Black Isle and the Tarbat Ness peninsula. Notable examples are at North Kessock and Hilton of Cadboll. Two levels at around 15 m (50 ft) and 30 m (100 ft) are seen at Munlochy in the south-east of the Black Isle. Stratified deposits of marine sand, gravel and clay occur on the raised beach terraces. A number of raised beach levels intermediate between 15 m and 30 m (50 and 100 ft) have been recorded, particularly around the Beauly Firth. These can usually be traced for short distances only, and probably indicate that the land was uplifted gradually, the uplift being punctuated by occasional stand-stills during which the sea was able to erode notches into boulder clay or Old Red Sandstone.

Examples of raised beaches and other post-glacial phenomena are rarer on the narrow, rugged and highly indented coast of Wester Ross. An exception to this is a very clear raised beach at Gruinard Bay (Plate 6) which can be seen to advantage from the roadside viewpoint on the hill going towards Laide.

The railway line between Beauly and Muir of Ord crosses a wide terrace thought to be formed by the highest raised beach at the head of the Beauly Firth. The high late-glacial raised beach is also well developed around the head of the Cromarty Firth and extends inland along the River Conon, where it merges with a large delta that formed at the edge of a glacier (Synge 1977). On the Black Isle this raised beach forms a 500 m (1,640 ft) wide terrace which increases in width inland. The terrace is built of finely laminated light-brown clays and fine silty sand, giving rise to well-drained, good quality soils. On the north side of the Firth this terrace is considerably narrower and it extends up the valley almost to Strathpeffer. The glacial and post-glacial beach deposits at Strathpeffer contain shells and whale bone fragments.

Beauly stands on a wide 7.6 m (25 ft) raised beach terrace which is composed of marine alluvium — finely laminated clay with beds of sand and fine gravel. Around Dingwall it is this same post-glacial beach which gives rise to the widest extent of carse land. The raised beaches around the firths are discussed in greater detail in a paper by Synge (1977).

Ferry Point and Ardjachie Point on the south shore of the Dornoch Firth, and Cuthill Links opposite these (on the Sutherland side) are raised post-glacial spit complexes made of well-rounded cobbles and pebbles with interlaminated lenses of coarse sand and occasional shell banks, now colonised by coastal plants and grasses. During the highest of the post-glacial sea levels there was a sea connection between the Cromarty and Dornoch Firths.

THE COAST

The three firths of Ross and Cromarty break the generally rectilinear coast of North-east Scotland, in stark contrast to the highly indented fiord-like west coast. The origin of these contrasting coasts depends on the relative hardnesses of the underlying rocks. On the east coast the NE-SW trend is parallel to the 'grain' of the country rocks which was imposed during the Caledonian mountain building period. In particular the coasts of the Black Isle and the Tarbat Ness peninsula facing the Moray Firth have been formed at the edge of the NE-SW trending Great Glen Fault. The eastern coastlands have been excavated from Old Red Sandstone mainly, which is a relatively uniform rock, so that the relief around the firths is of a uniform, low undulating plateau dissected by broad river valleys. Constructional shorelines occur, where wave action has shaped glacial deposits into long sandy beaches. Sand barriers built up by the action of wind since post-glacial times have caused the foreland of Morrich Mhor near Tain to advance out into the Dornoch Firth as the high-level post-glacial sea retreated. The Whiteness Sands have advanced, resulting in the silting-up of Tain harbour (Whittow 1977; Ogilvie 1923).

The rugged west coast of the District is a complete contrast to that of Easter Ross and the Black Isle. The long, straight, narrow, deep indentations on the west coast are glacially overdeepened Tertiary river valleys which were initially excavated along NW-SE fractures (faults and joints), fold axes and rock boundaries in the Lewisian Gneiss. The largest of these fractures is the Loch Maree fault and a magnificent view of the linear U-shaped valley occupied by Loch Maree can be had from NW of Kinlochewe. In the south-west of the District Loch Carron follows the line of a NE-SW Caledonian fault, while Loch Kishorn occupies a narrow belt where the relatively soft Durness Limestone is cut by a number of thrusts related to the Moine Thrust zone.

A further contrast can be seen in the nearly north-south coast of Torridon Sandstone that extends from Rubha Reidh to Applecross and beyond. Much of this coast facing the Inner Sound and The Minch is of high cliffs with numerous ledges (weathered-out bedding planes) inhabited by sea birds.

ECONOMIC GEOLOGY

The Old Red Sandstone of Easter Ross and the Black Isle was previously quarried on a large scale as masonry stone, but this industry has now disappeared. There are many fine buildings of this rock, such as Fortrose Cathedral (Plate 21) and Tarradale House. Flagstones of Moine schist were once worked at Raven Rock, near Strathpeffer, for local building purposes. Quarries in the granites are long since abandoned. On the west coast the Lewisian Gneiss and Torridon Sandstone have been used as local building stones. Extensive deposits of glacial and post-glacial sands and gravels are currently being extracted on a large scale in the east of the District for use as road metal and concrete aggregate.

There are no commercially important mineral deposits in the District being exploited now. Veins of silver-bearing galena (lead ore), zinc blende, barytes and calcite have been mapped in fault zones cutting Moine schists in Strath Glass. Lead mines did operate for a number of years in the first half of the 19th century. Copper and iron ores (haematite) have been recorded as occurrences in the Durness Limestone at Rassal (Loch Kishorn). The limestone itself is locally important as an agricultural material. Cassiterite (tinstone) occurs irregularly in magnetite-rich bands in granitic gneiss around the Carn Chuinneag intrusion. Recent prospecting of the copper deposits in the Lewisian Gneiss metasediments of the Gairloch area has failed to locate any worthwhile reserves, although the large number of drill cores has provided a massive amount of detail for research workers. Mica-rich pegmatites occur quite commonly in the Lewisian Gneiss and the Moine schist, but none is exploited. A vein of graphite was once worked in the Moine schist in Glen Strathfarrar. (For futher references see Phemister 1960 and Duff 1983).

The considerable deposits of oil and gas in the North Sea basin form the greatest economic asset in North-east Scotland. Production is now near its peak of almost 100 million tonnes per annum and the estimated recoverable reserves amount to 2,200-4,300 million tonnes (Duff 1983). Most of the deposits occur in association with graben structures, which are down-faulted crustal blocks containing thick sequences of sediments. The oil is mostly derived from the Jurassic Kimmeridge Clay, a black kerogen-rich mudstone. Oil has accumulated in traps beneath a caprock of Jurassic to Tertiary shales, whereas gas is usually restricted to the Palaeocene (Lower Tertiary, 63 million years old).

Another important fuel resource is peat which occurs in the east of the District as blanket bog deposits in many upland areas. The Aultnabreac deposit is being exploited using mechanised methods, but in the west the deposits are of local extent and the topography is such as to exclude mechanisation.

Over two hundred years ago the natural mineral waters of Strathpeffer were first investigated scientifically. Springs emerge from bedding planes of rocks and from fault lines and the underground circulation of water is shallow-level. The Old Red Sandstone contains fetid shales from which emerge sulphurous waters, while chalybeate springs (rich in iron carbonates) issue from glacial deposits and from muscovite-biotite gneisses in the Moine rocks (Phemister 1960).

SOIL TYPES

Most of the soils of Ross and Cromarty are developed on glacial drift deposits which have ultimately been derived from solid rocks. In the west the bedrock is gneiss, schist and sandstone which yield acid soils, although the Durness Limestone gives rise to local calcareous (lime-rich) soils. In the east there are frequent calcareous-rich layers in the Old Red Sandstone, as well as sediments with a limey cement, so that much of the soil of the Black Isle and Easter Ross is quite fertile. Fluvio-glacial sands and gravels, raised beach deposits and river gravel are other parent materials, most of which give rise to stony soils. In spring a glance at freshly ploughed fields will give some idea of the enormous volume of stone fragments present in the soils of the District.

Soil formation is affected by climatic factors, mainly rainfall and temperature, which interact with biological and chemical processes acting on the parent material. Agricultural activity over a period of time also has an important influence on soil formation.

There are many different soil types in Ross and Cromarty, by far the commonest being peat and peaty podzols and gleys in the western, central and high upland areas of the District where drainage is poor, rainfall is high, average temperatures are rather low and the parent material is coarse, stony, glacial drift derived from acid rocks such as gneiss, schist,

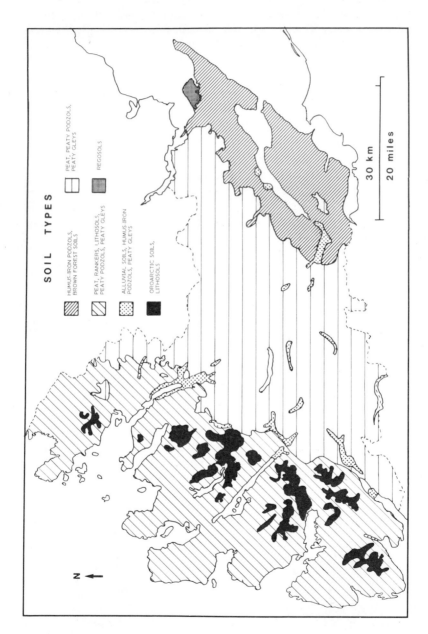

Figure 5 — Map showing distribution of soil types in Ross and Cromarty.

granite and quartzite. Peaty podzols and peaty gleys usually support wet heather moorland vegetation. Other soil types include rendzinas, developed from the Durness Limestone and found around Kishorn and other areas northwards to Elphin, just west of the Moine Thrust zone. These soils are shallow, freely drained and support grassland. Oroarctic soils develop on high upland areas where the climate is severe and the growing season is short. An open texture and large volume of stones is a characteristic feature due to the action of freezing and thawing. Rankers and lithosols occur where the parent material is acid and very stony, such as on scree slopes and mountain-top detritus. Alluvial soils form on river-valley detritus and occur mostly in the firthlands in the east of the District and at the head of Lochs Broom, Maree and Kishorn in the west. In the central parts of Ross and Cromarty, some of the larger straths have wide areas of alluvial soils, such as Strathcarron, Strathbran and near Achnashellach and Garve. These soils are shallow, coarse and fairly well-drained and support acid grassland.

On the Black Isle and the Tarbat Ness peninsula where the climate is rather warm and dry, humus-iron podzols have formed on fluvioglacial drift derived from the Old Red Sandstone and from raised beach deposits. Humus-iron podzols are very acid and fairly well-drained soils which show evidence of leaching of iron and aluminium from the soil layer immediately below the surface layer of raw humus. Arable and permanent pastures and dry heather moorland are supported on these soils.

In the lower parts of some valleys and lochs, especially in the west (e.g. Loch Carron, Upper Loch Torridon, Loch Maree and Loch Broom), brown forest soils occur. They are moderately acid with free or imperfect drainage and are developed on moderate slopes on top of glacial material and stony debris. Brown forest soils are shallow, fairly coarse-textured and support acid grassland with bracken or birch woodland and normally occur in association with humus-iron podzols.

Regosols are developed on windblown beach sand, such as on the south shores of the Dornoch Firth and around Balnapaling in Nigg Bay. Regosols do not show much of a soil profile due to their being unstable. For the same reason little vegetation is present, save for grassland on stabilised sites.

The distribution of the various soil types in Ross and Cromarty is summarised in Figure 5. Much more detail is available from the 1:250,000 scale Northern Scotland soil and agriculture maps and accompanying handbook (Futty and Towers 1982).

TABLE 1 — Monthly and annual average rainfall for stations in Ross and Cromarty

STATION	ALT (M)	JAN	FEB	MAR	APR	MAY	JUN	JULY	AUG	SEP	OCT	NOV	DEC	YEAR
ACHNASHELLACH	67	210	173	160	157	113	127	149	157	205	252	204	254	2161
APPLECROSS, BEALACH	396	237	184	163	161	126	148	177	191	248	287	236	285	2443
APPLECROSS HOUSE	21	156	120	107	104	83	97	115	123	161	188	157	187	1598
TORRIDON HOUSE	8	179	145	131	130	96	110	131	139	180	215	175	216	1847
LOCH CARRON	3	174	139	123	123	94	110	133	143	183	213	172	212	1819
KINLOCHEWE	23	195	161	149	146	105	118	138	146	190	234	190	236	2008
POOLEWE	6	154	127	117	115	83	93	109	115	150	185	150	186	1584
STRATHPEFFER	70	75	68	66	51	50	49	67	67	58	66	73	86	776
ARDGAY	55	106	85	71	76	86	82	95	115	95	110	110	120	1151
TAIN	43	66	53	45	48	57	55	65	78	63	72	71	76	749
ARDROSS	180	80	66	56	60	72	69	82	102	78	90	87	94	936
LOCH GLASS	219	122	107	87	90	83	74	87	103	107	130	120	157	1267
ULLAPOOL	12	139	118	97	99	75	80	87	96	125	154	143	171	1384
STRATHKANAIRD	14	157	133	110	112	85	91	98	109	140	175	161	194	1565
KNOCKANROCK	244	215	182	150	153	116	124	134	149	192	238	220	265	2138
INVERPOLLY	14	135	115	94	96	73	78	85	93	121	150	139	166	1345
FANNICH LODGE	268	187	160	132	135	109	106	117	135	163	202	189	237	1872
CROMARTY	6	50	42	37	41	54	56	67	86	59	65	61	61	679
FORTROSE	5	50	42	37	40	52	51	62	79	55	63	57	61	649
MUIR OF ORD	46	70	63	50	53	52	47	57	68	65	78	70	91	764
LOCH MULLARDOCH	217	218	180	166	163	117	132	155	163	213	262	212	264	2245
LOCH MONAR	213	197	163	150	148	106	119	140	148	193	236	192	239	2031

Figures supplied by the Meteorological Office, Edinburgh

CLIMATE

The western part of the District experiences a maritime climate, being located at the edge of the Atlantic Ocean in a predominantly southwesterly air stream. The weather systems of the west of Scotland are controlled by three main air sources, which vary greatly in intensity and frequency. Firstly, warm air from a high pressure area in the Azores arrives in depressions and often produces heavy, continuous rain. Secondly, cooler air from the North Atlantic brings showers to the coastal lowlands and more prolonged rain periods to the mountains. Lastly, polar airstreams travel south over the continental landmass and bring very cold, clear weather.

The west coast mountains present a barrier to the moist southwesterly winds from the Atlantic, forcing them to rise and lose their moisture. Drier, warmer air then descends and moves eastwards, to that the east coast of Ross and Cromary is much drier, sunnier and warmer than the west (Figs 6 and 7).

RAINFALL

The rain-shadow effect of the mountains is well illustrated by the average annual rainfall map for the District (Fig 6) which resembles the contour map. Around the lowlands of the east coast firths, the rainfall is relatively low, with only 600 mm (24 in) per year at Tarbat Ness. Easter Ross and the Black Isle are described as moderately dry and warm to fairly warm (Birse and Dry 1970). In contrast, rainfall in the mountains of the west and centre of the District, particularly the Torridon hills and the Fannich mountains is very high, usually in excess of 3,000 mm (118 in) per year, making this one of the wettest areas in Scotland. Throughout the District, October to January is the wettest period, April to June the driest, in common with most of Scotland. The western and central areas of Ross and Cromarty are described as wet, except for some of the low-lying peninsulas in the extreme west, such as Rubh Coigach and Rubha Mor, which are moderately dry. Average rainfall figures for stations in the District are given in Table 1. For comparison, Aberdeen has 830 mm (33 in), Glasgow 1,043 mm (41 in), and Edinburgh 660 mm (26 in) per annum.

TEMPERATURE

The average temperature in Ross and Cromarty varies with altitude and distance from the sea. Birse and Dry (1970) have produced maps of accumulated temperature, which is a measure of the total temperature above 5.6° over a period, expressed in day-degrees Celsius (day °C).

TABLE 2 — Averages of daily mean temperature (°C)

STATION	JAN	FEB	MAR	APR	MAY	JUNE	JUL	AUG	SEP	OCT	NOV	DEC	YEAR
INVERPOLLY	4.4	3.5	5.3	6.8	9.9	12.5	12.9	13.5	11.7	9.5	5.5	4.9	8.4
TARBAT NESS	3.2	3.5	5.1	7.1	9.3	12.1	13.7	13.4	12.1	9.6	6.0	4.2	8.3
POOLEWE	4.3	4.3	6.1	7.7	10.3	12.9	13.7	13.9	12.6	10.3	7.0	5.5	9.1
ACHNASHELLACH	2.6	2.7	5.0	6.9	9.7	12.4	13.3	13.3	11.7	9.0	5.3	3.7	7.9
KINLOCHEWE	3.1	3.2	5.4	7.4	10.2	12.9	13.9	13.9	12.3	9.7	5.7	4.3	8.5
FORTROSE	3.5	3.8	5.3	7.3	9.5	12.6	14.1	14.0	12.7	10.0	6.5	4.7	8.7

Figures supplied by the Meteorological Office, Edinburgh

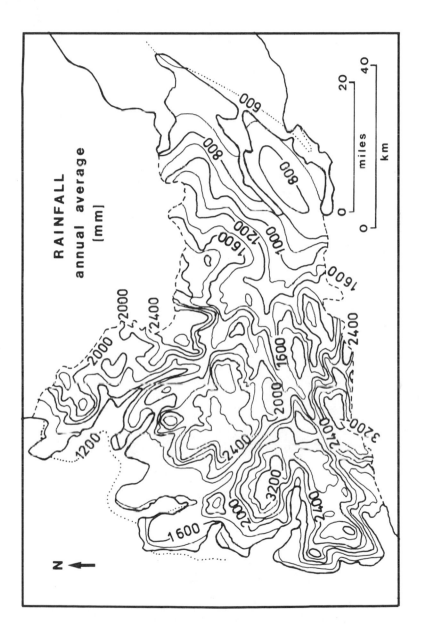

Figure 6 — Map of rainfall of Ross and Cromarty.

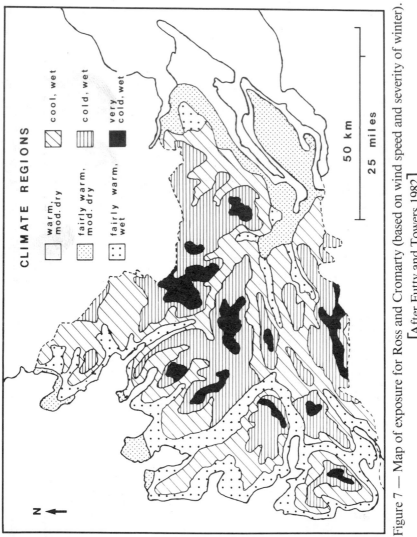

Figure 7 — Map of exposure for Ross and Cromarty (based on wind speed and severity of winter). [After Futty and Towers 1982]

The 5.6°C limit is the temperature above which plant growth (except alpines) becomes significant. Birse and Robertson (1970) have used accumulated frost (day-degrees below 0°C) to indicate the severity of winters. The lowest totals (and therefore mildest winters) occur on the west coast due to the important influence of the Atlantic Ocean. In the east, 20-50 day-degrees of frost are accumulated around the Moray Firth. In the centre, away from the maritime influence, 110 - 230 day-degrees are common, whilst mountain tops are of course coldest, with accumulated temperatures of 230 - 470 day-degrees of frost.

Values of accumulated temperature above 5.6°C are shown in a general way in Figure 7. Easter Ross and the Black Isle lie in the warm to fairly warm category; the west coast is fairly warm, whereas inland areas and mountains are cold to very cold. Throughout the District there is a small annual temperature range (Table 2). Mean annual temperature maxima are greatest in inland areas, away from the cooling effect of sea breezes. Lowest mean values occur in these same areas, whereas on the west coast the relatively warm sea in winter helps maintain higher average temperatures.

EXPOSURE

Exposure to the effects of wind is an important element of climate, especially in upland areas and on the west coast. The least exposed areas are in the east and in valleys. Birse and Robertson (1970) have assessed the climatic conditions in Scotland in terms of exposure (wind speed) and accumulated frost (day-degrees below 0°C). Their map shows that the Black Isle and the Tarbat Ness peninsula are sheltered (average wind speed less than 2.6 metres per second) or moderately exposed (2.6 - 4.4 m/s). The main straths are also sheltered or moderately exposed, with moderate winters (50 - 110 day-degrees C). The west coast is exposed (4.4 - 6.2 m/s) or very exposed (6.2 - 8 m/s) with mild winters, while the high ground in the west and centre of the District is very exposed or extemely exposed (wind speed greater than 8 m/s) with severe to extemely severe winters. The average annual wind speeds experienced on the west coast are among the highest in the world.

APPENDIX

GEOLOGICAL TIME SCALE

ERA	PERIOD	AGE OF BASE Ma	EVENTS IN ROSS AND CROMARTY
CENOZOIC	QUARTERNARY	2	Several ice ages
	TERTIARY		Deep erosion, tropical climate. Intrusion of dolerite dykes. Thick sediments in N. Sea and Minch. Final opening of Atlantic.
		65	
	CRETACEOUS	136	Erosion of land surface.
MESOZOIC	JURASSIC		Latest movements on Great Glen Fault. Subtropical seas flood Moray Firth and Minch Basins.
		190	
	TRIASSIC	225	Continental weathering; deserts.
	PERMIAN		Subsidence of Moray Firth and Minch basins. Opening of central North sea rift. Desert conditions prevail on land.
		280	
	CARBONIFEROUS	360	No sediments.
PALAEOZOIC	DEVONIAN		Old Red Sandstone continent, Orcadian basin. Caledonian mountains formed by collision of continents, intrusion of granite (420 Ma), folding and metamorphism of rocks at depth.
		420	
	SILURIAN	465	Caledonian orogeny
	ORDOVICIAN	530	Moine thrust movements.
	CAMBRIAN		Sedimentation in shallow shelf sea. Carn Chuinneag intrusion (560 Ma).
		600	
PRE-CAMBRIAN	PROTEROZOIC		Deposition of continental Torridon rocks and marine Moine rocks (up to 1000 Ma). Laxfordian complex — folding and granite intrusion, Lewisian, 1750 Ma.
		2200	
	ARCHAEAN		Formation of Scourian complex, Lewisian Gneiss, 2800 Ma, deformation, intrusion, metamorphism of existing rocks. Earliest continent formed.
		2800	

Chapter two

PLANT LIFE
Alexander Maclennan

INTRODUCTION

In common with other parts of the Highlands, knowledge of the plants of Ross and Cromarty is still incomplete, particularly for the less accessible central and western parts of the District. Certain groups of plants, particularly mosses, liverworts, algae, fungi and lichens have been poorly surveyed and considerable information remains to be gathered before a detailed knowledge of these is attained. Consequently this chapter concentrates on the better known flowering plants, though even these have not been comprehensively assessed. Druce's "Flora of Wester Ross" (1929) remains the only account of plants in the west and while Ursula Duncan's recent "Flora of East Ross-shire" (1980) provides excellent detailed information for the east, even that author points out that much information may yet be added.

Ross and Cromarty is a large District which contains a considerable variety of landforms, rock types, soil and climate. This diversity is reflected in the wide range of native plants present. A considerable proportion of the plants which comprise the native Scottish flora are known to occur, and it is likely that further species remain to be added. In addition there are many non-native species which have successfully naturalised.

HISTORY OF VEGETATION

The vegetation of Ross and Cromarty dates from the disappearance of the main ice masses over 13,000 years ago. The land emerging from the ice was colonised initially by lower plants, grasses, heaths and shrubs such as dwarf birch and dwarf willow, which were succeeded on lower, drier areas by woodland (initially birch-dominated), once conditions had stabilised further. By the end of the warm, moist Atlantic period (7500-5000 years ago), extensive pine forest had established with broadleaves such as oak, elm, alder and ash in the more favoured lowland valleys, and many of the Arctic and Alpine species which had once been widespread were now restricted to isolated mountain tops and other cool, exposed areas.

Conditions had become somewhat less favourable by the beginning of the present climatic period. The forests were declining and peat bogs, which had begun to extend during the Atlantic period continued to expand, as they do to the present time. The broad patterns of natural vegetation established at this time (some 2500 years ago) were reconstructed by McVean and Ratcliffe, (1959), who show that the bulk of the District (probably over 60%) was dominated by woodland. This was mainly of birch and pine in the central part of the area, with oak and other broadleaves in the lower valley sides and along the coastal margins, with thick alder and willow on the flood plains of the straths.

The only naturally unwooded areas within the tree line (below 600m; 1970ft) would have been those too mobile, wet, exposed or saline to support trees. Above this were shrubs like willow, dwarf birch and juniper with heaths on summit ridges, screes and exposed spurs.

Into this natural environment man had already appeared over one thousand years earlier, exerting his influence, tiny at first but with increasing effect over time. Native plants were utilised for food, clothing, building materials, medicines and other purposes and gradually new species were introduced to provide requirements which the native flora was unable to supply. Removal of trees for a variety of purposes and the gradual reclamation of land for agriculture soon made inroads to the native forests and other low ground habitats.

The late 18th and 19th century saw extensive reclamation of marsh, woodland and moor, particularly in the east, while in the central and western parts of the District an extensive sheep and deer grazing regime was introduced with burning as a major management tool greatly accelerating loss of habitats there. This period also saw major importation of non-native plants, particularly trees, which now, at maturity, form a major component of the Ross landscape.

Many of these activities continue through to the present, while more recent developments include the expansion of commercial forestry, and the construction of hydro electricity schemes, affecting numerous lochs and rivers in Mid-Ross and dramatically changing the plants within them as a result of diversion of water or great fluctuations in levels.

As a result of these centuries of change native woodland today comprises less than 3% of its original cover, while much of the moor which today covers most low ground in western central areas is an artificial, impoverished environment. Many of the original plant communities now survive only in pockets in marginal areas like remote glens, gorges, cliffs, islands or high ground. Plants in these communities have also been affected.

Casualties include the most famous Ross plant, the Alpine butterwort *(Pinguicula alpina)*, recorded in Britain only from one small area on the Black Isle. First discovered in 1831, within 50 years it was under severe pressure from agricultural reclamation, and by the second decade of the 20th century it was extinct. Many others, particularly those related to woodland, have been greatly reduced in their range and some may have been lost altogether. The beautiful twinflower *(Linnaea borealis)* one of the rarest Scottish pinewood plants, was once known from at least three localities in Easter Ross. One of these, on Brahan estate, was lost to cultivation over a century ago (Aitken, 1888). The other sites seem to have subsequently suffered similar fates and there is now no known site for this plant in Ross.

Ironically, by the late 19th century many species had become sufficiently rare to attract the attention of acquisitive Victorians. Duncan (1980) remarks that the Alpine butterwort may have been helped to extinction by the numbers of specimens collected, while Aitken (1888) records that at Invergordon, the last plants of the rare and attractive purple oxytropis *(Oxytropis halleri)* were seen being dug up by a man with a trowel. The same observer also notes that the decorative holly fern *(Polystichum lonchitis)* had been eradicated from the Raven Rock near Achterneed by summer visitors from Strathpeffer.

While many native plants were greatly reduced in their range, others nevertheless benefited, particularly heath species, while adaptive species like nettle *(Urtica dioica)* and couch grass *(Agropyron repens)* probably extended their range considerably. With the advent of modern herbicides and changes in agricultural practices however, many have now become rare, especially 'weeds' of arable ground and crops, like corn cockle *(Agrostemma githago)*.

Habitats and their plants

WOODLAND

The woods of Ross are described in detail in chapter 5. However, since they contain a high proportion of the plants of the District, a brief description is given here.

The majority of surviving native woods dominated by birch and rowan are on relatively acid soils, and have a restricted range of plants. Bracken *(Pteridium aquilinum)* and grasses like creeping soft-grass *(Holcus mollis)* are dominant, while in the moist western woods, mosses and lichens are abundant and the tiny, moss-like filmy fern

(Hymenophyllum wilsonii) is occasionally present on tree trunks and rocks.

Oak with a hazel understorey is found on richer soils and lower ground, particularly in the west. Ash is only present on the richest alluvial soils, becoming dominant on a small fragment of limestone at Rassal. These woods carry a diverse flora, and spring in particular can be a colourful scene with the ground a mass of wood anemone *(Anemone nemorosa)*, bluebell *(Endymion non-scriptus)*, primrose *(Primula vulgaris)* and lesser celandine *(Ranunculus ficaria)*.

Pinewoods are very fragmented. Many have open canopy, are heavily grazed and many of the characteristic plants are now scarce or absent. Most have a ground flora of heather *(Calluna vulgaris)*, with blaeberry *(Vaccinium myrtillus)* and cowberry *(V. vitis-idaea)*. Moss covers much of the ground surface and occasionally the white orchid, creeping lady's-tresses *(Goodyera repens)* is found among this. Juniper is a common understorey plant in the east but in the west is virtually restricted to islands, crags and gorges.

Probably the richest woodlands are in gorges and ravines exemplified by the chasm of Corrieshalloch (Plate 7) in the west and the Ethie ravine in the east. In these, oak, ash and elm are dominant and there is a good understorey of hazel, goat willow and bird cherry as well as uncommon shrubs like guelder rose *(Viburnum opulus)*. These dark, moist, often inaccessible areas are the ideal habitat in which to find a range of mosses, lichens and ferns, such as the elusive hart's tongue *(Asplenium scolopendrium)* and the hard shield *(Polystichum aculeatum)*. Indeed Corrieshalloch has a distinct flavour of rain forest. Grasses include the stately wood millet *(Milium effusum)* and some ravines, especially in the west, have good colonies of the mountain melick *(Melica nutans)* with its delicate nodding flower spikes.

Few woodland plants in Ross and Cromarty are nationally rare. Ironically one of the most threatened British plants, the pinewood rarity one-flowered wintergreen *(Moneses uniflora)*, survives in the District only in one known site near Strathpeffer, in an area from which tree cover was cleared decades ago. Species uncommon in Britain, but with good populations in Ross, include the easily overlooked coral-root orchid *(Corallorhiza trifida)* in damp birch woods, and in inaccessible ravines wood fescue grass *(Festuca altissima)*. A further group of interest consists of those which are at or near the northern end of their range, like toothwort *(Lathraea squamaria)*, near Dingwall; dog's mercury *(Mercurialis perennis)* by Loch Maree and near Evanton; and bird's nest orchid *(Neottia nidus-avis)* and herb paris *(Paris quadrifolia)* on the Black Isle.

MOUNTAINS

Ross and Cromarty has a considerable number of fine high mountains with much ground above 900 m (2950 ft) and a host of well known summits like Beinn Dearg, Ben Wyvis (Plate 38), Beinn Eighe and An Teallach (Plate 6). The majority of these mountains have nutrient-poor rocks. The best soils and associated plants are found where moist, hornblendic bands occur and on the small areas of Cambrian limestones and fucoid beds. The western mountains are moist and oceanic and, as a result of severe glaciation have much bare rock, while in the drier east the smooth slopes of mountains like Ben Wyvis are almost wholly vegetated.

The lower slopes of all the hills are dominantly peat-covered though in the west, often bare and littered with countless boulders. Here, plants like bog whortleberry *(Vaccinium uliginosum)*, Alpine bearberry *(Arctous alpina)* and dwarf birch *(Betula nana)* are found, the latter absent from the extreme west. Others include the lovely white-flowered dwarf cornel *(Cornus suecicum)* and red berried cloudberry *(Rubus chamaemorus)*.

Upper slopes, especially exposed spurs, tend to have much bare, stony ground in which typical species are mountain everlasting *(Antennaria dioica)*, the trailing mountain azalea *(Loisleuria procumbens)* and tiny dwarf willow *(Salix herbacea)*, while dwarf juniper *(Juniperis nana)* can be abundant in absence of burning. In the east, such spurs often have carpets of wind-clipped heather with much moss and lichen. Summit areas, particularly in the more westerly hills, have much bare ground, the home of 'cushion' plants like mossy cyphel *(Cherleria sedoides)* thrift *(Armeria maritima)* and moss campion *(Silene acaulis)*. Other characteristic species include three-leaved rush *(Juncus trifidus)* and the woolly hair-moss *(Rhacomitrium lanuginosum)*. In the eastern mountains, particularly on Ben Wyvis, large areas of summit are covered with this moss, forming a luxurious carpet along with stiff sedge *(Carex bigelowii)*.

Snow bed vegetation in upper corries is best seen in the central mountains like the Fannichs. Areas from which snow clears early are dominated by grasses, particularly mat grass *(Nardus stricta)* and tufted hair-grass *(Deschampsia cespitosa)*, while Alpine lady's mantle *(Alchemilla alpina)* is common and Sibbaldia *(Sibbaldia procumbens)* locally present. Near springs and runnels, starry saxifrage *(Saxifraga stellaris)* and Alpine willow herb *(Epilobium anagallidifolium)* may be encountered, often growing amid colourful moss mats. The longest-lasting snow beds do not disappear till the end of June; mosses and liverworts are the major constituents of these.

Rock faces and ledges are the best mountain areas to find a wide range of plants, particularly on rich, moist, friable rocks. These areas, largely ungrazed, can have a superb admixture of tall herbs and ferns and it is difficult to do justice to the range present. Typical species include globe-flower *(Trollius europaeus),* roseroot *(Sedum rosea)* and Alpine sorrel *(Oxyria digyna)* whose yellow flowers mingle with the white Alpine scurvy grass *(Cochlearia alpina)* and the purples of melancholy thistle *(Cirsium heterophyllum)* and Alpine sawwort *(Saussurea alpina).* Along with these are luxurious fern clumps, including Alpine lady fern *(Athyrium alpestre).* Smaller ledges may support less conspicuous but equally attractive plants like Alpine and Arctic mouse-eared chickweed *(Cerastium alpinum, C. arcticum).*

On lime-rich rocks, holly fern *(Polystichum lonchitis)* may be abundant along with one of the most attractive British plants, mountain avens, *(Dryas octopetala).* Screes have their own range of species like the aptly named parsley fern *(Cryptogramma crispa),* which has a western distribution.

Some of the rarest British plants are found in these mountains, most of these being remnants of a once widespread Arctic-Alpine flora. Many are known from only a few localities, while others are present on several mountains but nowhere occur in abundance. The list is extensive and includes the small Norwegian mugwort *(Artemisia norvegica)* which is found only on two summits, the curved wood-rush *(Luzula arcuata),* present on a few summits, mainly in the Torridon area and the rock whitlow grass *(Draba norvegica)* which occurs in the central massifs.

Rock and ledge rarities include the Norwegian cudweed *(Gnaphalium norvegicum)* which has almost half of its locations in Ross, the grass *(Poa glauca)* and the black sedge *(Carex atrata)* which is found on the higher central peaks. The Alpine saxifrage *(Saxifraga nivalis)* occurs sparsely on wet rocks in the central mountains while the even rarer brook saxifrage *(S. rivularis)* has a more western distribution, occurring on peaks like Beinn Eighe. The tufted saxifrage *(S. cespitosa)* is known from only three western summits. This is one of the rarest British plants and is given special protection by law.

High springs and flushes have notable species like the russet sedge *(Carex saxatilis)* and the sheathed sedge *(C. vaginata)* which have a distinct central distribution. The Alpine foxtail grass *(Alopecurus alpinus)* is recorded in Ross only on Ben Wyvis. Since many of these montane plants are inconspicuous and often occur in inaccessible places, it may be expected that additional sites or even species may be added.

MOORLAND AND PEAT BOG

Much of the surface of the District is covered by peat. In the west and central areas where rainfall is high and water tables are close to the surface, blanket bog has developed over much of the terrain, including areas once forested. This 'cold desert' is dominated by purple moor-grass *(Molinia caerulea)*, with heather *(Calluna vulgaris)*, cotton grasses *(Eriophorum vaginatum, E. angustifolium)* and deer grass *(Trichophorum cespitosum)*. *Sphagnum* mosses are abundant and the insectivorous sundews *(Drosera rotundifolia, D anglica)* and butterwort *(Pinguicula vulgaris)* are common.

Areas of bog which are enriched by water flow from springs or flushes are dominated by bog myrtle *(Myrica gale)* with bog asphodel *(Narthecium ossifragum)*, white beak-sedge *(Rhynchospora alba)* and few-flowered sedge *(Carex pauciflora)*. In richer areas the black bog-rush *(Schoenus nigricans)* is common, along with other indicators of higher nutrient status like broad-leaved cotton grass *(Eriophorum latifolium)*, and lesser clubmoss *(Selaginella selaginoides)* with its small yellow spikes. One of the tiniest and loveliest of Ross plants, the lilac-flowered pale butterwort *(Pinguicula lusitanica)* may be found scattered in these areas.

Swamp areas are dominated by *Sphagnum* mosses of several species bordered by bottle sedge *(Carex rostrata)* or the tall, slender sedge *(C. lasiocarpa)*. Bare areas of floating peat have tufts of bog sedge *(C. limosa)*, while any pools present will have the insectivorous bladderworts *Utricularia minor, U. intermedia)* along with bog bean *(Menyanthes trifoliata)*.

In the east heather and other dwarf shrubs are more abundant on drier, thinner peats. Petty whin *(Genista anglica)* is typically present along with bearberry *(Arctostaphylos uva-ursi)*. Other associates include tormentil *(Potentilla erecta)* and the small, blue-flowered, heath milkwort *(Polygala serpyllifolia)*. This type of community occurs only on very steep, often unstable slopes in the west, where petty whin is absent but the uncommon pyramidal bugle *(Ajuga pyramidalis)* may be found. Bog survives in the east only in deep glacial hollows. These areas have much floating sedge swamp, bog bean and marsh cinquefoil *(Potentilla palustris)*, which give way quickly to trees on drier ground.

What was the rarest plant in this habitat, the Alpine butterwort *(Pinguicula alpina)* is now extinct, but nationally rare species of today include the brown beak-sedge *(Rhynchospora fusca)* in the vicinity of Loch Maree, and the tiny bog orchid *(Hammarbya paludosa)*, a plant uncommon in Britain and considered endangered in Europe as a result of habitat loss.

LOWLAND GRASSLAND AND MEADOW

This habitat is much influenced by past human activity and has in many areas been lost to agriculture and forestry. Consequently the distribution of characteristic plants is very fragmented and often occurs only in small pockets. Herb-rich grassland is maintained by grazing and was often cultivated or cut for hay in the past. The main surviving areas are near crofting townships in the west, on richer coastal rocks away from extreme maritime influence and by lime-rich springs in the east. These areas have a varied flora which includes many grasses and herbs like hay rattle *(Rhinanthus minor)* and thyme *(Thymus drucei)*. Legumes are abundant, especially red and white clovers *(Trifolium pratense, T. repens)* and bird's foot trefoil *(Lotus corniculatus)*. Wetter areas are rich in sedges and have attractive herbs like the pink-flowered ragged robin *(Lychnis flos-cuculi)*, the yellow globeflower *(Trollius europaeus)* and white Grass of Parnassus *(Parnassia palustris)*. Summer presents a colourful scene in these areas enhanced by a range of orchids from the white greater butterfly *(Platanthera chlorantha)* to the deeply coloured Northern fen orchid *(Dactylorhiza purpurella)*.

In coastal areas, particularly on the rich sandstones of Easter Ross these grasslands include a further range of herbs such as the attractive bloody cranesbill *(Geranium sanguineum)*, rock rose *(Helianthemum chamaecistus)*, and purple milk-vetch *(Astragalus danicus)*. Flood plain grassland occurs by the margins of streams and rivers and is related to seasonal flooding. These are relatively species-poor and are dominated by sedges and tall grasses like tufted hair-grass *(Deschampsia cespitosa)*. Herbs include meadow sweet *(Filipendula ulmaria)* and angelica *(Angelica sylvestris)*.

Nationally rare plants of grassland include the purple oxytropis *(Oxytropis halleri)* which occurs in coastal grassland in Easter Ross. One of the rarest species in Britain today, the greater yellow-rattle *(Rhinanthus serotinus)* was once present in Ross but has not been recorded for over 50 years. It is almost certainly now extinct in this District. Uncommon plants include the large, trailing, bitter vetch *(Vicia orobus)*, present in a few localities in the west and wild licorice *(Astragalus glycyphyllos)* a very local species on the East coast.

LOCHS AND RIVERS

There is an enormous number and variety of water bodies in the District, from coastal edge to an altitude of over 700 m (2296 ft). Plants in these reflect nutrient status, the type of substrate (mud, sand, rock) the local climate (particularly exposure), stability of water levels and water

1. Ben Alligin, reflected in Loch Torridon   *(L. MacNally)*
2. Liathach, towering over Glen Torridon   *(L. MacNally)*

3. Loch Maree and Slioch   *(J. Campbell)*

4. Stack Polly and Cul Beg   *(J. Campbell)*

5. Ardessie Falls, Dundonnell   *(J. Campbell)*

6. Gruinard Bay and An Teallach   *(J. Campbell)*

7. Falls of Measach and Corrieshalloch Gorge, Loch Broom
                                              (J. Campbell)

8. Terraces cut in sand and gravel deposits at Achnasheen
(J. Campbell)

9. Munlochy Bay, showing a typical east coast salting   *(J. Smith)*

depth and clarity. In general, the higher the nutrient status, the richer and more varied the plants present. Gently shelving muddy shores also tend to have more plant life, and lochs or rivers with a variety of shore types have the widest range of vegetation. Exposure, low temperature, poor water clarity and extreme depth are all limiting to most plants as are great fluctuations in levels, a characteristic of many west coast streams.

The bulk of lochs in Ross are poor in nutrients, their catchments lying dominantly on hard, acid rocks which themselves are usually peat-covered. Some are exceptionally large and deep; for example, Loch Maree is 19 km (12 miles) long and reaches a depth of over 100 m (328 ft). These large lochs tend to be rather exposed and for their size are relatively poor in plants, which are concentrated largely in sheltered bays. Smaller lochs are often richer and more sheltered and many carry better plant cover. In these, stony and sandy shores contain plants like shoreweed *(Littorella uniflora)*, quillwort *(Isoetes lacustris)*, and often in slightly deeper water, the water lobelia *(Lobelia dortmanna)*, which raises its attractive lilac flowers above the surface on long slender stems. Areas of organic mud may have stands of bottle sedge *(Carex rostrata)* and in the west, scattered reeds *(Phragmites australis)* or bulrush *(Schoenoplectus lacustris)*, while species of open water include the white water lily *(Nymphaea alba)* which in flower can transform even the most dour peaty lochan. Others of deep water include the submerged long-stalked pondweed *(Potamogeton praelongus)*, which can sometimes be seen washed up on the shore, and the floating pondweed *(P. natans)*, a handsome plant with its burnished bronze leaves, and in many lochans the only visible sign of aquatic plant life.

Peaty lochs carry a further range of plants like bog bean *(Menyanthes trifoliata)*, with bog pondweed *(Potamogeton polygonifolius)* abundant. The grass-like leaves and spiky flower heads of the floating bur-reed *(Sparganium angustifolium)* are characteristic, and closer examination will often reveal the presence of one of the insectivorous bladderworts *(Utricularia Sp.)*. These poorer lochs have few uncommon or rare species. The marsh clubmoss *(Lycopodium inundatum)* is a nationally rare plant which is found on peaty shores in the Loch Maree area, while in a few peaty lochans of higher nutrient status in the west, robust stands of the uncommon fen sedge *(Cladium mariscus)* may be found. One other noteworthy feature in the west is the presence of small islands where in the absence of grazing or burning, lush herb and shrub cover has survived, in which the now uncommon royal fern *(Osmunda regalis)* is often abundant. These areas are a stark contrast to the impoverished flora of the man-made moors bordering the lochs.

The lochs of lowland Easter Ross, like Loch Ussie and Loch Eye, though very few in number are nutrient-rich, sheltered and have a good mix of substrates. Fringe vegetations in these is lush and can include thick beds of bulrush *(Schoenoplectus lacustris)* and the bottle and bladder sedges *(Carex rostrata, C. vesicaria)*. Bur-reed *(Sparganium erectum)*, water mint *(Mentha aquatica)* and amphibious bistort *(Polygonum amphibium)* are others typically present. Beyond this fringe, moist woodland is usually found, which adds to the diversity and appearance of these areas. Aquatic plants are very diverse and include stonewort *(Chara Sp.)* water milfoil *(Myriophyllum Sp.)* and many pondweeds *(Potamogeton Sp.)*. Indeed Loch Eye has more pondweed species than almost any other loch in Britain.

Plants of note include the dull but rare Marshall's rush *(Juncus nodulosus)* which occurs in only two sites in Britain, one of which is Loch Ussie, the Shetland pondweed *(Potamogeton rutilus)* and the least yellow water lily *(Nuphar pumila)*. Species more common in the south of Britain but very rare in the Highlands include the attractive greater spearwort *(Ranunculus lingua)*.

Few Ross rivers and burns support more than a restricted range of plants because most are spate streams with great fluctuation in level, and few muddy, slow-flowing sections. In the east, the better vegetated streams present are exemplified by the mouth of the Conon where islands and creeks support a wide and interesting range of plants. Of special note is the water plantain *(Alisma plantago-aquatica)* which is near the northern end of its range in Easter Ross.

THE COAST

Coastal plants are able to withstand saline, exposed and often unstable conditions. Many are fleshy-leaved to reduce desiccation, while others have large roots or a trailing growth form which enables them to trap or grow through sand or mud. The Ross coast has few large cliff areas. In the west, rocks abutting on the shore are mainly nutrient-poor in contrast to the Old Red Sandstone rocks which dominate the east. Cliff ledges, especially where ungrazed, include the tall daisy-like scentless mayweed *(Tripleurospermum maritimum)*, scurvy grass *(Cochlearia officinalis)*, named from its use as a source of vitamin C in days before citrus fruits became commonly available, the attractive thrift or sea pink *(Armeria maritima)* and sea campion *(Silene marinum)*. Rock crevices have sea spleenwort fern *(Asplenium marinum)*, while on poorer rocks many heath plants like crowberry *(Empetrum nigrum)* join the maritime species to form an interesting mosaic. Sheltered cliff areas have scrub in which willow, juniper and rose species are most abundant, though on the east coast hawthorn, blackthorn, and elder are additional species.

Areas of sand dune and shingle tend to be small. There is only one major complex, at the Morrich More, near Tain. Dunes are an exposed, unstable environment, in which resilient Marram grass *(Ammophila arenaria)* is abundant. In the east, the grasses sea lyme *(Elymus arenaria)* and sand couch *(Agropyron junceiforme)* are major constituents, though these are much less common in the west. More stable dune grassland is normally rich in herbs, many of which are legumes like clovers and vetches, with the yellow bird's foot trefoil *(Lotus corniculatus)* common. Creeping willow *(Salix repens)* is plentiful in damper areas. Others include trailing species like the purple flowered thyme *(Thymus drucei)* and the creeping sand sedge *(Carex arenaria)*.

Shingle beach areas have annual plants like orache *(Atriplex Sp.)* of which there are several species, but the most decorative, the frosted orache *(A. laciniata)* is only found in the east. Others include the beautiful oyster plant *(Mertensia maritima)* whose trailing stems, fleshy blue-green leaves and blue flowers are an unexpected contrast to the barren sand and shingle on which it grows. This uncommon and lovely plant seems, unfortunately, to be on the decline.

Rarities in this habitat include the Baltic rush *(Juncus balticus)* quite abundant in some eastern dune slacks and the curved sedge *(Carex maritima)* which occurs near Tain.

Salt Marsh occurs mainly as small fragments at the head of bays and exceptionally where sea sprays affects cliffs. The best examples in the west are in bays like Achnahaird and Kishorn while in the east, the Inver Bay area of the Morrich More has the most extensive saltings in the District. Plants in these areas are often covered at high tide and comprise species able to withstand this. Dominants include salt marsh grass *(Puccinellia maritima)* and the ubiquitous red fescue *(Festuca rubra)* which in this habitat often has handsome blue-grey leaves. The mud rush *(Juncus gerardii)* is abundant along with fleshy leaved herbs like sea plantain *(Plantago maritima)* and sea arrowgrass *(Triglochin maritima)*, while colour is added by the white flowered scurvy grass *(Cochlearia maritima)* and the pink sea milkwort *(Glaux maritima)* and sea spurreys *(Spergularia Sp.)*. Sea aster *(Aster tripolium)* is perhaps the most decorative of these, especially where ungrazed. Locally, beds of sea club-rush *(Scirpus maritimus)*, tall reeds *(Phragmites australis)* and in the east, the greater reedmace *(Typha latifolia)* add diversity of structure, while in the west, the saltings are often backed by colourful stands of yellow flag iris *(Iris pseudacorus)*.

Perhaps the most specialised plants occur in intertidal areas, where they have to withstand immersion at high water followed by desiccation at low tide. Here, the aptly-named eel grasses *(Zostera angustifolia, Z. noltii)* are abundant particularly in the east. In fact, the Cromarty Firth supports the largest concentration of these in Britain. Other species include beaked tassleweed *(Ruppia maritima),* and the glasswort *(Salicornia Sp).* whose fleshy leaves protrude from the mud like a forest of fingers. In summer, large areas of green algae like *Entermorpha sp* build up on the mud of sheltered estuaries while rocky shores are also dominated by algae, particularly seaweeds.

Non-native Plants

Many of the plants now found wild in Ross and Cromarty are not native to this area but have been introduced by human actions, some in recent times, others centuries ago. Many are a legacy of a useful or decorative past while others are unwelcome but often vigorous and adaptive species which have unwittingly or unavoidably been spread by man as he modified the land to his requirements. The plants which have had the greatest impact on the Ross landscape are undoubtedly trees and shrubs which are described in detail in chapter 5; there are many others less apparent than these but equally interesting.

Early introductions were associated with agriculture, and include cereal grasses and associated cornfield 'weeds' such as corn spurrey *(Spergula arvensis),* and corn marigold *(Chrysanthemum segetum).* Some of the earliest introductions have disappeared, though new agricultural plants continue to be imported and become established. Plants introduced as pot herbs include bishopweed *(Aegopodium podagraria)* and sweet cicely *(Myrrhis odorata).* Others had medicinal use like the poisonous deadly nightshade *(Atropa belladonna)* and henbane *(Hyoscyamus niger),* with alkanet *(Pentaglottis sempervirens)* and comfrey *(Symphytium officinale)* less dangerous legacies.

Species with a decorative function include the familiar snowdrop *(Galanthus nivalis)* which survives in areas like the Black Isle in places from which few remains of the original settlement now survive. Montbretia *(Crocosmia crocosmiflora)* is a similar successful garden escape. Others include butterbur *(Petasites sp.)* and the tall, iris-like sweet flag *(Acorus calamus).*

Other species of note include the American cord grasses *(Spartina sp.)* introduced in the last 50 years to the Cromarty Firth to help reclaim mud flats. These grasses have run rampant over whole estuaries in southern Britain, almost totally displacing all native plants but luckily the stands in the Cromarty Firth remain small and relatively stable.

Some plants have spread rapidly, like the attractive yellow monkey flower *(Mimulus guttatus)* and its close cousin, the red spotted blood-drop emlets *(M. luteus)* which were introduced to Britain from North America and Chile respectively in the first two decades of the 19th century. These spread quickly and are now quite common in Ross by coastal stream banks and are still extending their range today. Perhaps currently the most adaptive introduction is giant hogweed *(Heracleum mantegazzianum)*, a decorative plant which has spread over large areas of Grampian Region and is common in the vicinity of Inverness. Until recently it was spreading in parts of the Black Isle and had been recorded in W. Ross. This is a good example of an unwanted introduction since contact with the plant can produce nasty skin irritations in humans and for this reason Local Authorities have quite rightly begun to attempt its eradication.

The *Rhododendron ponticum* is another adaptive plant, introduced to decorate gardens and policies, which has spread widely and now dominates many hectares of ground especially in such areas as Torridon, Glen Carron and Upper Loch Broom. The dense shade and litter produced by these plants quickly displaces native species and in some areas the flora of native oak and pinewoods has suffered damage as a result.

The overwhelming majority of introductions have come from a source in South Britain or Europe. Consequently they have fared most successfully in Easter Ross where soil and climate is closer to their areas of origin. Many are found near the policies of older family seats where they were first introduced as garden plants. Road and railway lines have been major dispersal routes for many, while others have spread along the sea shore, across lochs or along river courses. Of particular interest in this context are the islands at the mouth of the River Conon which are a repository for many introductions washed downstream from the policies of Brahan Castle (the seat of the Seaforths), Conan House and from the Fairburn estate. Recent garden escapes from the growing villages of Maryburgh and Conon Bridge continue to provide further variety.

Chapter three

ANIMAL LIFE
Lea MacNally

The District of Ross-shire is exceptionally varied in habitat and, consequently, exceptionally rich in wildlife. It is only possible in the space available to give thumbnail sketches of this wealth of wildlife to act as some guide to readers.

RED DEER

Red deer are common throughout Ross-shire, more particularly in the relatively treeless mountainous areas of the north and west of the District. They are our largest surviving land animal in Britain and since most of them live on the bare hill nowadays, they are perhaps the one animal species one can guarantee to see, given the ability to look for them in their mountain fastness. In winter, indeed, it is not even necessary to climb high into the hills since, under stress of inclement weather, red deer may come very low into the glens and the stags (Plate 17), in particular may be seen quite near the roadsides.

Life for red deer begins in June with the birth of the calves to the hinds after a gestation period of eight months. Red deer hinds in the Highlands rarely give birth to a calf until they are three years old; the calves will weigh 6.4 to 6.8 kg (14 to 15lb) at birth and within half an hour of being born they will have struggled to their feet and, still wobbly-legged, be having their first feed of the mother's milk. They grow quickly and ten days after birth will be able to follow the hind wherever she goes. While the hinds are nurturing their growing calves the stags will be growing their new antlers, to replace the old ones, cast in late March. By mid-July the new set of antlers will be fully grown, but still covered in velvet and it will be mid-August before the new set is fully clear of this velvet and the stag is 'in hard antler'. By late September the hills of the red deer country find a voice of their own in the nerve-tingling roaring of the stags at the onset of the rut, seeking hinds from which, for the major part of the year they live apart. The rut, or mating time, has a pageantry all its own, set in the tremendous background of rocky hill and coire, tinted in vivid autumn colours and alive with the voices and presence of stags roaring, roaming and rutting in ceaseless activity. A fight between two such stags, in contention for hinds, is a thrilling spectacle then and ample reward for effort in reaching the red deer ground.

Winter brings the red deer lower, both for the better grazing available then on the lower hill, and for shelter from the type of winter weather more severe on the higher slopes. A herd of red deer, of either sex, seen against a background of snow, on a frosty, sunny day, is a magnificent sight and one only to be seen in the Highlands.

Since red deer when adult have no predators of any significance (fox and eagle will occasionally kill a red deer calf if opportunity offers) it falls to man to control the annual increase to the herds by exacting a levy on the deer numbers with his rifle. This deerstalking is very necessary for the well-being of the deer in balancing their numbers to the hill grazing available to them. A levy of 1/6th of the adult stock, in each sex, is generally accepted as adequate to keep deer stocks at a level. The stags are stalked in autumn, the hinds in the winter and hill walkers, at the autumn stalking time in particular, should liaise with estates as to where it is safe to walk without disrupting this necessary control work or of incurring the risk of a bullet whizzing by their ears.

ROE DEER

Roe deer are plentiful in Ross-shire but, in contrast to red deer, are more numerous in the wooded and cultivated areas of the District. Their preferred habitat is mixed species woodland, on the fringes of cultivated land, and in this Easter Ross qualifies admirably. The environment of the young trees stage of commercial afforestation affords an alternative habitat and the increase of this throughout the Highlands has led to an increase in roe deer numbers. Roe are unquestionably the daintiest of our native deer, true sprites of the woodland. They are much smaller than red deer of course standing only about 0.7 m (30 in) at the shoulder, though their long slender legs tend to make them look taller. They are not herd animals, as red deer are, though, in winter, an area of good shelter and feeding may have loosely-knit groups of two or more families each composed of buck, doe and their young. These young are born in late May and in June in the Highlands and, tiny dappled creatures of infinite appeal, weigh 1.8 to 2.3 kg (4 to 5 lb) at birth. Like red deer calves, the fawns of the roe deer are quickly on their feet after birth, seeking their first feed, and within ten days will follow the doe wherever she goes. Like red deer the males, known as bucks, cast and regrow their antlers, but at a different time of year. A mature roe buck will lose his 6-point antlers about the end of November and have his new set fully formed and free of velvet by the end of the following April. The roe mating time is different from that of red deer, mid-July to mid-August, and though a buck may mate with more then one adjacent doe at this time he is not as polygamous as the red deer stag. Roe are more nocturnal than red deer and the best time to see these attractive little woodland deer is around sunrise and sunset.

SIKA DEER

Sika deer are not indigenous to Britain, as are our red and roe deer, but are an introduced species. The first introduction into the District of these deer was in 1889, at Achanalt, near Garve. They were living in enclosed conditions until the 1914-18 war when feeding stringences culminated in the release of the Japanese sika deer to the hill, where these hardy, smallish deer adapted well and ultimately colonised adjacent wooded areas. In this area, between Loch Rosque and Garve, Japanese sika deer are probably at their greatest concentration in Ross-shire. They are also present however in Rhidorroch near Ullapool, and in Alladale, near Ardgay.

In size Japanese sika deer are between that of red deer and roe and are of noticeably compact, chunky build. Their summer coat is an attractive rich chestnut red profusely dappled with white, and, in complete contrast, their winter coat is one of almost jet black in the case of the stags, and a very dark brown in the hinds. The prominent white rump patch can be expanded at will to act as a danger signal as the alerted deer bounds away in alarm. The antlers of the stags are superficially similar to those of red deer but narrower in span and seldom exceed 8 points while their time of casting and regrowing these antlers, and their rutting time, also approximates to that of red deer. Their social habits however and their preferred habitat approximate more to roe deer. Their calves are also generally born in June, probably the best month for young deer to be born in the Highlands. The rutting cry of the stag is an eerie, thrice-repeated, high-pitched screaming whistle, while the alarm call is a single high-pitched whistle.

WILD GOAT

Wild goat herds, or more properly feral goat herds, are to be found in areas of West Ross-shire mainly, notably the Dundonnel area; on the mountain of Slioch above the shores of Loch Maree and in the Diabaig area adjacent to Loch Torridon. These scattered herds are all descended from one-time domestic stock kept by the Highlanders for the milk the nannies produced and, it is sometimes said, for their ability to eat out the high green ledges in rocky cliffs and so prevent sheep from straying into such tempting but dangerous grazing areas and becoming trapped there. The prevailing colour of the long, shaggy coat of our wild goats is either a dark, grizzled one, or one of black and white, with occasional cinnamon coloured ones. The billies are capable of growing quite spectacular horns (which increase in size with age) of two types, one which curves up and backwards, and the other, up and outwards. Nannies have much smaller horns. The young, the kids, are born at a notably inhospitable time of the year, in late January or early February, so that in exceptionally bad winters there is heavy mortality. Their summer habitat is on the high hill, but in winter, like red deer, they come much lower in the glens and may readily be seen near the roadside. These goats which live near the sea habitually eat tangle, a seaweed which is exposed only at low tide. The billy goats have an extremely pungent odour about their shaggy coats and one can smell their way-going through long heather hours after they have passed by. They are very keen-sighted, even more so than red deer.

Fox

The fox (Plate 16) is common throughout Ross-shire, some would say too common, no matter whether the terrain is bleak and mountainous or wooded and fertile. It is as handsome an animal as any we have in Britain yet a living epitome of the saying that 'handsome is as handsome does'. Probably no animal is more reviled in the Highlands, whether the land use is sheep-farming, crofting, deer forest or grouse moor. Nor is this reputation altogether undeserved for the fact is that this versatile, beautiful and supremely vital animal is quite capable of killing lamb, deer calf or roe deer fawn and of lifting a hen grouse from off her clutch of eggs. It is, indeed, a predator supreme and exceedingly adaptable in surviving where every man's hand has been against it for, literally, centuries. Nearly 2,000 foxes are killed annually in the Highland counties.

Foxes mate in late January-early February and at this time one may hear, in late evening or early morning, the staccato, sharp triple bark of the dog fox or the eerie skirl of the vixen. Cubs are usually born in late March or early April, five being a normal litter, though as few as one or as many as fourteen have been recorded. Dog and vixen are extremely good parents with the dog fox doing the majority of the hunting for food while the cubs are very young. Highland foxes often utilise those huge cairns of shattered rock, so common in the hills, for their dens, in contrast to the sandholes of the lower ground. Fox cubs will be old enough and strong enough to leave the parental care by August and at that time the entire fox family will split up and go their individual ways. Do not expect to see much of the fox: wariness, coupled with ultra-keen senses, ensures that the fox, more often, is aware of you first and has no desire to be seen, since its only predator, besides the golden eagle, is man.

BADGER

The badger (Plate 13) is present throughout Ross-shire with the exception of some of the more sterile and rocky mountainous areas such as Torridon. Its preferred habitat is deciduous woodland which is adjacent to pasture and arable and so again Easter Ross qualifies well. It is, however, found surprisingly far out in some hill glens where these are of green ground rather than heather and rock. The species is probably in a happier situation nowadays in the Highlands than formerly with a better understanding of its inoffensive habits and of course it is now a protected animal. Since it is of entirely nocturnal habit one might feel that it is a difficult animal to see. This is only true in a limited sense for, if one knows of an inhabited badger sett and is prepared to endure a certain amount of discomfort, it is possible to see the inhabitants, as they emerge in the dusk, especially in summer, by waiting out, in a position where one cannot be seen or scented. It is a tremendous thrill to see that white-striped, pointed snout materialise at the mouth of a deep shadowed hole, even if all one's joints are protesting after a long cramped wait.

The badger is omnivorous in its diet and indeed, perhaps surprising for such a large animal, a good proportion of its diet is composed of earthworms of which it is a more skilful finder than any human angler. In the Highlands it also eats carrion, more particularly in winter and early spring, at which period it is less active than in the warmer months. It does not hibernate however in winter. A tidy animal, the bedding it uses in its sett is renewed periodically and traces of this old and new bedding, of dead bracken and mollinia grass, will denote an occupied sett.

WILDCAT

One of our most interesting wild animals, a relic one might feel of a much more primitive era, the wildcat, is thinly distributed throughout Ross-shire though again absent, except perhaps as a transient, in some of the more barren rocky areas. It has an undeserved reputation for mindless ferocity, an illustration of the fact that a reputation is more easily acquired than lost. Its preferred habitat is marginal ground, wooded hill glens for instance, and it is seldom found above 457 metres (1,500 ft).

The wildcat's prey species consists of voles, mice, rats, rabbits and as opportunity offers, fledgeling or newly-fledged birds. Shrews it will kill as well but usually leaves them uneaten. Under stress of winter hunger a wildcat will occasionally raid a henhouse should this be inefficiently secured against such incursions, which, of course, brings down more invective on its head. Undoubtedly the wildcat was badly affected in the early years of myxomatosis, which decimated the rabbit population, for, like the buzzard in marginal hill areas, it relied heavily on rabbit as prey.

The wildcat, incidentally, is the indigenous cat of Britain and Europe, whereas our domestic cat is an introduced species. I look forward to the day when it is awarded some protection in the place of being almost universally reviled.

A necessarily, very wary species, there are probably more seen, in car headlights, in lonely wooded glens, at night, than in daylight hours. In looks it is a high-legged rangy animal, of tabby colouration, buff-grey, black-striped, with a broad head, and a rather bushy blunt-ended tail, ringed with black and terminating in black.

OTTER

The lengthy western coastline of Ross-shire, deeply invaded by long sea-lochs provides one of the best habitats left in Britain today for the otter (Plate 14). Unpolluted, relatively undisturbed by humans, with plenty of cover on their rocky shores and plenty of food in sea fish and crustaceans these sea lochs can be depended on to hold otters. The freshwater rivers and burns running into these sea lochs, often from sizeable freshwater lochs, afford diversity of habitat when required. Like the badger the otter is now a protected species and it is certainly worthy of this. The keen salmon fisher may not enjoy sharing a salmon river with an otter yet the otter does far less harm to salmon than the commercial greed of man.

A creature of great contrasts, an otter can be exceedingly wary or amazingly blasé of human presence. I watched an otter, in March one year hunting frogs in a muddy ditch which ran into the sea, and, though I was ultimately standing in full view, only some 4.6 metres (15 ft) away, the hunting otter paid no heed to me. It caught two torpid frogs and a 0.61 metre (2 feet) long torpid eel while I watched and after eating these made back for the sea. I have encountered an otter on land also, often crossing from one watershed to another, when this animal, so sleek and sinuously graceful in the water, looks rather buffoon-like.

Breeding can take place at any time in the year and two to three cubs are the normal. Very 'playful' animals, they may be seen at times en famille, enjoying a sliding spree down a steeply sloping, seaweed-slippery tidal rock. Indeed an otter was seen enjoying a game with an Irish setter on the shore of Loch Torridon this year (1983), for all of 15 minutes, a sort of otter versus dog hide-and-seek with no animosity on either side.

PINE MARTEN

Ross-shire has the distinction, arguably true, in such an elusive animal, of saving the pine marten (Plate 11) from extinction as a breeding species in Scotland. The evidence is strong that toward the end of last century the pine marten became extinct in Scotland except in an area of Wester Ross around Loch Maree. In this persecution era of all predators the polecat did become extinct in Scoland; the marten contrived to cling on somehow. From this toehold in Wester Ross the pine marten has now gradually re-colonised much of the Highlands, as good a re-colonisation feat as that of the osprey, if less publicised.

The marten is of the mustelid family, 0.76 to 0.91 m (2½ to 3 ft) in length, weighing 1.36 to 1.81 kg (3 to 3½ lb), dark-chocolate brown in colour but with an exceedingly handsome upper chest and neck colouration varying from lemon to apricot. The frontlet may be marked with dots and patches or streaks of dark brown by which individuals may be recognised. It is as at home in trees, or on near vertical rock faces, as on the ground and must qualify as our most agile predator. To see one race vertically down a conifer trunk, head first, is incredible. almost vertigo-inducing. Elusive and appealing little creatures of the twilight, one seldom sees much of them in full daylight. As omnivorous as the much larger badger, their diet ranges from wild fruits, such as blaeberry and rowanberries, through the eggs and fledgling young of nesting birds, to squirrel and rabbit. Carrion is sometimes taken. I have found appreciable red deer hair in pine marten droppings, and a well-documented habit is that of visiting the birdtables of houses adjacent to woodland. Their preferred habitat is wooded glens, but they are equally at home in long heather and shattered rock. They occasionally frequent unused eyries of eagles as daytime lying-up beds.

STOAT AND WEASEL

Both these mustelids are present and well, if thinly, distributed in Ross-shire. To this day one finds confusion in the general public in incorrectly naming these wee animals, stoats referred to as weasels and vice versa. Identification is easy. The stoat has a longish tail and the terminal end of this is black; the weasel has a mere wisp of a tail and this has no black tip to it. I do not believe that it is generally realised just what a tiny creature a weasel is, a mere morsel of restless energy and fearless, weighing only 0.085 to 0.142 kg (3 to 5 oz), and measuring, including tail, about 0.28 m (11 in) in length with a sinuous, boneless-seeming body hardly as thick as the human thumb. By contrast the stoat will weigh 0.255 kg (9 oz), measure in length, including tail 0.48 m (19 in) and is considerably thicker of body. The colour of each, in summer, is a rusty red, with the underparts of the weasel usually whiter, lacking the yellowish tinge, than the underparts of the stoat. A final diagnostic difference is that the stoat changes its summer red to a coat of white in winter, in which garb it is known as 'ermine'. The black tip of the tail is retained in summer and winter.

Both these mustelids will be scarcer in the more barren high ground of Wester Ross than on the more diverse woodland/arable mixture of Easter Ross, but they do occur sparsely for I have seen weasel and stoat feature as prey at eagles' eyries. This is only logical, for the main prey of both is mice and voles, fledgling birds and rabbit. Both share an insatiable curiosity and quicksilver flowing action and the weasel can, and does, pursue voles down their tunnels. Both do a fair amount of good in the countryside in preying on the rodent population.

RABBIT

It will appear strange to many people that the rabbit is NOT an indigenous wild animal of Britain since it now has a countrywide distribution in which Ross-shire is no exception. The ancestors of our wild rabbits came from the Iberian peninsula in Spain and were probably introduced to Britain, as a food species by the Normans. This must seem like heresy to those of us reared on childhood nursery stories of Peter Rabbit and Benjamin Bunny, but so it is. It was at a very much later date that the rabbit was introduced to the Highlands. In his history of the parish of Gairloch in Wester Ross, the author J. H. Dixon states "The common rabbit was quite unknown in Gairloch parish until about the year 1850 when it was introduced at Letterewe. It did not become general for many years after, but it is now common almost everywhere." The rabbit, then, has had a sojourn in Ross-shire of something over a hundred years. It is of course much more common in Easter Ross than in the mountainous areas of Wester Ross but even there, wherever there is sufficient green ground in the coastal glens, you will find the rabbit. Myxomatosis, introduced in clandestine manner from France to Britain in 1953, decimated the rabbit population throughout the entire country, the Highlands being no exception. Typically the rabbit staged a resurgence and it now appears to be slowly winning against the epidemics of this vile disease which still recurs. Though the rabbit in undue numbers can be a major agricultural pest it is also a valuable 'buffer' food-species for animals such as fox, wildcat and badger, birds, such as eagle and buzzard, and Man.

BROWN HARE

The brown hare is commonly seen on the better arable ground of the District, much of it concentrated in Mid- and Easter Ross. This is 'the mad March hare' of folklore due to its extrovert mating habits in that month. It is a much larger animal than either rabbit or mountain hare weighing an average 3.63 to 3.85 kg (8 to 8½ lb). This hare is a creature of green cultivated ground and has no seasonal change of coat in winter as has the mountain-living blue hare.

BLUE OR MOUNTAIN HARE

The smaller blue or mountain hare (Plate 15) weighs only 2.27 kg (5lb) or so due to an adaption to a much harsher living environment in which food and shelter are harder to come by than in the green ground habitat of the brown hare. In direct contrast to the brown hare the blue hare is distributed throughout the more mountainous country of West and North Ross-shire. Its numbers are fewer than at one time, possibly because it is at least partially dependent on good heathery ground and excessive muirburning, in the interests of hill sheepfarming over nearly a century and a half, has sadly reduced this type of ground in the West Highlands. Since it is a nocturnal species, however, there will generally be more blue hares in an area than is supposed. Certainly more hares turn up dead at the eyries of the golden eagles I study in the Torridon area than I ever see alive on the hill. The blue hare is a relict species of a much colder age, like ptarmigan, and like these birds, assumes a white coat in winter, as a camouflage aid against its main predator, the golden eagle.

RED SQUIRREL

It is confined to areas of mature conifers notably Scots pine. In Ross-shire, therefore, this charming little arboreal animal is much more likely to be seen in the coniferous woodland of Easter Ross and Mid Ross. The Pine marten is a predator on squirrels where both are present and it can overhaul and catch a squirrel in a tree-tops chase.

HEDGEHOG

The hedgehog is widely distributed over the lower ground of Ross-Shire even low in the glens of the North-West though the preferred habit is mixed woodland, scrub and arable mixture. Since it is a nocturnal prowler it can be in an area and remain quite unsuspected. It is a frequent casualty on the glen roads while travelling abroad on its nocturnal rambles its instinctive behaviour of curling up into a tight prickly ball is of little protection against a vehicle. Fox and badger are said to enjoy hedgehog and to be able to kill it even when it has rolled up into a seemingly impenetrable ball. While looking after a slightly injured hedgehog I discovered that if it was tipped over on to its back it would, after a few minutes, begin to uncurl. As soon as it began to uncurl, its vitals were immediately vulnerable to a quick snap from a fox or badger.

MOLE

Again it is widely distributed over the lower glens and particularly their arable or grassland stretches. It probably does little harm to farming interests but is disliked because of the large hummocks of soil which its tunnelling causes. It is preyed on by a wide range of four legged and winged predators but, like the shrews, though killed it may not be eaten. The common buzzard, in arable areas, catches quantities of moles. Fox and cat will kill them and, once only, I found a mole as prey at an eagle's eyrie.

BANK VOLE AND FIELD VOLE

Both species are common throughout Ross-Shire though less so in the mountainous areas. They can often be seen darting across the glen roads at night in the car headlights. The increase of young stage forestry plantations usually results in a consequent increase of voles which in turn attract short-eared owls and hen harriers.

WATER VOLE

This large aquatic vole is localised in its distribution in Ross-shire with the likelihood of finding its presence probably more assured in the west of the District where it favours wet green flats, at times among peat hags at altitudes up to some 366 m (1,200 ft). Its colour in the Highlands is a silky black and its curved incisors are a bright orange in colour. The existence of round holes and tunnels on such flats, and in the banks of drains crossing these, is a sure sign of its presence though the little animal is surprisingly wary and one more often hears the 'plop' as a water vole dives into the black peaty water than one actually sees it. It is an expert swimmer and diver yet this aquatic ability and its wariness does not always save it against predation by the golden eagle. In areas of mountainous country, where both are present, I have regularly found them as prey in an eagle's eyrie, particularly when the eaglets are small. This little animal is not a water rat, it is a vole with its chief diet consisting of grasses.

HOUSE MOUSE

As might be expected this little mouse is widely distributed throughout Ross-shire especially in urban areas. In more rural areas, which include the glens of Wester Ross, it is likely to be replaced by the wood mouse. Both these mice can be distinguished from voles by their pointed, instead of blunt muzzle and their much longer tails. The house mouse is greyer in colour than the wood mouse.

WOOD MOUSE

This rather attractive little mouse is browner in colour than the above and has larger ears, eyes and hind feet. It lives in varied habitats, but generally where tree, or shrub cover exists. It is herbivorous and, in Wester Ross seems to take the place of the house mouse in coming into outhouses, grain stores and even dwelling houses.

BROWN RAT

It is perhaps more common than is realised, tending to live outdoors in rural areas throughout spring, summer and autumn and to come into farm buildings and sometimes dwelling houses in winter. A destructive rodent and a very adaptable one, it is also a good swimmer which gives rise to the popular belief that there is a separate species, a water rat. This is incorrect; we have a water vole and a water shrew but not a water rat.

COMMON AND PYGMY SHREW

Both of these tiny creatures are present in Ross-shire, their long pointed snout and small size distinguishing them from mice and voles. They are of insectivorous rather than herbivorous habit.

WATER SHREW

This aquatic shrew is present in localised areas of Ross-shire and is black in colour rather than the grey of common and pygmy shrew. It favours burns and rocky beaches.

BATS

The common bat of Britain, the pipistrelle, is also common throughout Ross-shire and may be seen readily in the early dusk hawking for insects. It roosts in crevices and crannies in trees and often under the slates of buildings. The common long-eared bat also occurs but less commonly and may be recognised by its long ears.

SNAKES

The adder is our only snake in Scotland and it is widely if thinly distributed throughout Ross-shire but is probably more common on the drier Easter Ross areas. Its bite is poisonous but it is inoffensive towards man unless, very unluckily, you tread on one. If you see an adder, avoid it, if you will, but do not feel obliged to kill it.

The slow worm is much more common but though resembling a snake it is a harmless, legless lizard.

LIZARD AND NEWT

Both of these are widespread throughout Ross-shire but are unobtrusive little creatures which require sharp eyes to detect them.

FROG AND TOAD

Both are widespread, and readily seen throughout the District. Toads are of more lethargic habit than frogs and generally dry-skinned and warty of appearance whereas frogs are glossier of skin and leap actively when discovered. Frogs may be found surprisingly high on the hills, the highest I have personally seen was at 1006 m (3,300 ft).

Finally, around Ross-shire's extensive coastline, on both west and east sides, grey seal, common seal and porpoise may be seen, in western sea loch or eastern Firth.

Chapter four

BIRD LIFE

Roy Dennis

Ross and Cromarty has a rich and varied bird life, which is enhanced for the bird-watcher by the spectacular countryside. From east to
west the habitats are very different: in Easter Ross and the Black Isle the
land is fertile and low lying, a rich mosaic of farms and woodland with a
relatively dry climate: yet 130 kilometres (80 miles) away in Wester Ross
the landscape is wild and rugged, the real Scottish Highlands with large
freshwater lochs and high mountains, indented by the stormy waters of
the Minch. As elsewhere in the Highlands many of the bird species are
only summer visitors to the glens and mountains, so that these places are
rather quiet for birds in winter. In contrast, Ross and Cromarty is fortunate in that the firths and low ground in the east are an important
wintering area for wildfowl and waders, while some of the headlands,
such as Tarbat Ness are excellent places to observe bird migration.

The west coast has some attractive coastal scenery and islands: the
Nature Conservancy Council's Inverpolly Reserve includes part of the
coast as does the Scottish Wildlife Trust reserve at Coigach while the
RSPB has two island reserves at Isle Martin and Priest Island, the latter
holding one of Britain's most important Storm Petrel colonies. The sea
lochs hold interesting numbers of Great Northern Divers in winter and
the harbours are often good places to look for rare gulls in winter. The
large lochs of Wester Ross are important for the endangered Black-
throated Diver and the moorlands hold good numbers of waders such as
Greenshank and Golden Plovers. The mountains which stretch from
west to east hold important populations of Golden Eagles, Peregrines
and Merlins as well as Ptarmigan and Red Grouse. Alas, much of this
land has been very badly overgrazed by sheep and deer, and badly burnt
and eroded in the last couple of centuries, so that the biological productivity and wildlife is now greatly reduced.

The remaining birch woodlands which are valuable places for
wildlife, are often desperately in need of protection and regeneration. In

the east there are remnants of the original Scots Pine forest which still holds species like Capercaillie, Crested Tit and Scottish Crossbill but the trend has been to move towards commercial plantations which decrease the bird interest of these old woods. The rich low ground of the east is intensively farmed for cereals and stock, but because of the mosaic of woodlands some of the land is very rich in bird life. Grey geese and swans forage the stubbles in winter, while Buzzard and Sparrowhawks are common. The Dornoch, Cromarty and Beauly Firths are teeming with wildfowl and waders in winter, where these birds can feed on exposed mudflats; offshore there are important wintering sites for seaducks and sawbills. In summer the red sandstone cliffs of the Sutors have a very interesting seabird colony. Finally, the headlands can provide the bird-watcher with interesting seabird watching and migration. All in all, Ross and Cromarty is an absorbing District for birds and unlike most areas of our overcrowded island, there are plenty of places to visit and record new information. It is important to note that some species are rare and should not be unnecessarily disturbed when breeding. In fact, all bird-watchers should endeavour to observe nesting birds without causing disturbance.

The following account gives a summary of the distribution and abundance of birds in Ross and Cromarty.

DIVERS AND GREBES

Wester Ross is one of the most important areas for Black-throated Divers in the United Kingdom; these large beautiful birds prefer to nest on the bigger freshwater lochs, especially those with wooded islands. As the population is now fewer than 100 pairs in Scotland it is a very rare bird in need of special protection. Be very careful not to disturb it at nesting time and do not visit nesting islands by boat. In contrast, the smaller Red-throated Divers breed on smaller lochs and lochans throughout the upland areas; they are well dispersed and many of them flight to the sea, often over long distances, to fish. On only one occasion has the Great Northern Diver been proved to breed in Britain and that was in Wester Ross in 1970; single birds are occasionally seen in summer on freshwater lochs and with luck they may nest again.

The nesting divers return inland in late March and April and go back to the sea in August. In winter time, small numbers of Black-throated Divers occur off the east coast, while Great Northern Divers are regular winter visitors, especially to the west coast. Red-throated Divers winter in good numbers off the east coast. On a few occasions the rare White-billed Diver from the Arctic has been observed on the coast.

Small numbers of Little Grebe nest on richer lochs especially in the east and very rarely the beautiful Slavonian Grebe has attempted to breed. Outside the nesting season wintering Red-necked and Slavonian Grebes are seen in very small numbers off the east coast with the latter also in the western sea lochs. On rare occasions Great Crested and Black-necked Grebes occur on the sea in the east.

SEABIRDS

The Fulmar is common on our coasts. After starting to nest at the turn of the century, it is well distributed on headlands and islands in the west, with larger numbers on the coasts of Easter Ross and the Black Isle; there is an attractive colony on red sandstone cliffs at Rosemarkie and a few inland in the Fairy Glen. Manx Shearwaters do not breed, but occur in summer and autumn off the east and west coasts; with periods of strong easterly winds, large numbers may be observed off Tarbat Ness and the Black Isle. Sometimes Sooty Shearwaters occur with them and may be observed in hundreds on the best days. Cory's and Great Shearwaters have occurred as vagrants. One of the most important Storm Petrel colonies in Britain is on Priest Island, an RSPB reserve in the Summer Isles. These tiny black and white seabirds come ashore at night to their underground nesting burrows so that there is nothing to see during the day and it's uncanny to think that up to 10,000 pairs of petrels may nest in the Summer Isles. Occasionally some, along with Leach's Petrel, are seen off headlands in bad weather and occasionally they get blown inland. Gannets are regulars offshore and with onshore winds large numbers pass headlands like Tarbat Ness. At other times when large shoals of fish are close inshore, Gannets fish in west coast sea lochs as well as in the Moray Firth.

Cormorants and Shags are common along the coast; there are Cormorant colonies on both east and west coasts but the largest rookery is in Easter Ross. A small number of Shags nest at the Sutors of Cromarty with more scattered groups on the west coast. Cormorants occur in big flocks in the Moray Firth in winter with a large tree roost in Munlochy Bay. Small numbers of Cormorants also visit inland lochs and rivers.

The Grey Heron is not a seabird, but is well distributed throughout fresh and coastal waters with heronries in various place. The Black Isle heronry (30-40 pairs) is one of the largest in Scotland while in the west some pairs nest on cliffs.

The Great Skua has recently started to nest in the Summer Isles in very small numbers and the Arctic Skua may also do so occasionally. All four species are recorded on migration, especially in autumn on the east coast. With strong north-east winds in September, Tarbat Ness, Chanonry Point and the Kessock bridge can be excellent for these birds, with the best ever day being 27th September, 1976 when 186 Pomarine Skuas flew into the Beauly Firth.

Small numbers of Razorbills nest at the North Sutor and off Ullapool along with small colonies of Guillemots. A few pairs of Puffins occur at the Sutors, where there are also a few Black Guillemots; the latter are well distributed on the west coast. Larger numbers of Guillemots and Razorbills occur offshore and also winter in the firths.

Great Black-backed and Herring Gulls are common on the coast and at rubbish dumps and fishing harbours; Lesser Black-backed Gulls are summer visitors arriving in late March. They nest in other gull colonies. Common Gulls are widespread and in summertime breed on many inland lochs, rivers and moorland while Black-headed Gull colonies are mainly on lochs and marshes in the east. Both species occur in large numbers on the coast and coastal farmland outside the breeding season. Kittiwakes are common around the coasts but only breed in colonies at the Sutors of Cromarty. Glaucous and Iceland Gulls from the north are regular winter visitors in small numbers, although recently big counts have included 45 Iceland Gulls at Ullapool harbour in January 1984. The fishing harbours are certainly worth a visit for bird-watchers interested in rare gulls; Little, Ivory and Sabine's Gull have all been recorded in recent years.

Terns are summer visitors to the District; Common Terns are well distributed with small colonies on both coasts as well as small numbers nesting on inland fresh-water. Arctic Terns also have colonies on both east and west coasts, while Little Terns are scarce, with occasional nesting of a few pairs on the south shore of the Dornoch Firth. Sandwich Terns are regularly seen around the Moray Firth coast and very occasionally a big colony has nested at the Morrich More, but this nesting site is very irregular. Roseate and Black Tern occur as vagrants.

GEESE

Greylag Geese breed in very small numbers near Loch Maree and on the Summer Isles. Very large numbers arrive in October from Iceland. These birds feed on farmland stubbles in Easter Ross and the Black Isle and roost on Loch Eye, Munlochy Bay or the Cromarty and Beauly Firths. Numbers vary from year to year depending on the cereal harvest, with maximum numbers as high as 40,000, figures of 5-10,000 being normal. The Greylags migrate north in April. Pink-footed Geese also migrate here in large numbers and although only small numbers winter in the east, there is a noticeable spring arrival when several thousands land in the east in March before leaving again in May. Small groups of Greenland White-fronted Geese winter at Loch Eye and near Gairloch, while Brent, Barnacle, Bean and Snow Geese occur as stragglers. Up to 1000 Canada Geese arrive in late May from England to moult on the Beauly Firth; some of these birds also visit Munlochy Bay and the Cromarty Firth before departing in August.

SWANS

Mute Swans breed in small numbers in the east with very few in the west; non-breeding groups occur on the firths. Whooper Swans are common on autumn passage, with up to 1000 being recorded at Loch Eye. They feed on stubbles along with the geese and some remain all winter. Occasional birds, especially injured ones, may stay throughout the summer. Bewick's Swan is rare with occasional stragglers in winter.

DUCKS

Mallard, Teal and Wigeon breed in many areas and large numbers flock in winter. Teal flocks can reach 1000 in autumn on the firths and Wigeon numbers may reach 20,000 on the east coast inlets. The east coast is a very important wintering area for Wigeon from Iceland and Europe. Shelduck are common as breeding birds on the east coast with a few in the Summer Isles. Pintail regularly winter in Nigg Bay but Shoveler and Gadwall are rare birds. Vagrants include Green-winged Teal, Black Duck and American Wigeon.

DIVING DUCKS

Tufted Duck nest on some freshwater lochs, mainly in the east. Small flocks occur in winter and may reach 1000 on the Beauly Firth in severe weather. Scaup winter off Edderton where 200-400 may be seen; elsewhere the species is scarce. Non-breeding Pochard are mainly found at Loch Eye with small numbers at other lochs. Goldeneye winter in good numbers on many lochs and along the coast; at one time they were plentiful at Invergordon outfall with over 1000 being recorded; now they are much scarcer although up to 500 winter near the Kessock Bridge. Although some summer in the District, none as yet used nesting boxes erected in the area.

SEADUCKS

Eiders are well distributed along both coasts, mainly in the west. Scoters nest sparingly on a few mountain lochs but in winter the Moray Firth is very important for this species as well as Velvet Scoters and Long-tailed Ducks. These birds frequently pass Tarbat Ness and large numbers of Scoters may occur off Portmahomack and on the Riff Bank, between the Black Isle and Ardersier. Large wintering flocks (up to 5000) of Long-tailed Ducks also occur at the Riff Bank and off Shandwick. Flocks come into the Cromarty and Dornoch Firths, especially in late winter, while small numbers frequent the west coast. Red-breasted Mergansers are found as a nesting bird along the coasts and on inland waters, with flocks congregating along the coast in winter, when up to 2500 have been counted in the Beauly Firth. The Beauly Firth is the most important site for Goosanders in Britain with up to 2000 there in recent winters, feeding on sprats and herring. In summer, small numbers breed on rivers throughout the District. The Smew is a rare winter visitor.

BIRDS OF PREY

Ross and Cromarty is rich in birds of prey. The mountain country is ideal for Golden Eagles (Plate 12) and they occur from the mountains overlooking the Cromarty Firth through to the west coast. The adults are resident within their large home-ranges with immatures wandering onto uplands with no nesting areas. Breeding success is generally good although some areas are now very lacking in wild prey, and there are even places where eagles are still persecuted. The best chance of seeing eagles is to go along remote mountain roads and to scan the surrounding skylines. Nests should not be visited because of disturbance. Buzzards are very common; in fact a recent survey on the Black Isle suggested a population of at least 250 pairs. They breed in woods, mountains and on the coast; often they are mistaken for eagles; if the bird is perched on telephone poles and calling it is a buzzard, not an eagle. In recent years, with the reintroduction of White-tailed Sea Eagles on the Island of Rhum by the Nature Conservancy Council, some of the wandering young birds have been seen in Wester Ross, with even one frequenting the Cromarty Firth for a short time one winter. Ospreys are regular migrants to Ross and Cromarty, with occasional birds being seen on larger lochs and the east coast firths.

The Sparrowhawk is well distributed in the old woodlands, especially in the east. Often, especially in winter, it visits gardens and bird-tables. The larger Goshawk, which was exterminated along with the Red Kite last century, has returned and occasional birds are seen in forests in the east. Hen Harriers are scattered throughout the District, mainly on heather moors and especially on recently afforested moorland; their numbers are generally low but in autumn and winter they can regularly be seen on low ground hunting small birds, often over turnip fields. The Marsh Harrier is a rare migrant in spring.

Peregrine Falcons nest from coast to coast, but like so many birds they are commoner in the eastern half of the District where natural prey is more plentiful. Many old Peregrine sites have been recolonised and the species is generally doing well; this is reflected in the numbers which hunt the mudflats in winter for waders and wildfowl. The unobtrusive Merlin is widely but thinly spread throughout the uplands and occurs in small numbers in winter on the low ground. Most, however, migrate south. Kestrels are well distributed as a breeding bird but here in the Highlands they are not as common as Buzzards.

GAME BIRDS

Red Grouse is an important bird of the heather moors but in many areas it has become much scarcer this century. In fact it is quite a difficult bird to see in the west. Black Grouse and Capercaillie have also decreased in recent decades. The Black Grouse is thinly spread in pockets, mainly in Mid-Ross, but the Capercaillie is now restricted to a few old pinewoods on the edge of the mountains. Once it was quite common in the Black Isle forests but only a handful, if that, now remain. Ptarmigan are present on all the higher mountains and often in quite good numbers above 760 m (2500 ft). Partridges are restricted to the farming areas of the east, where quite good coveys can be observed; occasionally Red-legged Partridges have been released by game interests but they do not breed. Most summers a few Quail are heard calling, mainly in Easter Ross and the Black Isle, and in the best summers they almost certainly nest. Pheasants are well distributed on the low ground areas in the east where they are often reared.

CRAKES

Coot and Moorhen are regular as nesting birds in small numbers in the east, with very small numbers of the latter elsewhere. A good-sized flock of Coot occurs on Loch Eye in winter and sometimes in severe frosts the birds visit the firths. Water Rails and very rarely Spotted Crakes, are recorded, mainly in winter. Corncrakes still summer in very small numbers in the west, very much reduced from the old days, while occasional birds turn up to call elsewhere in the District. The occasional Crane is observed migrating through in spring en route for Scandinavia.

WADERS

Oystercatchers are widespread even into the remotest glens; the inland breeders return from England in March and depart in July and August, while the coastal breeders of the east winter in the firths where large flocks congregate. Lapwings are widespread and also occur in flocks on the coast. Ringed Plovers are scattered as nesting birds around the coast and on inland shingle and sand banks on rivers and lochs. Small flocks winter on the coast. Golden Plovers are well distributed on inland moors and mountain plateaux but are scarce in winter. Dotterel are scarce breeders on a few high mountains arriving as summer visitors in May. Snipe and Woodcock are well distributed throughout the glens, moors and low ground; Woodcock are a familiar sight in spring along woodland edges where they perform their attractive display flights. Good numbers of both species winter with us. Curlews are common as nesters especially in the east, where good-sized flocks winter on the firths. Common Sandpipers arrive in April from Africa to nest along most rivers and loch shores, and in some places, by the sea.

Redshanks are common in winter on the firths, with flocks of up to 800; most of these birds are from Iceland but reasonable numbers nest in the District in freshwater and coastal marshes. One of the special waders of the moorland is the Greenshank, a close relative of the commoner Redshank; it nests throughout the inland districts and adds greatly to the atmosphere of the glens with its lovely whistling calls. Dunlin also nest in the flow country but are generally rather scarce.

In winter, large flocks of Knot, Bar-tailed Godwit and Dunlin along with smaller numbers of Turnstone and Purple Sandpiper live in the firths and along the coast, mainly in the east. Grey Plovers, Sanderling and Whimbrel pass through in small numbers and occasional Black-tailed Godwit, Green and Wood Sandpiper, Temminck's and Little Stints, Curlew Sandpiper, Ruff, Spotted Redshank and Jack Snipe are also observed. Very rarely Wood Sandpiper and Temminck's Stint have been recorded nesting.

Doves, Owls and Woodpeckers etc.

The Wood Pigeon is common, nesting throughout the area and occurring in large flocks in the east in winter. Stock Doves are scarce with small numbers breeding in the east. Rock Doves are found along the west coast crofting areas but in the east they have been polluted by feral pigeons which nest commonly in the cliffs and farm buildings. The Collared Dove arrived near Portmahomack in the early 1960s and is now well established as a breeder but the Turtle Dove is only recorded as an occasional spring migrant. The call of the Cuckoo is a common sound throughout the District from April with good numbers breeding.

The most northerly breeding Barn Owls in the whole world occur around the shores of the Moray Firth where small numbers breed in the Black Isle and Easter Ross. Tawny Owls are widespread, with some even in isolated woodlands in western glens. The Long-eared Owl appears to be restricted to the eastern half of the District where it nests sparingly in woodland — a most unobtrusive bird; the best chance is to see or hear the young when they have left the nest but are still dependant on their parents. Short-eared Owls are even scarcer with just a few scattered pairs nesting on moorland and occasional wintering birds on coastal marshes. The Nightjar used to breed in certain wooded heaths in Easter Ross but now appears to be extinct. Swifts are common summer visitors in towns and villages in the east but do not nest in the west. The Kingfisher has nested once in Easter Ross but is usually a rare vagrant in winter. In fact, migrant Hoopoes are recorded more often with one every year or so. The Great Spotted Woodpecker became extinct in Ross and Cromarty in the last century due to the clearance of forests but it is now well but thinly distributed throughout the District, even in the west. In the last few years, Green Woodpeckers have reached the District and single birds have been reported at Ardross and on the Black Isle. This species is spreading north and since starting to breed in Strathspey ten years ago, it may soon nest in Ross and Cromarty. Wrynecks are occasionally heard singing in spring and have attempted to nest on at least one recent occasion.

SWALLOWS AND MARTINS

Swallows are common breeding birds throughout Ross and Cromarty while House Martins are scarce in the west but have good numbers in the east. Sand Martins are the earliest to arrive and they nest in colonies in river banks, cuttings and sand pits throughout the area. In late summer, hundreds gather over lochs and marshes where they often form communal roosts in reed beds before migrating to Africa.

PIPITS, WAGTAILS AND LARKS

The Meadow Pipit is the most common bird of the moorland and is found throughout the area; in winter very small numbers occur in the east. Birds from Iceland pass through the west coast on migration and quite big falls may occur on both coasts. Tree Pipits are well distributed in woodland as a summer visitor while Rock Pipits occur around the coast; they also winter on the Black Isle coast and along the firths. Pied Wagtails mainly return in March and April to nest throughout the area; in autumn they frequent the east coast firths before most of them leave to winter in England. A few winter in Dingwall and Tain. White Wagtails pass through in spring and autumn to Iceland, and very rarely one may breed with a local Pied Wagtail. Grey Wagtails are thinly distributed along all river systems and in most areas they are also only summer visitors, although small numbers do winter on the low ground where they favour farmyards. The Yellow Wagtail is a scarce vagrant. Skylarks are common nesting birds over farmland and also drier moorland, with small numbers wintering in the east. Great Grey Shrikes occur as migrants and winter visitors in small numbers, mainly in the east; some years several may arrive and in other years they are totally absent. Red-backed Shrikes have been rarely recorded on passage.

WARBLERS

The ubiquitous Willow Warbler is our commonest warbler; it arrives in mid April and suddenly every woodland and shrubby area is ringing to its delightful spring song. Willow Warblers nest throughout Ross and Cromarty, and in late summer they band together into loose flocks with tits and other passerines. Wood Warblers are scarcer but can be found in suitable deciduous woods, especially oak and mature birch. Chiffchaffs are heard singing in small numbers most springs but confirmed breeding is scarce. Garden Warblers and Blackcaps nest in small numbers in the east; occasionally Blackcaps sing in various places in the west and the species also occurs in small numbers at bird-tables in winter. Sedge Warblers are thinly scattered near freshwater and marshy ground, with small numbers also in the west. Grasshopper Warblers are scarcer but occur in rather similar places; small numbers probably nest most years. Whitethroats breed in drier, low ground situations in eastern areas and sparingly in coastal scrub in the west. Warblers also occur on migration at places like Tarbat Ness, especially during east coast falls. Numbers are never as high as in Caithness and Aberdeenshire but rarer migrants such as Lesser Whitethroat, Barred Warbler and Subalpine Warbler have been recorded. Finally, Goldcrests are widespread as a nesting species in coniferous woodland and also occur on migration on the coast.

CHATS AND THRUSHES

Spotted Flycatchers are summer visitors to many woodlands and larger gardens, although they are scarce on the Black Isle. Pied Flycatchers are occasionally recorded in wooded glens such as at Kinlochewe and Dundonnell where they have probably nested. On rare occasions vagrant Red-breasted Flycatchers have been recorded at Tarbat Ness. The numbers of Stonechats are very dependant on the severity of the winters; at present (1984) their numbers are very low but a decade ago when the population was high they were common in the west with smaller numbers scattered throughout the District. Whinchats, being summer visitors, are much less variable in breeding numbers and they are found in most glens, low lying moorland and forest clearings. Wheatears, which start arriving from Africa in late March, are among our earliest summer visitors; they are breeders throughout all moorland areas and even onto the high mountains. Good numbers also pass through on migration to Iceland, Greenland and Scandinavia. Redstarts are found thinly spread in mature woodlands throughout the area but not on the coastal plain. On the other hand, Robins are plentiful throughout all suitable habitats. The inland birds disperse to low lying areas in winter to join resident birds.

The common breeding thrushes are Blackbird, Ring Ouzel, Song and Mistle Thrush; they are all well distributed in suitable breeding habitats. The Blackbird is the commonest, followed by the Song Thrush which tends to be a summer visitor to our area with only small numbers wintering. Many Mistle Thrushes also move out for the winter after congregating in autumn to feast on moorland and rowan berries. Ring Ouzels are summer visitors to the glens and mountains; in areas of limestone outcrops they can be quite plentiful. Redwings and Fieldfares arrive in October from Scandinavia in very large flocks which roam through the glens feeding on berries, mainly rowans; in recent decades the Redwing has become a regular but sparse breeding bird in the glens and on rare occasions a pair of Fieldfares may also nest. Like several other Scandinavian species, they have started to colonise Scotland.

TITS

Great, Blue and Coal Tits are common birds; they frequent our bird-tables in winter and often nest in gardens as well as in woodland throughout the District. The Long-tailed Tit is also well distributed as a nesting bird in the coastal plain and along river sides in the glens. Crested Tits are rather scarce in Ross and Cromarty with small numbers in remnant Scots Pine woods on the Black Isle and around the moorland edge near Novar, Ardross and Ardgay. Willow Tits, which used to nest in small numbers, are now extinct. Treecreepers are well distributed from east to west and the Wren is abundant through many habitats ranging from sea coasts to mountain cliffs. The Dunnock is also widely dispersed while the Dipper is to be found on most rivers and, very occasionally, down to the seashore in wintertime.

BUNTINGS AND FINCHES

The Corn Bunting has decreased dramatically this century and is now restricted to a couple of areas in Easter Ross and on the Black Isle where even there it is likely to become extinct. Yellowhammers and Reed Buntings are much better represented, the former being found throughout agricultural areas and the latter near marshes, lochs and rivers. Snow Buntings arrive in autumn and many winter with us in small flocks both in the mountains and on the low ground; a few pairs occasionally remain to nest in the high mountains. Occasionally, migrant

Lapland Buntings are recorded on the coast and on three recent occasions single Little Buntings have been located in winter.

Chaffinches are one of our commonest birds; they nest in gardens and throughout wooded areas. In the forests they are principally summer visitors, congregating in winter in flocks on farmland. Some winters Bramblings occur with them and in years of good beech mast, flocks winter in the beech woods. Very rarely a singing Brambling may be heard in spring and one day it may remain to breed. Greenfinches are common in the east but rather scarce in the west, while Bullfinches are scattered throughout the area. They tend to be rather unobtrusive, except in winter, when flocks can be found feeding in the heather at the top edge of the hillside woods. Goldfinches are sparse but occasional pairs nest in Easter Ross and the Black Isle and small parties may be seen anywhere in winter. Siskins are now regular visitors to bird-tables in winter and spring where they seek out peanut bags; they nest throughout the conifer woods of the District.

The Linnet is principally found in the drier areas of scrub and gorse in the east of the District and its close cousin the Twite is found in the crofting areas of the west and in the mountains. Flocks of Linnets are found on the farmland in the east in winter, with occasional Twite with them. Twite flocks also occur on the salt marshes and in crofting areas. Redpolls are widespread and nest in woodland and birch scrub even in the highest glens; they also gather into flocks and in winter often frequent alder and birchwoods. Occasionally these flocks contain Mealy and Greenland Redpolls. The Crossbills are confusing: they are well distributed through pine and spruce forests with both Scottish and the smaller billed Common Crossbill nesting in the District. Invasions of Common Crossbills occur at intervals from Scandinavia and some of these birds remain to breed. In 1982 the first ever pair of Scarlet Rosefinch proved to breed in Britain nested in Ross and Cromarty, and if the westward spread of this bird continues it is likely to colonise Scotland. In early spring, 1984, a Hawfinch frequented gardens in Tain. Tree Sparrows nest in small numbers in various places in Easter Ross and the Black Isle although they were commoner about 20 years ago when some were also found in the west. House Sparrows are common and well distributed except in the uninhabited areas.

CROWS

Ravens breed throughout Ross and Cromarty but they are now relatively scarce in the east probably due to persecution. They occur from the mountains down to the coast. Hooded and Carrion Crows have a wide band of hybridization running north-east to south-west through Mid

Ross. Most of the birds in the east are black while pure Hoodies are dominant in the west. The Carrion Crow has been moving steadily north and west this century. Rooks are common in the eastern agricultural areas with large rookeries in many places; in the west they are scarce. Jackdaws have a similar distribution to the Rook and often nest together in the rookeries. The Magpie is a scarce nester in Easter Ross and the Black Isle with just a small number of scattered pairs which never seem to increase. Finally, the Starling is widely distributed as a nesting species and in winter large numbers arrrive from abroad, many taking up residence in towns.

Chapter five

WOODLANDS
Finlay MacRae

INTRODUCTION:

Ross and Cromarty which shoulders the North Sea and the Minch is about 125 km (78 miles) from east to west. From Brebag Tarsuinn in the north to Loch Loyne in the south is a distance of around 114 km (71 miles). Within these bounds lies a land whose beauty and diversity of scenery is unrivalled.

Woodlands of ecological, aesthetic, historical, and economic importance, both natural and artificial abound, and are well distributed from the dry eastern plain to the mountainous areas of high rainfall in the west. The trees we admire today as we travel by rail, by road, or on foot, date back over many centuries.

Long established estates such as Novar, Ardross, Fairburn, Brahan, Castle Leod, Rosehaugh and Flowerdale, to name but a few, have long been renowned for their fine woods, sylvan parklands, avenues and arboritae.

The Wester Ross groups of Native and Natural Pinewoods which have persisted since the Ice Age in a markedly oceanic climate are unique. the most prominent remnant of these ancient woods is Coille Na Glas Leitire on the southern shore of Loch Maree, while the Shieldaig pinewoods are the most westerly. Today these priceless relics from our sylvan past are carefully managed by the Nature Conservancy.

In the year 1600 a traveller in Wester Ross noted dense woods of Pine, Birch, Oak, Ash, Aspen, Elm and Holly on the south side of Loch Maree. In some places he said "ar fair and plentiful fyrrs (pines) of 60, 70 and 80 foot of good and serviceable timmer, suitable for ships masts, and in other places ar great plentie of excellent great oakes, where may be sawn out planks of 4 sumtyms 5 foot broad." Some of the earliest attempts at modern scientific woodland management were on Novar and Ardross estates where working plans prepared by eminent German silviculturists date back to the middle of the 19th century.

Arboritae at Castle Leod, Ardross and Novar display a splendid selection of conifers and broadleaved trees, native and exotic, planted in the latter half of the 19th century. Some are now very large trees. A Sitka Spruce *(Picea sitchensis)* planted in 1900 in Ardross was 40 m (131 ft) high and 5 m (16 ft 4 in) in girth when measured in 1980.

At Castle Leod near Strathpeffer a Douglas Fir *(Pseudotsuga taxifolia Douglasii)* planted at about the same time was 52 m (175 ft) high, and just under 5 m (16 ft 4 in) in girth when measured in 1980. Although the Native Pinewoods and broadleaved woodlands are much depleted, sufficient evidence exists to illustrate the diversity, geographical distribution and ecological and historical significance of the great forests that once spread over large areas of Ross-shire.

Let us now take a glance back into forest history:

The Ice Age which removed every vestige of tree growth from Highland Scotland makes a good starting point. The ice sheet, at least 1000 m (3000 ft) thick in places, finally retreated about 8-9000 BC, and the climate gradually became warmer.

The liverworts and mosses, followed by dwarf woody shrubs, were among the first significant colonists of a virtually sterile landscape. Then came Birch and Pine, and eventually Oak, Alder, Ash and Aspen — the first woodlands, highly diversified in composition.

When the post-glacial optimum emerged around 5000 BC Ross-shire was forest clad, with the exception of the rock-bound lands of the west. Here, the warm, moist, well-sheltered glens, often highly enriched, display today on a small scale, attractive natural broadleaved forest such as Rassal Ashwood on the lime-rich soils by Loch Kishorn. Under the deep peats of the poorly-drained central interior lies evidence of a once thriving forest, with large pine stumps entombed for centuries, yet remarkably well preserved.

The narrow, dry, eastern heathlands fall gently to the North Sea, through mixed woodland, interspersed with pasture, to rich highly productive arable farmland. It is claimed that; "Before man there were the forests, and after man the deserts". Neolithic man regarded the forests as an enemy, something to be conquered and subdued, and the land on which they grew, put to better use. The mixed Oak forest on the rich brown soils was probably the first to be cleared to extend the pastureland.

At that time reindeer, elk, and red deer were plentiful, their meat valuable food, and their skins vital protection in a hostile climate. Lynx, wolf, and bear, formidable predators, roamed the forest while early man kept to the fringes and open glades.

Yet, with simple cutting tools, with fire and flocks, man's conquest of the forest progressed purposely and assuredly. Peat and moorland

10. Loch Achnacloich, Easter Ross   (A. Maclennan)
The diverse plant range contrasts markedly with the
lochs of Wester Ross

11. Pine Marten   (L. MacNally)

12. Young Golden Eagle   *(L. MacNally)*

13. Badger   *(L. MacNally)*

14. Otter   *(L. MacNally)*

15. Mountain or Blue Hare   *(L. MacNally)*

16. Fox   *(L. MacNally)*

17. Red Deer Stags (L. MacNally)

18. Carnurnan, Clava-type Cairn, Black Isle (R. Gourlay)

spread as woodland decayed and man, abetted to some extent by nature, laid large tracts to waste.

The Bronze and Iron Ages saw continued extension of forest clearance and with the development of more sophisticated cutting tools the forest dwindled. Around the year 100 AD the spine of the Black Isle was clad in dense Oak/Pine forest, but clearance of the valleys to pasture had commenced and progressed up the more gentle slopes. Yet in 400 AD the Romans found Scotland "fearful with woods" *(horrida sylvis)*, so we can assume that about this time the greater part of the Ross-shire forests were untouched.

By 900 AD Norse depredation of the forests in the Northern and Western Isles and Sutherland spread into the North Ross forests and their clearance continued into feudal times. History records that during the feudal period (1110-1400) the clearance of forests in Scotland was on a scale never experienced before or since. Records for Ross-shire are scanty but we can assume that the more readily accessible areas were under threat.

Although hunting remained the primary forest use, the provision of in-grazing and winning constructional timber was gaining importance. In this period forest managers were mentioned for the first time. They supervised large tracts of hunting land all over Scotland. Some of the earliest forest laws were introduced, but again little is known about the position in Ross-shire. During the Stuart Dynasty (1400-1603) there are numerous interesting records regarding the Ross-shire woodlands. In 1480 there were "forester crofts" at Ardmeanach, Culbokie and Pitlundy in the Black Isle. Presumably such lands were part forest and part pasture, and held under tenancy.

Even the small islands such as Isle Ewe and Gruinard were densely wooded. An historical entry revealed that "northwards from Loch Ewe lyes the ile of Graynorde (Gruinard), miare nor ane myle long, full of wood, good for fostering of thieves and rebellis". A wild country indeed at that time!

Of the Loch Maree basin it was written that "all their bounds is compase'd and hemd in with many hills, thair skirts being all adorned with wood, even to the brink of the loch for the most part". In 1538 Andrew Wright who skippered the barque "Huey" was paid in full for sailing to Dingwall in Ross for gun timber (wood for gun stocks) . . . Exploitation was under-way.

The beginning of the 17th century saw a definite turn in the tide of deforestation in Scotland and the first attempts to make good the harmful effects resulting from the destruction of forests. Yet, in Ross-shire, this period marks the start of surveying the less accessible areas such as

Glencarron in the east and the Loch Maree woods in the west, with a view to their exploitation. In 1610 Sir George Hay obtained the use of the woods in Letterewe to win fuel for iron smelting, and this marked the beginning of their decline on a large scale, each furnace consuming the timber from 48 hectares (120 acres) per annum. The smelting lasted until the woods were exhausted. Cannons made from the iron were cast at Poolewe.

Balnagown was well-wooded at this time and the Meikle Wood of Oak and Birch stretched through the parish of Edderton from the Struie road down to the sea and west to Fearn. The wood was bought by English brothers who cut it down, and converted it to charcoal which was shipped out through Tain. The finest pines in Strathcarron, farther west, went to make ships' masts, while crooked material was used for ships' planks and barrel staves. Even the bark was used in the leather-tanning industry. The whole enterprise was highly profitable for the forest owners of the time, who generally cared little for conservation.

As always a few recognised the need to replant and there are records of Beech, Oak, Ash and Elm being planted on Kilcoy in the Black Isle in 1685. A good deal of this planting was by way of adornment in the policies of "big houses". The late 17th century also marks the first steps in forest education and literature, the first book being published in Scotland in 1683. It was concerned with forest trees — "The Scots Gardn'ner" — and came from the pen of John Reid, gardener to Sir George MacKenzie of Rosehaugh. In it, he dealt with nursery work and transplanting, pit planting, weeding, cleaning, and even some of the common diseases of trees. He was a man well ahead of his time.

In 1748 Hugh Munro, surveyor on the Cromartie estate, noted that while houses had formerly been made of wood the material was now so scarce that people began to build with stone.

The Highlands were now pacified and serious inroads were made into the remaining Oak, Birch, and pinewoods for commercial purposes. A small turn of the tide took place toward the end of the 18th century, when landowners began to take stock of the denuded landscape. Eager to restore the balance they took to planting on a reasonable scale. Fine woods were planted at Brahan, Novar, Newhall, Foulis and Balnagown, with reports of millions of transplants being used. Wright (1778) called Foulis "the best planted estate in the country", the Hill of Foulis and Swordale being particularly large and fine.

Owners vied with one another as to who should possess the finest woods. In the west at Flowerdale extensive planting was carried out by Sir Alexander MacKenzie. He planted Oak, Ash, and Scots Pine, "covering precipices and deep declivities, and even beginning to cover the rocky summits".

In the early 19th century some semi-mature woods were even being offered for sale: the beginning of plantation forestry as we know it today was recognised. Intensive ground preparation and careful selection of planting stock soon provided well-grown woods. These were well-cared for, cleaned, pruned, thinned and subjected to other skilled management techniques available from the forest literature emerging at that time. This welcome upsurge in forest activity continued well into the 1850s when prizes were awarded for large scale projects — eg to the 210 hectares (519 acres) of mixed Oak, Pine, and Larch created by MacKenzie of Kilcoy in 1822.

The industrial revolution which followed saw many changes. Metal replaced timber in ship building, and with improved sea communication, timber and timber products were cheap to import. Large estates passed into the hands of wealthy industrialists, who managed them for pleasure and sport rather than profit. The end of the century saw increasing apprehension about the state of our woodlands, the general lack of investment, and interest, in home timber supplies.

Particularly active in the early 20th century to increase the woodland area, was Mr Munro Ferguson of Novar, who recognised the need for state involvement and investment in forestry. He also recognised the need for forest education at university and forest school level.

The Great War of 1914-1918 brought the need for a home-based forest policy into sharp focus with the German blockade necessitating further inroads in our reserves of standing timber. The Forestry Commission was established in 1919 and this marked the beginning of a new and powerful interest in forestry in Scotland, in which Ross-shire has played a valuable role. Fittingly, Lord Lovat, who with Munro Ferguson (then Lord Novar) had championed the cause of forestry, became the first Chairman of the newly-formed Commission. The beginnings were small and insecure with the depression in full swing, but the outbreak of World War II soon illustrated the need for a strong expansive forest policy, when our remaining woodlands were severly depleted.

Following upon the war the upsurge in large-scale afforestation both state and private was spectacular and this has continued until the present day. Table 3 helps to illustrate the increase in the woodland area of Ross and Cromarty since the first national census of woods in 1947-1949.

TABLE 3 – FOREST LAND USE

Classification of High Forest and Scrubland:

Year	Private Woodlands		FC Woodlands		Total
1947	Conifers	6091 ha (15,045 acres)	Conifers	7111 ha (17,565 acres)	13,202 ha (32,609 acres)
	Broadleaved	1087 ha (2,685 acres)	Broadleaved	11 ha (28 acres)	1,098 ha (2,713 acres)
	Total	7178 ha (17,730 acres)	Total	7122 ha (17,593 acres)	14,300 ha (35,322 acres)
1947	**Scrubland (Private)**		**Scrubland (FC)**		**Total**
		8208 ha (20,276 acres)		950 ha (2,346 acres)	9,158 ha (22,622 acres)
	Devastated (Private)		**Devastated (FC)**		**Total**
		1265 ha (3,126 acres)		166 ha (410 acres)	1,431 ha (3,536 acres)
Year	**Private Woodlands**		**FC Woods**		**Total**
1954	Conifers	5754 ha (14,213 acres)	Conifers	13,024 ha (32,171 acres)	18,778 ha (46,384 acres)
	Broadleaved	368 ha (909 acres)	Broadleaved	40 ha (99 acres)	408 ha (1,008 acres)
	Total	6122 ha (15,122 acres)	Total	13,064 ha (32,270 acres)	19,186 ha (47,392 acres)

Percentage of forest cover 1954 = 3%.

1983
(March 31st)

Conifers	10,500 ha (25,935 acres)	30,195 ha (74,581 acres)	40,695 ha (100,516 acres)
Broadleaved	550 ha (1,358 acres)	950 ha (2,346 acres)	1,500 ha (3,704 acres)
Total	11,050 ha (27,293 acres)	31,145 ha (76,927 acres)	42,195 ha (104,220 acres)

Percentage of forest cover 1983 = 6.6%

Percentage of forest cover
Scotland   1983 = 7.3%

Summary Ross-shire:

1947	14,300 ha	(square miles = 55)	(sqare kilometres = 142.4)
1954	19,186 ha	(square miles = 74)	(square kilometres = 191.7)
1983	42,195 ha	(square miles = 162)	(square kilometres = 419.7)

In 35 years an increase of 27,895 ha or 107 sqare miles (277 square kilometres)
Percentage of Scottish Total Forest area in Rcss-shire = 8.2%.

(The above figures are in some cases approximations, their main value lies in depicting the great advances in afforestation in Ross-shire over the last 35 years).

THE NATIVE PINEWOODS (Pinus sylvestris var scotica)

H M Steven, late Professor of Forestry at Aberdeen University and co-author with Dr A Carlisle of "The Native Pinewoods of Scotland", put our forest history into perspective when he said that "to stand in a native pinewood is to feel the past". We are fortunate in Ross-shire to be able to stand amid such ancient trees, and to take note that they are separated from their earliest predecessors some 9000 years ago, by only 30 generations.

The Wester Ross group embrace the stands at Loch Maree, Coulin, Achnashellach and Shieldaig, the remnants of a once extensive forest. The Glas Leitire woods once described as some of the best woods in the west of Scotland, were heavily exploited in the early 17th century. The remnant that survives today is carefully managed by the Nature Conservancy. When Lord Elphinstone acquired Coulin in 1881 he built the staircase and other woodwork from timber cut from native pine growing on the south shore of Loch Clair. Some of the old pines in this area show signs of resin tapping, resin being used with butter and tobacco juice for smearing sheep before the days of sheep dips.

In all the open Wester Ross pinewoods red deer, roe deer, and sheep do considerable damage by browsing pine regeneration up to 1.8 m (6 ft) in height. The Shieldaig native pinewoods at 5° 38′ are the most westerly in Scotland.

THE PRESENT SATE OF ROSS-SHIRE'S WOODLANDS

Since the end of the 1939-45 war there have been tremendous advances in afforestation, particularly at state level, although the contibution by private landowners has been very significant, particularly on the former well-wooded estates — such as Novar. Grant-aided plantations managed under plans agreed between the owner and the Forestry Commissioners take up almost the entire effort.

With the advent of mechanical ploughing and drainage, areas of the poorer deep peats previously regarded as unplantable are now made available to tree growth, the limiting factor often being exposure rather than soil poverty. The introduction of exotic species has boosted the volume production on the better sites and on the poorest sites cultivation, drainage, and the use of fertilisers spread from the air have improved tree growth beyond expectation. On good soils in the west, Sitka Spruce *(Picea sitchensis)* remains the firm favourite producing a heavy crop over a relatively short period of time — ie 50 years.

On the deep acid peats, Lodgepole Pine *(Pinus contorta)*, used as a pure crop or in mixture with Sitka Spruce, also produces timber at an early age, on land previously regarded as unfit for trees.

In the east of the District the hard gravel heaths are committed to the traditional native conifer Scots Pine (*Pinus sylvestris;* Plate 36), a well-tried species that has stood the test of time. The use of broadleaves has declined and apart from their use in landscaping no significant areas of broadleaved trees are now planted.

The power saw is in common use, while the horse is seldom seen in the woods; extraction is by highly sophisticated custom-built machinery such as the Forwarder and the Cable-crane. Some of the machines used cost in excess of £100,000. A network of high-grade forest roads ensures that timber is transported by lorry from the heart of the forest to the source of use. Advances in sawmilling have been equally spectacular, electricity often providing the power source for modern automated machinery capable of producing high volumes of sawn timber with minimal input of labour.

Forest education and management is at a high level, and the employ-ment of professional foresters is now normal procedure both in state and private forestry. In addition to timber growing, the modern forest manager is involved in the ancillary techniques of forest design, land-scaping, forest recreation and wildlife conservation and control.

Public access to the forests is encouraged through a system of forest walks often accompanied by interpretative material. School children and adults are given an opportunity to learn about forestry through visits and lectures, and in due course it is hoped that the forest orientated public will increase. A traveller by road, or rail, from Dingwall to Kyle of Lochalsh across the district cannot fail to be aware of the extent of the new "green mantle". Much remains to be done and there is still con-siderable scope to increase the woodland area of Ross-shire with only minimal disturbance to what we have come to regard as traditional land use, such as sheep farming and deer stalking.

Clearly every attempt must be made to achieve a sensible balance so that the Ross-shire of the future will maintain its sylvan character, and that its heritages of fine landscape and wildlife conservation can march in step with all other land uses.

Part two

HISTORICAL

Chapter 6

THE ANCIENT PAST
Robert Gourlay

INTRODUCTION

Any attempt to describe or explain the early human history of Ross and Cromarty has first to overcome several problems, and these are such that a full and detailed account is at present impossible. In spite of this, the following chapter attempts to do this within the limitations imposed. The first of these problems lies in the obvious physical disparity between Easter and Wester Ross. In terms of landscape and resources they are remarkably different, and the effect that this has had on early human communities as reconstructed through the processes of archaeological investigation is far from fully understood. In order that the reader is familiar with the physical background, it is recommended that the chapters of this volume which deal with the natural environment are read prior to this one. This will help to explain the dramatically skewed distribution maps which follow.

In essence, the eastern part of the District, including the Black Isle and the lower parts of the east-flowing river valleys, is low-lying, easy of communication and relatively fertile. By contrast, the west — and much the larger portion — is hilly or mountainous with difficult routes for communication and very restricted areas of good quality cultivable land. As a consequence, human response to the environment has given rise to an archaeological record which, at first glance, suggests that the two areas were almost mutually exclusive. Distributions of monuments of all types show a marked preference for the kinder terrain of the east, but it is worth pointing out that while this may seem reasonable on the surface, the limited areas of good land in the west have almost certainly led to the destruction of most earlier remains within them, and concealed the evidence of sizeable prehistoric communities.

The difficulty outlined above is compounded by a second, and infinitely more serious, problem. For reasons which the author is at a loss to explain, Ross and Cromarty has been much neglected by archaeologists and historians. As a result, the basic stuff of early human studies — the data upon which to begin a reconstruction of man's way of life — is scrappy at best. Because of lack of research, it is certain that many more sites remain to be discovered, while excavation of those already known is sorely needed to provide detailed information upon which to build a picture of the past.

A further point worthy of consideration is that the Ross and Cromarty landscape known to its early inhabitants would have been strikingly different from that of today as changes in both climate and sea level acted upon the countryside. Over the 10,000 years or so since the final retreat of glacial ice from the area, the bare and barren land which it left in its wake has been undergoing a continuous modification due principally to changing climatic conditions. The accompanying table (Table 4) outlines these changes and presents a simplified account of their effect on the vegetation. Perhaps the most important effect, archaeologically, has been the irregular accumulation of peat over much of the District. This important resource contains a great deal of recognisable remains from the distant past and is the principal source of the information contained in the climatic chart. Peat may also cover parts of the landscape which were previously suitable for agriculture, and this aspect will be dealt with later in more detail. Finally, as part of this introduction, we must see the landscape occupied by a range of dangerous, but now extinct, predatory animals. It is infinitely more easy to understand the need for hedges, ditches, or other defences around house sites or stock enclosures when the prospect of the wolf at the door — or a bear — is a very real one.

MESOLITHIC HUNTERS AND GATHERERS

No trace of Palaeolithic (Old Stone Age) man is known from Ross and Cromarty, while the controversy which still surrounds the finds of pre-glacial animal bones supposedly bearing evidence of human activity, from caves near Inchnadamph (NC 275 206) in Sutherland, is such that discussion of this remote period can be ignored here. For Ross and Cromarty, present evidence points to the arrival of the first colonists after the retreat of the ice. The pre-glacial land surface would have been completely scoured away by ice movement, so that evidence of earlier human occupation can only come from caves whose recesses were protected. Caves of this kind are rare in the District.

The final retreat of the ice can be taken to have occurred around 8,000 BC, leaving a landscape scraped clean of soil and vegetation which only slowly began to recover. It is impossible to say when conditions became sufficiently amenable to have supported first the plants, then the

TABLE 4 — CLIMATE AND VEGETATION CHANGES FROM THE END OF GLACIATION TO THE IRON AGE

Climate Zones and Approx. dates b.c.	Vegetation	Climate
Sub-Atlantic	Increasing ash, birch and beech. Large tree clearances	Deteriorating
1,200		
Sub-Boreal	Tree clearance	Stable
3,200		
Atlantic	Mixed oak woodland and alder	Optimum
5,300		
Boreal	Mixed oak woodland with pine and hazel	Improving
7,500		
Pre-Boreal	Birch and pine	Improving
8,300		
Immediate post-glacial	Tundra and some readvance of ice	Generally Improving
10,000		

game animals, upon which men must have preyed. Nevertheless, it is possible that a few intrepid hunters penetrated the area at a very early date, perhaps only during the summer months, although their transient, nomadic way of life has left no trace. It is not until much later, perhaps 5,000 BC or so, that recognisable traces begin to appear in the archaeological records. These almost invariably consist of 'middens' or heaps of food debris, most often recognised along the raised beaches where they are intermittently revealed by shifting sand. Because of their coastal location, they usually consist of massive piles of discarded shells, which though abundant are not particularly nutritious and may indicate temporary winter or early spring camp sites when other food was not easily available. At other times of year, migratory animals such as deer were hunted, most probably by following the herds, with the diet supplemented by smaller mammals, birds, fish and so on, with wild fruits gathered in season. At times of dearth they appear to have retreated towards the coast, where abundant shellfish provided an ample, if monotonous, diet.

Only a few midden sites of this kind occur in Ross and Cromarty, and those principally in the east. Because most of them can only be seen from time to time, and because they are very sensitive to disturbance by visitors, they have not been mapped. The bulk of them are known from the coast between Tarbat Ness and Nigg and between Cromarty and Rosemarkie, where occasional sea-caves may have provided additional protection from the elements. In the west, only one or two sites have been confirmed, but continuous occupation of the larger beach areas, and the practice of using shell as fertiliser, has probably removed many of them, while those remote beaches which may have been suitable are beyond the reach of all but the most intrepid archaeologist. A recently-discovered cave-shelter between Red Point and Craig Youth Hostel lies some 125 m (c. 400 ft) above the sea and almost 1 km (0.5 miles) away. In front lies a large mound of discarded and broken shell. Excavation is needed to confirm its Mesolithic date, but should it prove to be so, sites can clearly be expected away from the traditionally-recognised areas.

Few of the known sites have produced artefacts, principally because so few have been examined, and it is necessary to draw on evidence from outside the District to understand this hunter-gatherer way of life. Much of the best evidence derives, surprisingly, from the west coast, in various caves in and around Oban in Argyll. This shows that they were skilled hunters who possessed a remarkable kit of tools of wood, bone, and stone ideally suited to a people on the move. Spears, bows and arrows and harpoons were made to exploit the rich game resources on land and in the sea. In spite of abundant game at times throughout the year, the presence of wild animals like lynx and boar would have made life hazardous, and it may be that even an area as large as Ross and Cromarty would only have supported a few nomadic bands, perhaps only a hundred people in total. It may well be that future work will locate more of their camps, inland as well as coastal, so that much more can be learned. In Ross and Cromarty, the evidence is still very scant.

THE FIRST FARMERS

The Mesolithic way of life appears to have continued virtually unchanged until around the middle of the fourth millennium BC (c. 3,500), when an influx of new settlers began to arrive in Scotland. These were the first farmers, families of the Neolithic (New Stone Age) who derived from northern Europe where increasing pressure on the available land forced some of their number to seek new areas for cultivation. Although their way of life was dramatically different from the native Mesolithic people, they continued to coexist for some time until they at last merged to become settled farmers.

A settled existence, based on the growing of crops and the keeping of domestic livestock, brought great changes. While hunting still played a large part in the economy, grown or stored food surpluses meant sedentary habits, the building of permanent houses and the adoption of crafts impossible for the nomad. Objects which were too heavy or too fragile to carry around could be made, allowing the development of the skills of the potter and the weaver. In spite of this, traces of these early settlements are rare. It is likely that, in a forested landscape being cleared for cultivation, buildings were of wooden construction, unlike the famous village of Skara Brae in Orkney, where the treeless islands forced the occupants to build in stone. No domestic sites of the period are known in the District, and for much of our information we are made to turn to the study of the dead rather than the living, and the great stone chambered tombs.

A glance at the distribution map (Fig 8) of chambered tombs shows the large number which still survive in Ross and Cromarty, and the almost total occurrence of these in the east. This would have been less marked before the reorganisation of the county boundaries, as several tombs lie over the border in what is now part of Sutherland, principally in Strath Oykel and around Ledmore junction. As with other types of monument, however, chambered cairns may have been totally removed by later communities and so distorted the pattern. In Easter Ross, where cultivable land was plentiful, recognition of their religious importance — or perhaps mere superstition — has allowed many of the tombs to survive.

The vast majority — all but one or two — of the chambered tombs of Ross and Cromarty belong to a group known as passage graves, because of the occurrence of a narrow passage within the cairn leading to an internal burial chamber. Tombs of this general type are found throughout the Western Isles; in Orkney and Shetland; and in the northern counties of Sutherland and Caithness. The forms of passage and

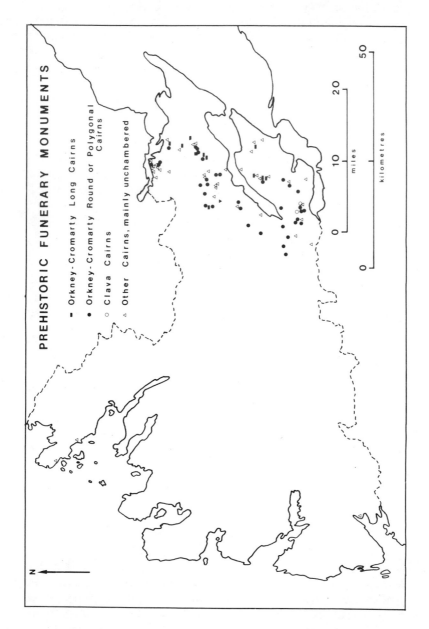

Figure 8 — Prehistoric funerary monuments.

chamber are varied, while the ruinous state of some preclude detailed plans. One or two have been excavated, with interesting results.

The cairn at *Kilcoy South,* on the Black Isle (NH 570 515), excavated by Woodham in 1956-58, proved to be a more complex structure than its superficial appearance suggested. The plan of the interior suggests that a small, round cairn was first constructed. This was then superseded by a secondary phase of a similar, but slightly larger form. In turn these structures become incorporated into the present cairn, with the passage slightly extended to open into the newly-created V-shaped forecourt. This development of cairns over long periods of time has been demonstrated elsewhere, notably at *Camster Long* in Caithness (ND 259 262), and at *Mid Gleniron* in Wigtonshire (NX 186 610), where two adjacent cairns revealed multi-phase building evidence. Such development indicates that many of the tombs remained in use for a time which has been reckoned as 1000 years or more. While the earliest phase at Kilcoy South may date to perhaps 3,000 BC, fragments of *Beaker* pottery found within it may demonstrate its continuing use until as late as perhaps 1,800 BC. Close to Kilcoy South are the remains of two other tombs, *Kilcoy North* (NH 570 517) and *Carn Glas* (NH 578 520). The latter has also been excavated by Woodham, and also produced remains of Beaker ware. It measures some 21.5 m (70 ft) in diameter and stands to a height of 1.3 m (4 ft). The chamber, divided into two compartments, is entered from the ENE.

Another example is at *Balnaguie* (NH 628 547), near Munlochy, where only the massive support stones for the chamber and passage now survive beneath towering oak trees which lend a dramatic atmosphere to the site and account for its occasional description by locals as a 'druidic temple'. Further cairns can be seen throughout the Black Isle, for instance at *Belmaduthy* (NH 644 559); *Easter Brae* (NH 661 628), where a much-battered long cairn has a small, circular cairn of later type only 50 m (160 ft) or so to the west; *Muir of Conan* (NH 576 567), with a circular cairn covering a rectangular, two-compartment chamber approached by a passage from the ENE.

Farther north, in Easter Ross, many other sites can still be seen. Along the hillslopes above the Alness-Tain road via Scotsburn are no less than eight chambered tombs, three of which are long cairns, four circular, and the eighth only surviving as a mutilated chamber, at *Scotsburn House* (NH 715 761). The long cairns are at *Kinrive East* and *West* (NH 699 754) and *Wester Lamington* (NH 747 780). In none of these can the form of the chamber now be distinguished. At *Millcraig* (NH 658 710); *Scotsburn Wood East* (NH 726 768) and *West* (NH 721 767); and *King's Head Cairn* (NH 697 751), are round cairns. The last example incorporates both a two-compartment chamber and a cist, or stone coffin of later date, set into the NW part of the cairn.

The valley of the Alness River provides several more, the best preserved being at *Stittenham* (NH 649 743), where a much-disturbed 12 m (40 ft) diameter cairn surrounds the remains of a polygonal chamber entered from the SE. A group of three, in various stages of mutilation are at Lechanich, about 4 km (2½ miles) north of Edderton. Of these, the best is *Lower Lechanich South* (NH 684 858) where the remains of a chamber can be distinguished on the E side of a cairn measuring some 22m (70 ft) in diameter.

The odd men out of the chambered tombs of Ross and Cromarty are those which belong to the class of tombs known as 'Clava' passage graves after the type site at *Clava,* near Culloden on the banks of the river Nairn (NH 757 444). While Clava itself, much restored and open to the public, is the best example, that of *Cairn Irenan* (NH 566 522) near Muir of Ord exhibits many of the diagnostic features of its type. These are much later cairns, perhaps dating from a cultural overlap of Neolithic and early Bronze Age peoples in the centuries immediately after 2,000 BC. Circular in shape, they are usually surrounded by a 'kerb' of large boulders which were graded in height from the SSW, near the entrance to the passage. In addition, most sites are surrounded by stone circles, a feature which is otherwise unknown except for a few rare instances such as the great tomb of Newgrange in Ireland. Cairn Irenan itself is typical of this style, consisting of a passage grave 12 m (40 ft) in diameter contained within a graded boulder kerb. The encircling ring of standing stones once numbered nine, of which only four remain standing and a further four lie where they have fallen. The 4.3 m x 3.4 m (14 ft x 11 ft) oval chamber is entered through a passage from the SW some 4 m (13 ft) in length. Clava tombs rarely occur north of the Beauly Firth, their main distribution clustering around the inner Moray Firth and along the Nairn and Findhorn valleys. Outliers occur around Aviemore. The only other known example from our area stood at *Croftcrunie* (NH 611 519), but it has now been totally removed.

THE BRONZE AGE

Other burial cairns shown on the distribution map (Fig 8) represent either chambered tombs too mutilated to be recognised as such, or burial monuments of early Bronze Age date, many covering stone coffins or 'cists'. The latter, together with an entirely new form of burial in which a cist is simply inserted into a dug pit with no above-ground cairn, marks a change in the treatment of the dead — and as we shall see in religious practice generally — which seems to coincide with the arrival of a new group of people. Around 2,000 BC, burials begin to be accompanied by 'Beakers', a richly-decorated form of pottery made principally for this purpose, and probably designed to hold food or drink for the journey of the deceased into the afterlife. The people associated with these burials, known conveniently as the 'Beaker' people, appear to have been responsible for bringing the techniques of copper, and later bronze, working from their European homelands. Beaker burials in unmarked graves were found during railway construction at *Dalmore,* Alness (NH 666 687) in 1878. Some of the burials were unaccompanied, as were a number of examples found during house building, earlier this century, in the heart of Balintore village where at least five have been found. 'Cemeteries' of this period are obviously difficult to locate, and depend to some extent upon the techniques of aerial photography, which will be touched upon later. None of the cemeteries can now be seen, but of the unchambered cairns the most dramatic example is the *Grey Cairn,* Glenurquart, on the Black Isle (NH 733 624), which is some 20 m (65 ft) in diameter and still standing to almost 2.5 m (8 ft). A small modern cairn 'decorates' the summit. A single cist, which produced skeletal remains, several flints and an almost intact beaker, was recently found at *Fodderty* (NH 511 595). The finds are in Inverness Museum.

Other elements of the changes in religious practices can be seen in the area. Earlier Neolithic 'temples', or religious enclosures survive as 'henge' monuments, much smaller than the great enclosures of Stonehenge itself, Avebury, or the Ring of Brodgar in Orkney, and without the latter addition of standing stones. Examples of these can be seen at *Loch Achilty* (NH 441 569) and *Conon Bridge* (NH 542 550; Fig 9). While in other parts of Scotland henges have the later stone circles added, none of the Ross and Cromarty examples have been developed in this way, perhaps indicating that they went out of use. Freestanding stone circles, without the earthwork of the henge, are also rare. With the exception of that surrounding Cairn Irenan and a possible example at *Carriblair,* Edderton, (NH 709 851), standing stones in the District are confined to single examples such as *Inchvannie* (NH 500 593) near Strathpeffer, and at *Windhill,* Muir of Ord, where one can be seen either side of the main road (NH 532 483 and NH 530 483).

All the types of monuments just discussed — henges, stone circles and standing stones — have been closely linked with prehistoric astronomy and the presence of a priestly element in early societies. This is a complicated and controversial topic which cannot be entered into here, although many of the sites *ARE* clearly related to the movements of the sun, moon and stars. Most of the huge literature on this subject tends

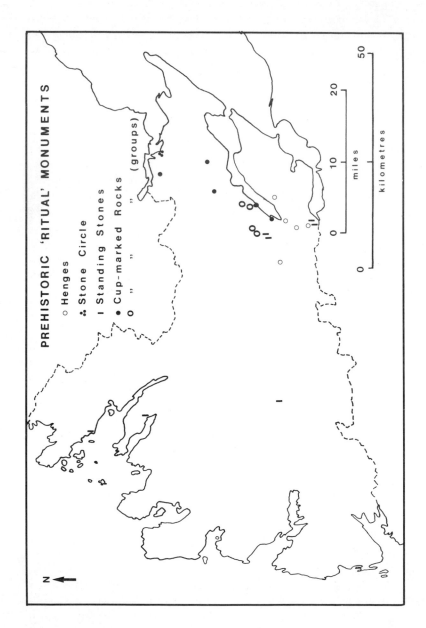

Figure 9 — Prehistoric "ritual" monuments.

to vary on one fundamental point — the *ACCURACY* of the sites as solar, lunar or astral observatories. Nevertheless, through the mists of speculation and complex mathematics, something of their real importance can be seen. The monuments appear to mark the seasons in some way, principally mid-winter and midsummer. These crucial points at the turning of the seasons would have been of paramount importance to an agricultural society, and probably linger on today as spring and harvest festivals, midsummer and midwinter rites and customs.

No discussion of religion in the Bronze Age would be complete without mention of the enigmatic 'cup-marked' rocks, which although once thought rare in the Highlands are now beginning to be discovered in increasing numbers. Most consist solely of a number of small, saucer-shaped depressions on the surface of large boulders or rock outcrops. A few have 'rings' surrounding some of the cups. The meaning and purpose of these stones is a mystery, although they do seem to be found often in situations with a clear view of the sea. A very large example can be seen on the standing stone at Inchvannie; several occur on the Pictish stone in *Dingwall churchyard* (NH 549 589); while another bearing some 30 'cups' and a symbol rather like a spoked wheel, from *Ardjachie* (NH 746 845) now lies at Tain Museum.

While clearly much remains of the Bronze Age in Ross and Cromarty, it is not until the later part of this period, perhaps until 800 or 700 BC, that identifiable domestic dwellings are to be found. The appearance of metal tools would have done very little to alter the essential way of life established by the Neolithic farmers. Crops such as barley and oats were still grown, and stockraising of cattle, sheep and pigs. Timber, gathered from land cleared for cultivation, might still have been the principal material for house-building. By the late Bronze Age, however, the climate appears once more to have been deteriorating into colder, wetter conditions. A dramatic increase in the formation of peat begins to occur around this time also, perhaps reducing the amount of land available for cultivation and certainly reducing the quality and quantity of accessible timber. This combination of effects may have, in part, given rise to a new type of site, at rather higher altitudes than those already established. These are the 'hut circles' which lie scattered almost everywhere across the landscape. Because of their profusion, and their often rather unimpressive appearance on the ground, they have not been mapped. Nevertheless, a good example can still be seen at *Driminault* (NH 723 750), measuring about 12 m (40 ft) in diameter with a simple entrance in the SE. At *Ardvannie,* 4 km (2½ miles) NW of Edderton are numerous examples set in heather moorland and surrounded by small stone heaps which may represent material cleared from their accompany-

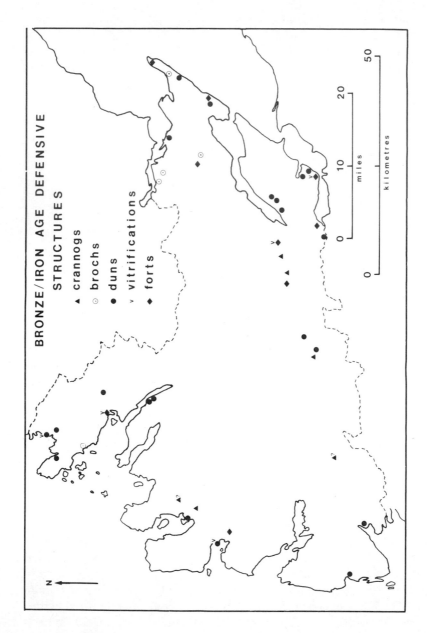

Figure 10 — Bronze/Iron Age defensive structures.

ing fields (NH 672 874). Many examples can also be seen in the west, often in groups and accompanied by clearance heaps and occasional traces of field walls, notably on the north side of the *River Sand,* above the road, and about 7 km (4½ miles) NW of Gairloch. Here, over 20 hut circles, two or more larger enclosures, field walls and clearance heaps cover an area of almost 20 hectares (50 acres) of the hillside. Amongst them are considerable remains of later settlements, with shielings, stock enclosures and later buildings. Unfortunately, a visit to this area involves a rather energetic walk, but more accessible sites can be seen at *Gleann Crom* (NG 850 885), just above the road between Poolewe and Aultbea and marked as 'settlement' on the Ordnance Survey map (Sheet 19). Here three huts are visible in moorland.

While a few excavated examples of these settlement complexes of huts and field systems have been shown to develop in the later Bronze Age, perhaps as early as 800 BC, they appear to have continued in use or to have been built well into the ensuing Iron Age. In general terms they should be regarded as belonging not to a named 'period' but to the first millennium BC.

Also originating in the Bronze Age, but more often seen as a phenomenon of the Iron Age, are the hillforts (Fig 10) — particularly those which demonstrate the process of *vitrification.* Settlers from North-eastern Europe appear to have migrated to Northern Scotland in the 9th or 8th centuries BC, bringing with them a new technique in defensive architecture generally known as the *timber-laced* fort. This involves the construction of massive stone ramparts in and around a supportive framework of pegged timbers which had the effect of locking the structure together. Within these walls, buildings of timber appear to have been built both free-standing and as lean-to structures against the inner wall-face. Probably thatched or turf roofed, it may well have been the accidental firing of these structures which set alight the wall timbers and led to the intense heat which in places has melted the stones of the ramparts into the vitrified masses which can be seen today. The clearest example of a vitrified fort can be seen at *Knock Farril* (NH 504 584), on a dramatic knife-edged ridge above Strathpeffer and with panoramic views in all directions. The importance of this fort as a strategic lookout can easily be appreciated. Occupying a level summit area of some 130 m x 40 m (425 ft x 125 ft), the fused masses of vitrified ramparts can be clearly seen at the break of slope with, here and there, gaps where portions of the wall have fallen away downhill. At either end are curious outworks, also vitrified, which are seen as linear protrusions along the spine of the hill. A deep depression in the interior marks the position of a sump, or well, which would have provided the water supply for the inhabitants.

Further examples of vitrification occur on the fort at *Ord Hill,* North Kessock (NH 633 490), now completely obscured by a forestry plantation; and in the west at *An Dun,* Gairloch (NG 802 753), where a small fort of perhaps different origin occupies a promontory on the shore near the village. At the latter, which is about 20 m (65 ft) in diameter, the vitrified material is to be seen flanking the entrance on the southern side. On the east side, natural gullies have been artificially deepened to form defensive ditches. Also in the west is the magnificently spectacular *Dun Canna* (NC 112 008) at the mouth of the River Kanaird and looking westward across to the Summer Isles. Set on a promontory which drops precipitously to the sea, the defences are concentrated on the narrow neck on its landward side. Here a massive, perhaps vitrified, wall protects the promontory from attack, while a second wall, possibly slighter but also vitrified, may represent a later defensive element on the western end. A third west coast example, presently the most northerly vitrified site on the west mainland, is at *Inverpolly* (NC 066 155). As the promontory on which it stands is cut off at high tide this site is very difficult to visit.

THE IRON AGE

Although, as we have seen, many of the types of site traditionally linked with the Iron Age in Northern Scotland — namely the hillforts and hut-circle settlements — owe their origins to Bronze Age peoples, perhaps the monuments most closely associated with this period are the brochs (Fig 10). These tall, windowless, dry-stone towers are seen as characteristic of their time and place. Ross and Cromarty, however, has very few within its boundaries, as most of our brochs lie to the north and west in Sutherland, Caithness and the Northern and Western Isles. Nor, in fact, are there many hillforts compared with areas to the south. For some reason as yet unexplained, Ross and Cromarty lies across the 'frontier' zone between these two great classes of defensive monument. Why they appear to confront each other in this way is uncertain, as the forts should predate the brochs by some centuries. However, recent work has indicated that some brochs may be considerably earlier in origin than the traditional century or so either side of the birth of Christ, and that their mutually exclusive distribution may reflect some kind of cultural confrontation in the earlier Iron Age. Further studies on the development of brochs may also shed some light on this, as the discussion of Dun Lagaidh (Plate 19) below will show.

Anyone searching for the classic broch tower in Ross and Cromarty will be disappointed. Most examples in the District survive as large stony mounds whose structural features can only be guessed at without excavation. A glance at the companion volumes to this publication, the *Sutherland Book* and the *Caithness Book* will indicate where brochs can best be seen to the north, while to the south the best-preserved examples on the mainland, cleared and presented to the public, can be visited at *Dun Telve* (NG 829 172) and *Dun Troddan* (NG 834 172), close together in Glen Beag, Glenelg.

The architectural origins of the brochs remain obscure, and several current theories fail to reach satisfactory conclusions on this important point. What is certain, however, is that many of the features most closely associated with the brochs themselves can be identified in other types of structures, however they may be related. This can best be demonstrated with reference to the excavations at *Dun Lagaidh* (NH 142 913) and *Dun an Ruigh Ruaidh* or *Rhiroy* (NH 149 900), both lying above the south-western shore of Loch Broom opposite Ullapool. Here Dr Euan MacKie revealed the existence of sites closely related to the brochs but deserving of a different descriptive term, and a continuity of occupation which may well exist elsewhere and be of importance in understanding their development.

At Dun Lagaidh, Dr MacKie's work revealed three separate phases of building which began with a timber-laced fortification whose origins lie in the Bronze Age tradition previously discussed. Radiocarbon dates related to the burning of the fort, which produced vitrified material, placed its destruction in the earlier part of the 7th century BC. A thick occupation deposit associated with this phase perhaps suggests a fairly long period of use. A second phase, which may represent the arrival of new settlers, took the form of a circular, solid-walled, defensive structure. Despite having many of the features contained in brochs, such as an intra-mural staircase, mural guard cell, and door-checks in the entrance passage, the site is now described as a 'galleried dun', related also to similar stone-walled fortifications found scattered along the west coast as far south as Kintyre. Finds from this phase place it firmly in the Iron Age. In turn, after a period of abandonment, the dun walls were refortified by adding mortar to create a crude and simple castle. Coins recovered date this phase to the 12th or 13th centuries AD.

Nearby, at Dun an Ruigh Ruaidh, a further site was excavated by Dr MacKie which contained architectural features that led him to classify it as a 'semibroch', a type of monument which he sees as lying midway along a developing tradition between the stone-walled duns of the west coast and the brochs proper. Excavation revealed that the curve of the otherwise circular wall nearest to the cliff above which it stands had been flattened or straightened, and the wall built thinner and less substantially, presumably as strong defences were less needed on this side. No intramural gallery existed in the reduced part of the wall, suggesting that it had never been a free-standing tower. In a second phase, the defensive nature of the site appears to have become less important, and was converted into a dwelling after removal of the raised floor which had rested on a ring of posts in the interior and a ledge, or 'scarcement' around the inside of the wall. Elsewhere in the District, broch remains are rather obscured by collapse and the ravages of time.

The remaining type of defensive site of the period consists of the *duns,* usually small, but enclosed within a stone or earthen wall of a size which seems out of proportion to the area contained within them. Including, for convenience, the sites of Dun Lagaidh and Dun Ruigh Ruaidh, some twenty duns survive in Ross and Cromarty. However, with the lack of systematic fieldwork referred to in the introduction, this number could well increase. Many of these sites are now relatively featureless, surviving only as vague enclosures within a noticeably substantial, but tumbled and spread, wall. Perhaps the best of these is *Carn Mor,* Culbokie, (NH 603 585), where a much-spread wall encloses an area of only 18 m (60 ft) in diameter. The whole is surrounded by outworks consisting of two earthen ramparts with an intervening ditch, and this defence 'in depth' perhaps owes something to hillfort traditions from farther south. Some human bones were recovered last century from this most interesting site, which is probably of several constructional phases encompassing a long occupation. A similarly laid-out site, though in much more ruinous conditions, can be seen at *Dun Mor,* near Beauly (NH 512 471), within a few yards of the District boundary. At *Drummondreach* (NH 581 575), the outer defences are confined to the N and E of the main enclosure. At *Wester Rarichie,* near Shandwick (NH 840 736), the relative disproportion of wall and enclosure can be seen where a wall spread to 6 m (20 ft) or more encircles an area only some 10 m (33 ft) in diameter.

In the west, the vitrified dun at Gairloch has already been referred to, while further north, another vitrified example stands close to the shore of Enard Bay. Known as *Meall an Iaruinn* or 'Iron Hillock' (NC 066 155) it comprises a circular enclosure some 18 m (60 ft) in diameter within a vitrified wall still standing to a maximum height of about 1.5 m (5 ft). An outer annexe stands on the south-west.

The more mundane domestic dwellings continued to be the hut circles. Here and there, remains of field banks seem to radiate out from the brochs, indicating that they formed focal points for at least some of the agricultural societies who lived around them. Only a few of these sites have been examined in detail, none in Ross and Cromarty, and the paucity of finds has added relatively little to our understanding of the people who lived in them. Farther north, some of these settlement systems contain examples of a monument known as a 'burnt mound'. For a long time believed to be confined almost exclusively to the Northern Isles, examples have been found in large numbers in both Sutherland and Caithness. At present, only two are recorded in Ross and Cromarty, but this is certainly to be remedied by future fieldwork in the area. The burnt mounds are fundamentally just that, mounds of a circular or kidney shape composed of burnt stone, ash and charcoal. In some instances they have a hollow in one side which gives them a double-humped look. In the hollow area, large stones occasionally indicate a structure below ground. Excavation in Orkney and Sutherland in recent years has shown these to represent communal cooking-places. The cooking is carried out in a pit, carefully built and lined, into which hot stones were thrown. If dry, the covered pit then baked the food placed above the stones. If it contained water, the food would have been boiled or steamed. After cooking, the cooled, cracked stones were discarded from the pit, ultimately building up around the pit to form the 'burnt' mound. Their dating is very similar to the huts, and it seems likely that they form part of the general settlement pattern of that time. Burnt mounds are almost invariably found close to supplies of fresh water. Two possible examples at *Balnacraig*, just north of Alness (NH 646 707), lie close to a small stream which flows into the Averon.

Also associated with fresh water are the 'crannogs' or small artificial islands which appear to date from the Iron Age although they can be demonstrated to have continued to be built, or at least used, as late as the 17th century. There are four certain, and two possible, examples in the District. The largest of these lies in *Loch Kinellan* (NH 471 575) on the outskirts of Strathpeffer village. Investigations in the past have shown that it has a substructure of massive timbers, now invisible, which elevated it above the loch surface. A late medieval brooch from the island suggests its occupation until a very recent date. Not far away, in *Loch Achilty* (NH 430 563) is another, smaller, example. Farther west, at the head of Strath Conon is another in *Loch Beannacharain* (NH 243 508), now only visible when the level of the loch is low. A fourth crannog can be seen in *Loch Kernsary* (NG 882 802) a short distance east of Poolewe, loosely associated with a curious boat-shaped building which stands on the loch shore. Crannogs make good defensive sense, as they are difficult to attack by both man and beast, and dispense with the perennial problem of the occupants of hilltop defences — that of ensuring an ample supply of fresh water, particularly during attack. Furthermore, their position leaves cultivable land, usually on the adjacent shore, free of buildings. Some may have been reachable only by boat — wooden dug-out canoes are sometimes associated with crannogs — while others were approached by a causeway of stone or timber set below the water surface and following a curved or sinuous line to deceive those unfamiliar with its position. The fluctuating levels, damming and drying up of many of our lochs has meant that some crannog sites are now lost forever. Nevertheless, work carried out on inland waters elsewhere, particularly Argyll, suggests many more sites may be discovered in the future.

THE PICTS

The people known to us as the 'Picts' go back in time to the first references to them by classical writers in the late 3rd century AD, and have always been something of an enigma. Until relatively recently, both writers and map-makers have described the brochs as 'Pict's Houses', although these structures clearly have their origins long before the emergence of the Picts in the historical record. In all probability, the term 'Pictish' should only really apply to a politically-recognised element represented by the higher social strata of the tribal societies in the north and north-east, as archaeology has yet to recognise anything characteristically 'pictish' in terms of the more mundane aspects of their culture. The English historian Bede, writing in the 8th century, mentions both 'northern' and 'southern' Picts, and it is likely that Pictland was simply a confederation of quite different tribal groups held together by an aristocracy responsible for the only truly recognisable facet of Pictish culture — its art.

The majority of inhabitants of Pictland probably descend from the native Bronze Age population, modified by incoming groups such as the builders of the timber-laced forts, and perhaps, the brochs. Until they emerge into written history, we can regard these people as 'proto-Pictish'.

What emerges quite clearly from the few available historical references is that Pictish political power in the 6th century at least was firmly based in the north. At other times, notably during the 4th century and the great raid of 367 AD on the Roman frontier, and later with the Pictish-Scottish confrontations, the focus of power may have lain in the south. However, when St Columba attempted to convert the northern Picts about 563 AD, the ruling king, Brude or *Bridei,* appears to have been all-powerful, with hostages at his court from subject tribes in the Orkneys. Note here that the traditional conversion of the Picts much earlier, by St Ninian, probably only refers to those south of *Druim Alban,* the Cairngorms and their eastern extension.

Where King Brude's fortress lay is not certain. The most popular contenders for the honour are *Urquhart Castle* (NH 531 286) where an earlier fortress probably underlies the present castle ruins, and *Craig Phadrig* (NH 640 453) on the outskirts of Inverness, at which occupation during this period has been demonstrated by excavation.

It seems certain that the Picts frequently re-used earlier hill-top fortifications, some of which would already have been vitrified at this time. They may also have reoccupied the sites of brochs and duns, all occupying the best defensive locations. No Pictish artefacts are known from the majority of these sites, but both Ord of Kessock and Knock Farril may well have been used.

Beyond the speculated re-use of earlier forts, evidence of Pictish occupation in domestic terms is entirely lacking. No house sites dateable to this period are known, nor can any burial deposits be located with certainty. To try to recognise the areas occupied by the Picts we are forced to turn to other evidence. One of the most commonly-used pointers to Pictish occupation concerns the place-name element 'pit' meaning a 'parcel' or 'share' of land. This element is to be met with frequently in Ross and Cromarty, at least in the east where a glance at the Ordnance map will reveal many. All lie on the better-quality land, but it is presumptuous to assume that the more marginal lands lay empty. Also, place-name evidence must be treated with care, as intrusive elements constantly appear as land ownership changes. What might be made of a name such as 'Jindalee' (NH 545 576), between Dingwall and Maryburgh, a thousand years from now?!

By far the most lasting legacy of the Picts has been their art and sculpture. Ross and Cromarty contains some of the very finest examples of this work, and none should be missed. They begin, chronologically, with simple 'symbol stones' bearing beautifully-executed incised decoration, often depicting animal life. At Strathpeffer is the Eagle Stone or *Clach an Tiompain* (NH 485 585). As well as the eagle, the stone carries an enigmatic symbol known as the 'horseshoe'. In *Dingwall churchyard,* a re-used cup-marked stone bears several symbols including the 'V-rod and crescent'. Just outside *Edderton* (NH 708 850) is a tall pillar, probably Bronze Age in origin and known as *Clach Chairidh,* bearing a fine representation of a fish and the symbol known as the 'double-disc and Z-rod'. At Rosskeen is the *Clach a'Mheirlich* (NH 681 690), whose symbols are now much eroded, but where traces of a crescent and perhaps a 'tuning fork' can still be made out. All these are known as

'Class I' stones, as they bear only non-Christian symbols *incised* on the rock. Three more fine examples from Ross-shire can be seen in an important collection of Pictish sculpture in *Inverness Museum and Art Gallery.*

While the stones above may represent the best of Pictish sculpture at an early stage in the development of the art, perhaps when the height of Pictish power lay in the north, its final flowering is also well-represented in the District. By this time, perhaps during the 9th century, the Picts had become Christian and were producing a form of religious art emphatically their own, although it owes much of its style to Irish and Northumbrian influences. These are the great *cross-slabs* of which the three principal examples remaining in Ross and Cromarty represent the very pinnacle of Pictish sculptural art. Mere description cannot compensate for a visit to these monuments, which can be seen at *Shandwick* (Clach a Carridh) (NH 855 747); *Nigg Church* (NH 804 817; Plate 20) and *Rosemarkie* (NH 737 576) where the great slab and other carved stones of the period can be seen in the museum at *Groam House* in the main street. Other fine examples from the area, from *Rosemarkie, Tarbat Ness* (NH 914 840) and *Hilton of Cadboll* (NH 873 768) now rest in the *National Museum of Antiquities,* Edinburgh, where they form part of a recently-established display of Early Christian sculpture. A single example survives in the west, where Pictish influence and rule seems to have been less well-established, at *Achtercairn* (NG 807 756), where a Class I stone bearing a fish symbol and part of a goose was built into the new cemetery wall in 1964.

THE VIKINGS

Many people still regard the Vikings as principally a violent and bloodthirsty race of hooligans intent on rapine. Certainly, they are known to have carried out savage attacks around the coasts of Britain, particularly during the late 8th and the 9th century, and most notoriously the sacking of undefended monastic settlements such as that on the island of Lindisfarne off the Northumbrian coast. In spite of this reputation, new archaeological evidence suggests that this was not always so, and that in some areas the intention was peaceful settlement and co-existence with local communities. The picture is varied, and the total lack of sites in Ross and Cromarty which can be attributed to the Viking period mean that, at present, we cannot be sure of the nature of the Viking presence in this area. That there *was* a presence is not in doubt — the abundance of Norse-derived place-names in both the east and west of the District testify unequivocally to Norse settlement. It is possible that rather different circumstances obtained in east and west, as excavations at the *Udal* (NF 82 78) on North Uist clearly indicate a violent take-over in the mid-9th century, while work at *Buckquoy* (HY 243 282) on the mainland of Orkney suggests integration with the indigenous Pictish people.

To add to our difficulties, only one proven Norse settlement is known on the Scottish mainland. At *Freswick* (ND 376 676) in Caithness, a late Norse settlement has recently been investigated by the University of Durham, but earlier levels which would indicate the nature of the Norse arrival are unfortunately not yet located. It cannot, therefore, be said what form the occupation of our area took.

As no sites are known in Ross and Cromarty, little can be said here to describe this period, and with the notable exception of a hoard of Viking silver found during the digging of a grave at *Tarbat Church* (NH 914 840) in 1899, a Norse occupation migh never have been recognised without the insurmountable evidence of the place-names, which survive in some profusion. Most are discussed in detail in W.J. Watson's excellent volume, *Place Names of Ross and Cromarty*, published in 1904, so that only a small selection will be discussed here. The reader is also referred to chapter 12 of this volume. Perhaps the best-known is *Dingwall* (NH 55 58), from Old Norse 'Thing-vollr', meaning 'place of the court of justice'. Local tradition places the site near the town at a later, and now vanished, 'moot-hill,' mentioned in 1503 but now untraceable. However the presence of such a judicial site suggests that Dingwall may have been of some importance at this time, prior to its elevation to the status of a Royal Burgh in 1227 by a charter of King Alexander II. *Tain,* another early burgh, has an obscure, non-Gaelic name which may also be of Norse origin. Smaller settlement elements include the Old Norse 'bolstadr', a homestead, which survives in abbreviated form in *Cadboll* (NH 87 77) and *Hilton of Cadboll; Arboll* (NH 88 82 and surrounding area); and *Culbo* (NH 63 60) on the Black Isle, recorded as *Culboll* in 1560. The first elements of these names are also Norse, meaning 'ark' or 'seal'; 'cat'; and 'ball' or 'knob' respectively. The 'bolstadr' element also appears in the west in slightly variant form as the 'pool' in *Ullapool* (NH 12 94). The prefix appears to derive from a personal name, *Ulli,* perhaps also seen in *Ulladale* (NH 47 58) behind Strathpeffer.

Old Norse 'dalr', a dale, demonstrates the Norse naming of natural features, but this applies only when the 'dale' element forms the final part of the present name as in *Swordale* (NH 57 65), 'sward-dale'; and *Strathrusdale* (NH 57 77). The latter, with the Gaelic 'srath' added as an unnecessary prefix — giving 'dale-ram's-dale' — indicates just how far inland Norse settlement may have penetrated. On the coast, from Old Norse 'vik', a bay, derives *Shandwick* (NH 85 74), 'sand bay'; and in the west two examples of *Shieldaig,* from 'sild-vik' or 'herring-bay' in Applecross and near Gairloch. Several other bays containing this element can be seen on the maps of the west coast of Ross and Cromarty, notably *Diabaig* (NG 79 60), 'deep bay', and *Cuaig* (NG 70 57), 'cow bay'.

Finally, a most interesting place-name occurs in the lower part of Strathconon as *Scatwell* (NH 39 55). This name comes from Old Norse 'scat-vollr', meaning common grazing land, and points out that 'scat' — a form of land tax associated with the Norse but more familiar in the Orkney and Shetland Islands — was being paid here. This suggests an established and settled community whose legislation owed rather more to the 'Thing' at Dingwall than native Scottish law.

Many traditions and legendary tales surround the Viking era, but with the lack of identifable sites on the ground and almost no excavation work, most of these must remain, for the time being, legends. Perhaps the most relevant of these concerns the battle of Torfness, fought between King Duncan (of 'Macbeth' fame), and the Norse Earl Thorfinn. Often placed at *Tarbat Ness* (NH 94 87), it is by no means certain that this was, in fact, the battle site. Other contenders are the large fort at *Burghead,* in Moray (NJ 11 69). Wherever the true battle site lies, that Thorfinn was the victor is not under dispute. Gradually, the Norse presence would have become more and more assimilated into a society which by the 11th century had become part of Medieval Scotland, leaving behind only a tantalising glimpse of their former renown in what is now Ross and Cromarty.

THE EARLY CHURCH

While it seems likely that the Picts were the first to introduce Christianity to the area, the evidence is sadly lacking. Controversy rages anmongst scholars of the period as to precisely how, and when, the Christianisation of this part of Scotland began. Records are few and far between and sometimes of doubtful authenticity. What follows can only be a personally-slanted summary of the multifarious publications and counter-publications which deal with this problem.

Bede, writing in the 8th century, tells us that his 'southern' Picts had been converted by Nynias (Ninian), who traditionally lived in the southwest of Scotland during the 5th century AD. He further tells us that the 'northern' Picts had been converted by St Columba about 563 AD, and that he had been given the island of Iona by them to found a monastery. Adomnan, Abbot of Iona, writing in the late 7th century a *Life* of St Columba, describes the saint's visit to Pictland in some detail but although he describes miracles performed by the saint and describes King Brude's 'high esteem' of Columba, he nowhere states that he, or the

Picts, were converted. Nevertheless, he later describes the monasteries 'within the boundaries of both people' (Picts and Scots as being responsible for their saviour from pestilence).

It is likely, then, that while the northern Picts were still pagan after their southern neighbours' conversion by Ninian, and perhaps even after Columba's visit, that Christianity had spread to our area by the end of the 7th century. Nevertheless, with the exception of those Pictish sculptures which carry Christian symbols and iconography, there is practically nothing, in the absence of documentary sources and dateable sites on the ground, upon which to reconstruct the development of the early Christian church in Ross and Cromarty. While some rather obscure references may provide clues for the specialist historian, these are rather beyond the scope of this volume, and instead we shall turn to the problem of the archaeological remains, linking them, when possible, to the other sources of evidence.

Ross and Cromarty contains well over three dozen sites which are possibly attributable to the pre-Reformation period — a period which spans some 900 years. Some remain as upstanding monuments in various stages of ruin; others exist only as churchless graveyards; as place-names; or as part of a folk-memory which may not always be trustworthy. In its early stages, the church was based on Celtic monasticism which derives ultimately from Ireland, and it is to Ireland that we must look for information about monastic layout and style. This gives us the monastic 'enclosure', known variously as 'lis' or 'rath', and less usually 'caisel'. The monasteries consist of an area of sanctified ground in which all the daily needs of the monks were accommodated — a place to pray and contemplate, a place to eat and sleep — set within an enclosing wall or 'vallum' of stone or earth construction. Many monastic sites of early date in Ireland conform to this general pattern, and sometimes internal features may be distinguished such as cells for the monks and small oratories. Their highland counterparts can be seen at *Iona* (NM 248 243), founded by St Columba; and *Applecross* (NG 714 458) a later foundation by a monk called Maelrubha in the later 7th century AD. At both sites, the monastic area was surrounded by a wall in this fashion, but these two only have adequate documentation, and we should seek sites of a similar type in our search for further examples in the District.

Such an arrangement may exist at *Hilton of Cadboll* (NH 873 768) where the footings of a chapel can be seen within an irregular-shaped enclosure which might relate to monastic occupation. A Pictish cross-slab, now in the National Museum of Antiquities, Edinburgh, may have come from a semi-circular annexe at the west end of the chapel. A somewhat similar arrangement can be seen at *Cille Bhrea* (NH 576 614) on the shore of the Cromarty Firth (near the north end of the bridge) and now suffering from erosion by the sea. At Nigg, the placing of the present churchyard between two stream channels, and certain slight indications on the ground, might suggest that here is another example, to some extent supported as at Hilton of Cadboll by the presence of a sculptured cross-slab. In the west, a chapel of 18th century date may overlie a much earlier, and perhaps monastic, church at *Laide* (NG 902 920).

Within the second category comes the graveyard at *Annat,* at the head of Loch Torridon (NG 898 547), where no trace of a church can now be seen, although the hill behind the site is known as *Beinn na h-Eaglaise,* 'church hill'. The name itself, in Gaelic *an Annaid,* means 'the mother church', and is perhaps indicative of an early foundation of which no trace now survives. There are many Annats or Annaits in the Highlands, some with churches, some without. Ross and Cromarty has at least four others; as a field name at Castlecraig, near Nigg; on *Carn na h-Annaid* and *Clach na h-Annaid* (NH 340 547) where there is a burial-ground; and at *Annat Bay,* Lochbroom (NH 01 97). All of these sites need further investigation for evidence of the early church, particularly as Annat has been defined as 'a 9th-10th century term for a church site abandoned during that period and not subsequently re-used as the site of a focal church'. (See also Chapter 12).

Other place-name sites, some with surviving remains, contain the element 'cill', a cell or church. Of these, now written as 'Kil-' that at *Kilmuir* on the Black Isle (NH 676 501) is well worth a visit. Originally *Cill Mhoire,* 'Mary's Church,' the remains of a medieval church survive in a most picturesque setting. It is unlikely to be of very early date. Also note *Cille Bhrea,* above. A most interesting example occurs at *Kildonan,* 'Donan's Church' (NH 078 908), on the east shore of Little Loch Broom. Here, a small graveyard of oval shape lies beside the stream which bisects the deserted township of Kildonan. A few curious graves are visible when not concealed by rank bracken. These consist of three or four smallish flat slabs laid end to end on either side of apparently shared headstones which are rude and unmarked. What may be an open paved area within the graveyard may mark the site of a preaching cross, where local services were conducted in the open for want of a church building. Across the stream are the impressive remains of the crofting township.

Lastly, with regard to place-names, the author was recently informed of some curious enclosures of unknown purpose at *Inver Alligin, Loch Torridon* (NG 842 573) apparently called, respectively, *Lismore* and *Lisbeg* (Lis Mhor and Lis Bheag), or the large and small 'lis', which as already explained, may refer to early monastic sites. The island of *Lismore,* in Loch Linnhe, contains just such a site. While the enclosures bear no resemblance to those, for instance, at Iona and Applecross, we might possibly have an indication of some early ecclesiastical presence in the vicinity. There is a great deal of fieldwork to be done!

By the early 8th century, things were changing, and with Pictish power then in the south, King Nechton expelled the Columban clergy and admitted the Roman church under St Peter in its place. From this time the church tended towards a diocesan form, under the rule of Bishops, and monasticism retreated. The spiritual focus of the north moved to Dunkeld instead of Iona, although some Scottish kings continued to be buried in the precincts of that Abbey. Under this system a more complex and organised church system became established with the formation of parishes and parish churches.

Churches, relatively speaking, were still few in number and very isolated from the centres of the papacy under whose rule they lay. This may be why so few records have survived and thus why so little is now known of them. Only a small number of tantalizing references have left clues to the organisation and effectiveness of the pre-Reformation church in the Highlands.

Only one certain monastic house outwith Applecross can be identified with any certainty in Ross and Cromarty. This is at *Fearn* (NH 837 772). Originally established about 1221 AD at *Old Fearn* (NH 631 784), it was removed to New Fearn shortly after — about 1238 AD — traditionally because of its proximity to hostile tribes farther north. The first abbey appears to have been colonized from Whithorn in Galloway; indeed, relics of St Ninian are supposed to have been brought there by the two canons who established the house for Ferquhard, Earl of Ross. The Whithorn connection seems to have continued at least until the abbacy of Finlay McFaed, who died in 1485. His monument now lies in St Michael's Aisle, on the south side of the church. While all traces of the cloister and domestic buildings have long since gone, parts of the church still survive among later additions and alterations. Many of the lancet windows are likely to date from the rebuilding of the abbey in the mid-14th century, while St Michael's Aisle may have been built by Finlay McFaed himself.

An early foundation, possibly monastic, may have existed in *Rosemarkie* (NH 737 576). The site was founded by one *Curitan,* but it is not known if he was the same as one of that name present at a council in Ireland in 697 AD, nor can his association with Saint Boniface be established. Whatever its origins, it seems clear that by the mid-15th century, when Fortrose and Rosemarkie became a combined burgh, the focus of church life centred on *Fortrose Cathedral* (NH 72 56, Plate 21). Some fine remnants of the cathedral, principally the south aisle of the nave and the undercroft of the chapter-house, can still be seen in a charming setting. Much of the detail of the nave is of 14-century date, including the fine stone vaulting of the roof. It is the only monument within the rearranged boundaries of Ross and Cromarty in the guardianship of the Secretary of State for Scotland.

Finally, for this discussion of the pre-Reformed church must needs be brief and selective, we turn to those churches dedicated to St Duthac (or Duthus) in Tain. There are three dedications to this much loved saint who is said to have lived about the year 1000. Of these, reputedly the oldest lies on the links close to the mouth of the River Tain (NH 785 822). While its foundation is obscure, the present remains appear to date only from the 14th century. It was destroyed by fire in 1429. In the centre of the town the two other dedications to Duthac survive side by side, both much restored. The smaller building may have been the original parish church, although it may not be earlier than its larger neighbour, the *Collegiate Church* (NH 780 821), as the ruins appear to date from the 15th century while those of the Collegiate church derive from the mid-14th century.

The Collegiate church gained its status in 1487, but probably deserved this rather earlier, possibly at the chapel site on the shore before it was destroyed. The shrine of St Duthac was a famous place of pilgrimage, particularly by King James IV, and became one of the most important ecclesiastical centres in the Highlands. What may be a statue of St Duthac can be seen in the right-hand of two niches in the west gable, while the fine tracery of the windows has been embellished by memorial stained glass inserted during restoration of the church in 1877.

POSTSCRIPT

While a good deal is already known of the early inhabitants of Ross and Cromarty, much remains to be investigated and analysed. New approaches and techniques are being devised by archaeologists all the time, and doubtless a revised edition of this chapter could be written within a very short time. Aerial photography in particular is likely to play a major role in finding the remains of buildings made of perishable materials such as timber and turf. Agricultural occupation is being found at higher altitudes and in more remote situations by the same method. Infra-red air photography will soon be attempted, with as yet unknown results. Archaeology is a continuing and expanding study, and closely related to the many branches of science which can help us to learn more and more about our distant forebears. The future is an exciting one.

Please note that references to sites in this chapter *do not* assume that there is right of access to them. Permission should always be sought from the landowner or tenant prior to a visit. In particular it has been requested that the Clava Cairn at Carnuran (Plate 18) should not be visited on Sunday. Please also remember to close all gates and respect crops and livestock, as without the co-operation of landowners many of these sites would be completely inaccessible.

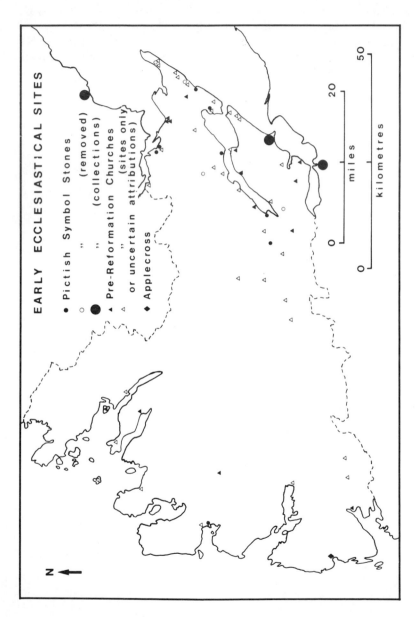

Figure 11 — Early ecclesiastical sites.

Chapter seven

THE CLAN PERIOD

Jean Munro

There seems to have been an earldom of Ross as early as the 12th century when it was apparently held by someone called in chronicles Heth (or Aed or Adam), and later by his son Malcolm. Norse influence, so marked in the west, was felt also in Ross but Magnus Barefoot did not include Ross or Caithness when he formally claimed the Western and Northern Isles for Norway in 1098. Malcolm MacHeth had links with the Norse world, however, for he married a daughter of Somerled and their daughter married Harald earl of Caithness and Orkney. Malcolm's grandson Aed was involved in rebellion against William the Lion in Moray where he was killed in 1186 and Kenneth son of Aed was killed in similar circumstances in 1215 by Farquhar Macintaggart. This later rebellion proved to be the last and King Alexander II awarded the earldom of Ross to Farquhar, with whom it is possible to begin a coherent story. Farquhar described as the son of the priest *(Mac an t-Sagairt)* is said to have been lord of the secularised monastery of Applecross, and perhaps was already lord of other lands of the west. Whatever his exact origins he was certainly of native stock and prepared to support the King's authority in his earldom.

There is no ready-made definition of the extent of the earldom at this time. The earl's lands covered the east of the modern District, but not the south part of the Black Isle, the southern march being the river Beauly and the northern probably the Kyle of Sutherland. But on the west it is much more difficult to follow. The bounds of the earldom of Moray were described in 1324 as '. . . the lands of Locharkaig and Glengarry and Glenelg, then by the march of Glenelg to the sea towards the west, and by the sea to the bounds of North Argyll which belongs to the Earl of Ross: and so by those marches to the marches of Ross and by the marches of Ross to the water of Forne (Beauly) and thence to the sea'. This Moray definition seems to tell us two things — first that North Argyll was a geographical description which has no relation to the modern county of Argyll and indeed had no common boundary with it: and second that in the 14th century the western coastlands were not part of the earldom of Ross although held by the earls.

Farquhar seems to have been often with the King; for example he was in Galloway in 1235, but in the early 1220's he founded the abbey of Fearn on a site in Kincardine parish which some 15 years later, with the consent of the abbot and brethren, he moved to the parish of Tarbat 'for the more tranquility, peace and quietness'. Farquhar's son William was acting as King's justiciar north of Forth by October 1239, and his position was much strengthened when after the treaty of Perth in 1266 he received the lordship of Skye, recovered for Scotland with the other western isles from the King of Norway.

With William the third earl of Ross who succeeded his father in 1274 we reach much firmer ground. During the early stages of the war of independence William was a supporter of John Balliol and it was this that led him to capture Robert Bruce's wife, daughter and sister when they took refuge in the sanctuary of St Duthac at Tain in 1306 and hand them over to King Edward of England. But Edward's son and successor could not or did not support the earl when he was pressed by Bruce in 1308 and in the autumn of that year he submitted to Bruce at Auldearn. He was given easy terms, getting all his lands back with the addition of Dingwall, until then a royal burgh, with its castle. Nor was this all, for William's sons Hugh and John were singled out for honours. Hugh married the King's sister Maud and thereafter added to the lands his father owned — getting Cromarty and Nairn and extending south into Strathglass. John his younger brother also made a profitable marriage through royal influence — to Margaret niece and co-heiress of John earl of Buchan. John and Margaret had no children and in 1316 Margaret's lands which lay north of the watershed between the rivers Ythan and Don, were entailed on John's elder brother Hugh. This brought a great extension of wealth, power and influence to the earls of Ross.

Hugh was earl of Ross for only ten years and fell at the battle of Halidon Hill in 1333. Shortly before he died he gave a charter of the lands of Rarichies between Balintore and Nigg to his younger son Hugh, along with some lands in Buchan which he later exchanged with his elder brother for west coast property in Ross including Eilean Donan castle. These grants were not only confirmed by the next earl William but Hugh of Rarichies was given more lands in Easter Ross.

But during the 1360's William earl of Ross became a supporter of his relative by marriage the Steward, later King Robert II, and John lord of the Isles in their defiance of David II's financial policies. This was probably the background to the marriage in 1366 of William's elder daughter and heiress Euphemia to Sir Walter Leslie, younger son of a Fife laird and soldier of fortune in high favour with King David. After David's death earl William sent a complaint to his brother-in-law Robert II saying that his daughter's marriage had been arranged quite against his will and that only by compulsion of King David and through fear of his anger had William agreed to her succession to his lands and title. The Leslies did not last long in the earldom of Ross for Euphemia's son Alexander, having married a daughter of Robert Duke of Albany, died quite young in May 1402 leaving an only daughter also called Euphemia. Her maternal grandfather soon became regent of Scotland on behalf of James I a prisoner in England, and by 1415 he had arranged that his granddaughter should resign the earldom of Ross in favour of his son John earl of Buchan.

This was not done without a struggle. Alexander Leslie earl of Ross had a sister who was married to Donald lord of the Isles, and Donald challenged Albany's dealings with the earldom. In 1411 he invaded Ross, seized Inverness and marched east to fight a battle at Harlaw near Inverurie in Aberdeenshire. His exact objective is not clear for the result of the battle was indecisive and Donald withdrew to the west. Albany occupied Dingwall and had begun to raise more men when Donald submitted and agreed to keep the peace. But Donald did not abandon his wife's claim and until his death some ten years later he called himself lord of the Isles and of the earldom of Ross (the latter being a style used at the time by husbands of heiresses), while his wife was described in a document of 1420 as lady of the Isles and of Ross. Their son Alexander succeeded as lord of the Isles on his father's death about 1423 and in 1426 and 1427 was describing himself as lord of the Isles and master of the earldom of Ross. By this time Buchan was dead, James I had been released from England and on his return had almost wiped out the Albany family. After some years of changing allegiance to and from James, Alexander was finally recognised as earl of Ross before the end of 1436.

For the next 40 years the earldom of Ross was held jointly with the lordship of the Isles, first by Alexander until 1449 and then by his son John. During this time the west coast lands seem to have been absorbed into the earldom — in 1463 John granted his natural brother Celestine the lands of Lochalsh, Lochbroom and Lochcarron 'within our earldom of Ross' while in the same year lands in Skye, also given to Celestine, were described as being within the lordship of the Isles. Oddly enough there is no record of the lords of the Isles visiting these western areas. Alexander and John both spent a good deal of time in Easter Ross, mainly at Dingwall and they also dated documents at Tain, Balconie and

Delny. Alexander served for a period as King's justiciar north of Forth, as his great grandfather had done, and based himself in Inverness.

In the end the union with the lordship was to bring about the forfeiture of the earldom. The lords of the Isles had already rebelled on a number of occasions against the kings of Scots and in 1462 John, acting as an independent power, made a treaty with the Yorkist King Edward IV of England at a time when the official policy of the Scottish crown was support for the Lancastrian Henry VI. John agreed to divide Scotland with the disinherited earl of Douglas and to receive a regular pension from England. This treaty remained a secret from the Scottish court for a number of years. John went to work and captured Inverness and confiscated the burgh customs but before he could penetrate farther the Scottish crown — at that time a regency for the young James III — abandoned the Lancastrians and in June 1464 signed a 15 year truce with York. Two months later John admitted his attack in Inverness (but not the treaty) and was forgiven when the court visited Inverness. A period of comparative peace led to a full treaty between James III and Edward of York in 1474, following which James apparently found out about the earlier treaty with the lord of the Isles. John was summoned to appear before Parliament, failed to do so and had his life and lands forfeited on 1st December 1475. Dingwall castle was captured by the earl of Huntly and in July 1476 John did appear before Parliament and renounced his earldom of Ross and the offices of sheriff of Inverness and Nairn which he had held, though he was allowed to keep part of his lordship of the Isles. The earldom of Ross was formally annexed to the crown.

So far we have been looking at the rulers of Ross, but what of their followers? We do not know much about the early native inhabitants of Ross but by this time some familiar names had begun to stand out. A variety of families had settled into lands within the earldom and were gradually developing into what we recognise as modern clans.

The first of these was, of course, the Rosses who descended from Hugh of Rarichies and who, after 1372, represented the male line of descent from Farquhar and the earls of Ross. During the period of the lords of the Isles Hugh's descendants held their lands from them as superiors, and as early as 21 January 1439/40 Alexander as earl of Ross granted a charter to John Ross as heir to his father Hugh lord of Balnagown in lands including Balnagown, Rarichies, Easter Allan and Culcairn. John acted as a witness to documents by Alexander and his son John on many occasions until at least 1466. These same lands were confirmed to John's grandson and heir David Ross by the crown in 1490. An essential part of any clan was the circle of relatives formed around the chief and the first of these to appear seems to have been William brother of John Ross of Balnagown who held lands at Little Allan and from whom descend a number of cadet or minor landed families. Gradually the circle widened with churchmen, merchants and small farmers all claiming to share the blood of Ross of Balnagown.

Also early established in the east of Ross was the founder of the clan Munro, whether native or incomer is uncertain. Hugh earl of Ross (1323-1333) apparently granted lands in the Black Isle 'for faithful service' to the father of Robert Munro. Robert, who was said in 1369 to have been lately killed in defence of earl William of Ross, had a charter from the earl of Easter Foulis in exchange for the Black Isle lands, to be held as freely as any other land within the kingdom of Scotland granted by any other earl or baron for good deeds. Soon more lands followed with, specifically included in the charter, the liege-men, natives and in-habitants of the lands. The Munros like the Rosses were frequent witnesses of the earls' charters in the 15th century, being designated Munro of Foulis by 1437, and soon more Munros begin to appear in records with cadet families established along the shores of the Cromarty Firth. Gradually the natives and inhabitants were absorbed into the clan and by constant inter-marriage came to share Munro blood as well as loyalty.

The early history of the Mackenzies, later probably the most numerous and powerful of the Ross-shire clans, is not so clearly documented. There is no surviving record of an ancestor before about 1400 but a recent historian has argued that the progenitor Kenneth was living in the early 14th century and that it was in his time that Randolph earl of Moray on behalf of the king attacked and captured Eilean Donan castle and, according to the chronicler, exposed the heads of 50 'misdoaris' on the walls. Moray in fact sent his 'crowner' to act for him in Kintail and it is possible that this was the earl of Ross. Certainly Kintail was in Ross hands by 1342 for in that year earl William granted a charter of part of Kintail to Reginald son of Roderick of the Isles and in 1350 he dated his charter of his 'Argyll' lands to his brother Hugh at Eilean Donan. It seems that the Mackenzies thereafter undertook a rearguard action and a battle, probably that called Bealach na Broige, fought by the earl of Ross with the Munros and Dingwalls against the western Mackenzies and their friends, though traditional accounts make exact dating very difficult. Fairly soon after this it seems from Mackenzie traditional history that the chief was established in an island castle in Loch Kinellan near Strathpeffer and it was from this base that they once again advanced west to Kintail. A family historian records a charter (now lost) dated January 1463/4 in which John lord of the Isles and earl of Ross gave Alexander Mackenzie of Kintail the lands of Garve and

Kinlochluichart, said to be 'to defray expenses in making peace between the king and the earl'. From the same earl came a charter unfortunately undated, of lands in Strathconon later confirmed by the king. Exactly when Kintail was returned to the Mackenzies is not clear but Alexander Mackenzie OF KINTAIL appears as a witness in a charter of November 1471 and in 1508/9 his grandson resigned into the king's hands all his lands including, with Garve and Strathconon, the 40 merkland of Kintail with the castle of Eilean Donan, all which were regranted to him as the barony of Eilean Donan. So it would seem that the Mackenzies were established in the eastern central lands of Ross and probably back in Kintail once more before the forfeiture of the earldom of Ross in 1476. They had also begun to establish the wide spread of cadet families soon to make the chief so powerful, when Hector, a younger son of Alexander of Kintail, founded the family of Gairloch.

Before leaving the Mackenzies it should be recorded that the ancestors of the Macraes probably came from the east of the county of Ross about the time of the Mackenzie loss of Eilean Donan in the mid 14th century, more probably to help the Mackenzies than to garrison Eilean Donan for the earl of Ross, though they later performed that task for the Mackenzies. Of the blood of the Mackenzies, or rather descended from a common ancestor, were the Mathesons who came into some prominence in Lochalsh in the 17th century.

To the north of the Mackenzies the lands of Coigeach were the property of the Macleods of Lewis. This family, descended from a Norse ancestor, was in close touch with the lords of the Isles and well established in Lewis, but it is not clear exactly when they acquired Coigeach. It was certainly forfeited by Torquil Macleod of Lewis before March 1507/8 and returned to his brother Malcolm in June 1511. Lochbroom, of which Coigeach may have been a part was owned, as we have seen, by Celestine, brother of John lord of the Isles by 1463 but whether the Macleods of Lewis were established in mainland Ross by 1476 is not certain.

In the extreme east of Ross were the lands of the Urquharts of Cromarty. The sheriffdom of Cromarty covering an area of only about 310 km² (120 miles²) was probably established before 1300, and in 1316 king Robert gave it to his brother-in-law Hugh Ross. Sir William de Monte Alto or Mowat the hereditary sheriff for the king and then for the earl of Ross died in 1327 and his son Richard, described as 'capellanus' or chaplain, agreed to give up the office. In November 1358 the king gave the office to Adam Urquhart who already held lands from the earl of Ross. The Urquhart lands, never extensive, were strategically important at the mouth of the Cromarty Firth and the port and the burgh added to its value. William Urquhart of Cromarty was given a royal licence to build and fortify a castle on the motte hill at Cromarty in 1470.

The fertile lands on the promontory between the Cromarty and Dornoch Firths were for a long time held by smaller families — Mac-Cullochs, Denoons, Corbetts, Dunbars and Vasses who remained independent units as vassals of the earls of Ross. It was partly from Andrew Denoon that Thomas Dingwall, sub dean and later chancellor of the diocese of Ross obtained the lands of Kildun near Dingwall in 1460. He was closely connected with the earls, being treasurer and then chamberlain in the earl's household and was followed in Kildun by a namesake who had brothers John, Alexander and William. The Dingwalls of Kildun, already established, were to play a short but important part in the years after 1476.

Dingwall Castle was of course the headquarters of the earldom of Ross although the earl's court of law was described as meeting at Kinnairdie just to the north of the town across the Peffery. This may have been due to the fact that Dingwall had been created a royal burgh by Alexander II as early as 1226/7, but in 1321 was alienated by king Robert in favour of the earl of Ross and remained associated with the earldom until the forfeiture of 1476. In 1497/8 its royal status appears to have been returned, though it was later challenged. The status of the burgh of Cromarty, also alienated by Robert I, was also confused during the century following the fall of the earldom. Tain claimed immunity from paying taxes either to the king or the earl as early as 1439 and in 1457 a royal charter, granted to the collegiate church and the inhabitants of the town, ratified the privileges already held but did not actually call it a burgh. It was clearly a community formed around the early sanctuary of St Duthac.

Also dependent on the church in Ross was the burgh of Rosemarkie whose original charter was granted in the 13th century. A charter by James II in August 1455 erected the nearby settlement of Fortrose or Chanonry into a bishop's burgh and united it with Rosemarkie. This area was the seat of the bishops of Ross and the site of the cathedral church from at least the mid 13th century. The diocese was apparently co-extensive with the earldom and the six parishes on the west coast, Applecross, Kintail, Gairloch, Lochbroom, Lochalsh and Lochcarron, which were transferred from Argyll to Ross at an unknown date, as the lands were added to the earldom.

This, then, was the state of Ross at the time of the forfeiture of the earldom. So far, with reasonably firm control from the centre and with enough land available to satisfy the growing ambition of the vassals, there had been comparatively little conflict within the earldom. But now there was a vacancy in the leadership and the fierce rivalry between the contestants for power led to almost continuous unrest. This rivalry was between the clan leaders already established in Ross — there were no significant incomers taking part in the struggle.

X X X X

The first part of the 16th century in Ross was dominated by attempts to re-instate the lordship of the Isles, forfeited in 1493 soon after Sir Alexander Macdonald of Lochalsh, nephew of the last lord, had tried to re-occupy Ross and was beaten by the Mackenzies at the battle of Blar na Pairc in Strathconon.

Donald dubh, grandson of the last lord of the Isles, a prisoner from his birth, escaped from Inchconnel in 1501 and was only taken again after 6 years and three government campaigns against him. Donald took refuge with his mother's sister who had married Torquil Macleod of Lewis. The earl of Argyll operated against the lordship vassals and their allies in the south and the earl of Huntly with Fraser of Lovat and Munro of Foulis in the north — the latter party being ordered to capture and garrison the castles of Strome and Eilean Donan said to be 'richt necessar for the danting of the isles'. Campaigns were directed by land and sea and by 1507 all the island clans submitted except Torquil Macleod of Lewis who was forfeited and his land given to his brother Malcolm. Donald dubh returned to prison for another 30 years but raised a rebellion in the Isles in 1545 during which he died. After his first rising Huntly remained as king's lieutenant for the north and hereditary sheriff with deputies including one for Ross holding courts at Dingwall and Tain.

Soon after Flodden in 1513 a new rebellion was led by Donald, son of Sir Alexander of Lochalsh. Mackenzie of Kintail and Munro of Foulis were deputed to deal with events in Ross and the former seized the royal castle of Dingwall and threatened to keep it for himself. This was the constant problem of the crown, that with no standing army or police it had to rely on loyal (or presently loyal) neighbours to proceed against rebels and wrong doers and then could not always control the resulting feuds. The death of Donald of Lochalsh in 1519 ended the rebellion and the male line of Celestine of Lochalsh.

This was important in the history of west Ross as Donald had been lord of Lochalsh, Lochcarron and Lochbroom. He was survived by two sisters Margaret wife of Alexander Macdonell of Glengarry and Janet who had married William Dingwall of Kildun. Each part of the lands was divided between them. The Dingwall half of the lands was gradually and fairly peacefully acquired by the Mackenzies, although William Dingwall of Kildun was killed in 1527 by a son of Kintail — Lochbroom was exchanged for Fodderty in 1543, Lochalsh by wadset in 1554 and final sale in 1571, and Lochcarron by sale in 1579, by which time the Dingwalls had lost Fodderty also. The Glengarry half of the same lands caused a long and bitter feud with the Mackenzies. In 1546 Grant of Freuchie was awarded the lands among others as compensation for losses suffered in a Glengarry raid on Urquhart and Glenmoriston two years earlier. By contract of marriage with Colin Mackenzie of Kintail in 1570 Barbara Grant took as part of her dowry the half share of the lands of Lochbroom. Similarly in 1571 Donald MacAngus of Glengarry retrieved his half of Lochalsh and Lochcarron by a marriage with Barbara's sister Helen Grant. But the Mackenzies were not satisfied and the feud between them and Glengarry became acute between 1580 and 1603. The end came with the death of Glengarry's son and the capture of the castle of Strome by the Mackenzies, and the traditional story of the burning of the church and congregation at Kilchrist by Glengarry was in retaliation for this. It proved to be the climax of the whole long affair. Glengarry was forced to yield the half lands of Lochalsh and Lochcarron, with Strome castle now and for ever a ruin, entirely to the Mackenzies — the charter of 1607 stated that he had 'resigned' the lands in the Mackenzies' favour.

In the east of the county there was also disturbance during the 1570's. Again the bone of contention was land and power, this time on a smaller scale — the former property of the bishop of Ross, the castle at Chanonry. There was trouble immediately after the Reformation as Bishop Sinclair complained of the cost of guarding his castle and said that when he was absent on his duties as president of the Court of Session it had been attacked and held for nine months. Sinclair's successor as bishop was John Leslie who in 1567 gave a charter of his lands including the castle to a cousin Leslie of Balquhain whose rights were purchased by Colin Mackenzie of Kintail, whose clan was expanding very fast in the east as well as the west of Ross. Meanwhile the Regent Moray, acting for the infant James VI, had appointed Andrew Munro of Newmore to be bailie and rent collector of the bishop's lands with occupation of the castle as a base for repressing rebels. On the death of Moray the new Regent tried to give the castle to another bailie who attempted to dislodge Munro by force with the help of the Mackenzies already gathered there. The feud between the Munros and the Mackenzies in Chanonry lasted for three years and, after some bloodshed, was decided in favour of the latter who had captured and held the steeple. But the Privy Council ruled that Munro was to be awarded suitable compensation for the expense of his original occupation of the castle.

A third feud also concerned the Mackenzies but began with divisions in the family of Macleod of Lewis and led to chaos and their downfall. Roderick Macleod of Lewis had married a daughter of Kintail but later divorced her and their only son, brought up among his mother's people in Strathconon, was known as Torquil Cononach. Roderick married twice more and had more sons. The second son was drowned in 1566 and this opened up the succession and led to violent quarrels between the two remaining legitimate sons as well as several illegitimate ones. In 1568 Torquil Cononach even invaded Lewis, captured his father and held him for some two years. The feud dragged on and after Roderick's death in 1595 his youngest son Torquil dubh was declared heir. Within two years he was abducted and handed over to his half brother to be executed at Ullapool on the Coigeach lands which Torquil Cononach had been given by his father. The later events which ended with Lewis in Mackenzie hands do not concern us, but Coigeach does. Torquil Cononach's sons died before him and his heir was his daughter who was married to Roderick Mackenzie, second son of Kintail, the Coigeach lands being settled upon them and their heirs.

The general lawlessness of the country, as illustrated by these events could be turned to their own use by any clansmen. Alexander Ross of Balnagown entered enthusiastically into the scramble for land and power after the Reformation and the succession of Regents which had produced the crisis at Chanonry. This earned the displeasure not only of the Privy Council in Edinburgh but also of the cadets of his own clan Ross led by his son and heir George. They met in Tain on 2 August 1577 and wrote to Alexander their chief exhorting him to serve God and be obedient to the authority of the Regent, urging him 'maist earnestlie to do the same rather nor perish his hous kyn and freinds and tyne the riggis that his elders wan'. Alexander paid no heed to them, and was outlawed and imprisoned in Tantallon. Released on promise of good behaviour he was no better, and in 1583 his son George was directed by a royal letter of fire and sword to collect his clan and pursue him. When he succeeded to the chiefship George was not all that much of an improvement, but he was forced to fall in with the new regulations for imposing law and order.

We have seen the problems posed by widespread clan rivalry and part of the solution tried in the 15th and 16th centuries. When an offender refused to surrender to Parliament to answer for his crimes a commission was issued to a neighbour to proceed against him in the king's name. Every chief had the basis of an army in his kin, friends, servants and the tenants on his lands. The king would create one of these as his lieutenant and give him wide powers for a specified time, as Huntly had had in the north in 1502 and on many later occasions. The more powerful the lieute-

9. DunLagaidh,
multi-period defensive
site, Wester Ross
(R. Gourlay)

0. Nigg Stone
(I. Campbell)

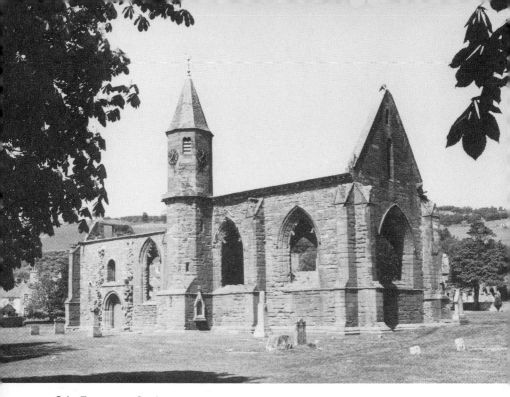

21. Fortrose Cathedral   *(J. Campbell)*

22. Castle Leod   *(R.C.A.H.M.S.)*

23. Tain Parish Church (Former Free Church) c.1890
(Tain and District Museum)

24. Hugh Miller's Cottage, Cromarty
(R. Gourlay)

25. Meikle Tarrel Farmhouse, Tarbat Parish   *(SDD (HB))*

26. Foulis Ferry Storehouse   *(SDD (HB))*

nant the more efficiently he could carry out the king's work. But by setting one clan against another and exploiting private rivalries the king was
laying up trouble for the future. Gradually the Privy Council and the
king began to realise that this was only an *ad hoc* solution. Under the
regents for the infant James VI the highland chiefs had to ask lowlanders
to find security for them — for example James Scrimgeour, constable of
Dundee, agreed to be one of the two cautioners for Colin Mackenzie of
Kintail coming to Edinburgh to appear before the Council, which he did,
but later the constable stood to lose some £5,000 when Alexander Ross of
Balnagown failed to appear when similarly charged. In 1587 the king
turned to the use of the general band which had proved successful earlier
in the century on the border with England. This was based on the principle that the chief or landlord was responsible for the good behaviour of
his clan or tenants and cash sureties had to be put down by the chiefs. An
act of Parliament listed those chiefs to be held responsible and included
Mackenzie of Kintail, soon to become a Privy Councillor himself, the
laird of Foulis (Munro), the laird of Balnagown (Ross), the tutor of
Cromarty (Urquhart) and Torquil Macleod of Coigeach — the last not
perhaps the best example of a law-abiding citizen. This proved to be fairly
successful and a more determined effort directed at curbing the power of
the island chiefs lessened the general tension.

X X X X

The events of the next century and a half can best be followed by
tracing the fortunes of the clan leaders in peace and war, but it must be
remembered that every leader carried with him a following of his own
clan and allies. With the arrival of the 17th century there came a short
period of calm in the northern highlands. Constant pressure by an increasingly efficient Privy Council gradually combined with a wish for the
rule of law and order, though inter-clan rivalries were never deeply
buried and constantly broke through. The Mackenzie chief, now a
member of the Privy Council, was raised to the peerage as Lord Mackenzie of Kintail in 1609 and in 1633 advanced to earl of Seaforth. He had by
now acquired an importance both nationally and locally comparable
with the giants Argyll and Huntly. Personalities within the clans were
playing a greater part than before and the line-up in future contests was
not to be on quite such clear-cut lines. One reason for this was individual
response to the Reformation — a response not always predictable by
family loyalty. On the whole the Munros and Rosses were staunch
Presbyterians while the Mackenzies took a more moderate line usually
within the reformed church and the Urquharts agreed with them, but

there could sometimes be division within the clan or even between father and son or brother and brother. From this religious division sprang the Covenanting bias of the two former clans and the Royalist and later Jacobite leaning of the latter. In the 1620's and 1630's there was widespread recruiting in Ross for the army of Christian IV of Denmark and later of Gustavus Adolphus of Sweden for their wars in Germany. This was part cause and part effect of the new attitude towards law and order at home.

After a period of uncertainty over Charles I's religious policy which tried to impose English forms upon the Scottish church, a party in Scotland drew up the National Covenant which was signed by many up and down the country. In April 1638 a meeting at Inverness brought in 'the whole gentry of Ross' except Sir Thomas Urquhart of Cromarty. The Urquharts were still holding Cromarty at this time but the family was in great financial difficulties owing partly to the general eccentricities of an early 16th century ancestor and partly to his large family — he is said to have had 25 sons and 11 daughters. His ultimate successor, another eccentric Thomas, was knighted in 1617 by James VI but was generally incompetent and brought the Ross-shire part of the family into deep trouble, while a junior branch which had moved across the Moray Firth, made good at Craigston near Turriff.

Following the signing of the Covenant war broke out early in 1639 in which Cromarty followed Huntly for the king and Seaforth garrisoned Inverness castle for the Covenant for whom at that stage Montrose also fought. The complicated story of the 1640's cannot be told in detail here but events in Ross and concerning Ross-shire clans can be mentioned as far as evidence goes. Attendance at Lord Lovat's funeral in the early 1630's by 900 Mackenzies, 900 Munros and 1,000 Rosses gives some idea of the numbers that could be involved in clan regiments. The atmosphere was evidently full of military preparation and in 1644 the minister of Wardlaw wrote 'There is nothing heard up and down the kingdom but alarms and rumores, randevouzes of clans, every chiften mustering his men' and later 'all the clans . . . were ingaged in dayly randivouzing'.

By 1644 Montrose was trying to raise the country for the king but Seaforth was not to be drawn out. He led a band of Covenanters which blocked the northern exit of the Great Glen forcing Montrose to fight the battle of Inverlochy, and three months later Seaforth and the Mackenzies were again with the Covenanting army, as were the Munros and Rosses. The Mackenzies suffered badly in the defeat at Auldearn and Seaforth made an uneasy peace with Montrose. He and his clan were not involved in the defeat of Montrose at Philiphaugh near the English border on 13

September 1645, but soon Seaforth was trying to bring about a compromise by suggesting that the king be invited to Scotland so that his presence could dispell 'the Clouds of mistakes' and there might be peace in the exhausted country. Many must have sympathised with this sentiment but his plan, or 'remonstrance' as it was called, though extensively subscribed in Ross, held no practical solution and Montrose was forced to leave Scotland. Another attempt at a compromise was the Engagement signed by the king in December 1647 and offering military aid from Scotland in exchange for concessions on religion. The Engagement has been described as 'the biggest turn-over of opinion in the century' and was supported by many former Covenanters including Munros and Rosses. An army was raised in the early summer of 1648 but the leading Scots Covenanters would have none of it. An interesting sidelight on clan loyalty appears when 24 Mackenzies stated that though the clansmen wanted to fight for the Engagers they would serve only under Seaforth who was not acceptable to the leaders for fear he would alienate hard line Covenanters. The Engagers' army invaded England but surrendered in August 1648. Seaforth later escaped to Holland and died there.

The execution of Charles I in January 1649 produced a quick reaction in the north in the form of a rising led by Seaforth's brother Thomas Mackenzie of Pluscardine, supported by Sir Thomas Urquhart of Cromarty, several Munro cadets under John Munro of Lemlair (the chief was a minor) and many Mackenzies. On 22 February 1649 they attacked Inverness, expelled the garrison, and kept the town for about a month before retreating to the hills of Ross when an army marched up from the south. Cromarty and Lemlair submitted on 21 March but Pluscardine and his Mackenzies stayed together, briefly took Chanonry and Inverness again when they were left unguarded, but were finally beaten in a battle at Balvenie in Moray on 8 May. The leaders were imprisoned and later ransomed but the clansmen were marched to Inverness and then 'dismissed every man armless and harmless to his own home.' Garrisons were placed at Chanonry and at Brahan, the Mackenzie castle in the east, and Eilean Donan. Meanwhile negotiations dragged on between the Scots Covenanters and the young king Charles II in exile in Holland where both Seaforth and Montrose had joined him. The talking continued over the winter of 1649/50 and at a point where they seemed to have failed Montrose set out for Scotland to make a show of force. He spent the winter in Orkney and crossed to Caithness in April 1650 expecting help from the Mackenzies but the presence of the garrisons and the lack of directive from Seaforth in fact kept them away. The Rosses and Munros remained as Covenanters and formed part of the force which defeated Montrose at Carbisdale on the eastern border of Ross and

Sutherland on 27 April 1650. Montrose was captured and executed in Edinburgh on 21 May and a month later the king signed the Covenant on board a ship at anchor at Speymouth.

Charles II was crowned at Scone on 1 January 1651 but in England Cromwell had collected an army and crossed the Tweed as early as July 1650. An English victory at Dunbar that September was not immediately followed up, but in the summer of 1651 Cromwell advanced again and, dodging the Scots with a movement into Fife resulting in the battle of Inverkeithing, occupied Perth. Charles and his army marched from Stirling into England and reached Worcester before Cromwell caught up with him and routed the royalist army on 3 September 1651. This army included many Ross-shire men — David Ross of Balnagown was captured and later died in London — Sir Thomas Urquhart of Cromarty was also imprisoned and died in exile in Holland. Many prisoners were taken — king Charles was one of the few to escape — and groups of them were sent to slavery in America, joining those sent after earlier battles. After Worcester Cromwell had no difficulty in over-running Scotland and it was soon after this that the citadel at Inverness was built and many great houses had soldiers quartered in them.

The last major royalist rising of the civil war period began early in 1653 on the border of Ross with a meeting of royalist clan leaders in Strathglass, and in April Seaforth, who had been one of the first chiefs to take action, presided at a royalist council of war at Glenelg. Over the summer Highlanders gradually came together under the earl of Glencairn. By the autumn it was believed that 7-10,000 men were in arms but split into small groups scattered about the country and anxious to avoid direct confrontation. On the whole the royalist groups operated south of Inverness and in December the main party was in Badenoch. During February 1654 the earl of Middleton landed in Caithness and joined forces with Glencairn at Dornoch. But soon General Monck arrived in Scotland with more men from Cromwell and the campaign he undertook in June and July 1654, after he had sealed off the highland frontier with garrisons, led him through Glenmoriston into the heart of Kintail and back to Inverness by Glenstrathfarrar. In the face of this military and some political show of strength the royalist rising seemed to fragment and waste away amid much marching and counter marching and disputes among the leaders. By January 1655 Seaforth and some of his Mackenzies had made terms which allowed them 'to carry theire arms for theire owne defence against broaken men and theaves within theire owne bounds', as were other highland chiefs who submitted a few months later.

From then until the Restoration of 1660 Scotland was firmly governed by General Monck but Ross-shire and the whole north suffered severely from having troops quartered on them, being 'plundered be the soggeris' after the country had already been laid waste many times by different bands of men. As early as 1646 Strathglass had been raided and a local minister wrote: 'betuixt the bridge end of Inverness and Guisachan (at the head of the glen) 26 miles there was not left in my country a sheep to bleet or a cock to crow day, nor a house unruffled' and things certainly got no better during the following years.

The Restoration brought further extension of the power of the Mackenzies. The main line of the Urquharts of Cromarty died out soon after 1660 but even before that the junior branch of Urquhart of Craigston had acquired part of Cromarty and they inherited the rest in 1667. By 1684 the barony was in Mackenzie hands and the lands followed ten years later. These hands were not those of Seaforth but a junior but quickly rising family descended from Roderick Mackenzie and the heiress of the Macleods of Lewis. Roderick inherited Coigeach through his wife and had been given lands not far from Dingwall by his father on which he built Castle Leod (Plate 22). In 1623 he bought the lands of Tarbat which had only 13 years before passed from the Dunbars to a Munro cadet. Roderick's grandson bought lands at Milntoun, formerly the seat of another Munro, and transferred the name of Tarbat to the house he built there. Another change of name, which did not last, was decreed in 1678 when the 'city and town of Portmahomack' was in all time coming to be known as Castlehaven. Roderick Mackenzie's grandson George was the most successful member of his family with a career in law and national politics. After participation in the Engager and Glencairn risings he became a lord of session at the Restoration and was created Viscount Tarbat in 1685 and Earl of Cromartie in 1703.

In the Highlands the years following the Restoration saw a gradual return to order with the re-introduction of the system by which chiefs were responsible for keeping the peace within their clans and were answerable for the good behaviour of their followers. For a variety of reasons this was a time of acute financial crisis for many highland landlords. We have seen the Urquharts of Cromarty go down before it and Ross of Balnagown was to suffer also. For the first time on any scale outsiders had a measure of control over Ross-shire estates as security for essential loans.

This situation was in no way improved by the Jacobite struggle which lasted on and off from 1689 until 1746. As with the civil war the Ross-shire scene was often a diversion from the main events taking place elsewhere but at times that diversion was crucial. When king James VII and II left London the leading Mackenzies were divided in their response. Seaforth went abroad with the king and was with him later in Ireland before returning home to recruit for him, while Tarbat, a Privy Councillor, helped to put William and Mary on the throne of Scotland and advised them on a plan to win over the clan chiefs by buying up their feudal superiorities — something that was partly done in 1747. The Munros and Rosses followed their Presbyterian line and supported William. David Ross of Balnagown commanded 300-400 men in the garrison of Inverness with the Munro chief's son under him, while General Mackay marched south against the Jacobites in the summer of 1689 to defeat at Killiecrankie and victory at Dunkeld. Mackay had tried to recruit Mackenzies into his army but found them 'partly disaffected and partly irresolute and indifferent, and all of them more apparent to joyn against than with him'. Seaforth's return in July 1690 did not make much difference as by then the rising had virtually failed but he was imprisoned in Inverness and Edinburgh for some years and then returned abroad where he died.

After alarms and excursions the next major rising took place in 1715 after the death of Queen Anne. By this time the immediate family of Ross of Balnagown had died out and the estate had passed to Ross of Halkhead in Ayrshire, described by the earl of Cromartie as 'ane old west country laird' and not known to be any relation. The clan was led by a Ross-shire cadet Ross of Pitcalnie. The Ross-shire line-up for the '15 was virtually the same as before. The first earl of Cromartie had recently died and his successor took no part but Seaforth was an ardent Jacobite. He called 1500 men to Brahan in September 1715 and against them were gathered at Alness a force including 300 Munros under the chief's son, and 180 Rosses under Malcolm of Pitcalnie, all commanded by the earl of Sutherland. Before a full-scale confrontation could take place Seaforth was called south by the Jacobite leader the earl of Mar, who delayed the vital battle of Sheriffmuir until the northern army arrived. The loss in casualties and prisoners to the Mackenzies in the indecisive battle was high and Seaforth immediately turned for home where things were going badly for the Jacobites. As soon as Seaforth had marched south Sutherland and his force attacked the castle of Inverness which fell on 13 November when young Munro of Foulis was made governor. Sutherland was able to show enough strength to force Seaforth to submit by the beginning of 1716, but news of the arrival in Scotland of king James caused him to take up arms again and plunder his neighbours. When all was over Seaforth was attainted and his lands forfeited.

The brief rising of 1719, which took place in Seaforth's country of Kintail, was intended only as a diversion while Ormonde launched an invasion of England. Again Cromartie took no part and there were

Munros in the government army. Seaforth returned to the west of Scotland by ship with the earl Marischal and some 300 Spanish troops. They landed in Lochalsh and occupied Eilean Donan castle. There was little reaction from other Jacobites and General Wightman was able to march quickly across country from Inverness to defeat the small force in Glen Shiel. Seaforth's castle of Eilean Donan was blown up in a bombardment from the sea but he himself escaped once more abroad.

It was following this rising that the loyalty of Mackenzies to Seaforth was demonstrated when they continued to pay rent to their forfeited and exiled chief and drove the government factor, a Ross from the east of the country, and his military escort from the estate. By 1725 General Wade reported that the Mackenzie tenants once the richest in the Highlands were now poor through neglecting their business and applying themselves to the use of arms. He might as justly have said that they were poor through having their houses and crops burnt by government troops as a lesson. The Seaforth estates were sold back to his son, known by his courtesy title of Lord Fortrose, in 1741. While in the north in 1725 General Wade went to Brahan where at a formal ceremony he received 'the chiefs of several clans and tribes' (mainly Mackenzies) and their men who 'marched in good order through the great avenue that leads to the Castle; and one after another laid down their arms in the Court Yard, in great quiet and decency'. This was following the Disarming Act and some 50 Mackenzie lairds had asked Wade not only to be allowed to give up their arms at their clan centre of Brahan but that the Highland Companies (in which many Munros and Rosses were serving) should not be present.

Clan rivalry was carried from the battle field to the political scene especially at election times. Ross-shire was represented in Parliament after the Union of 1707 by a member for the shire and one for the northern burghs which comprised Dingwall, Tain, Dornoch, Wick and Kirkwall. The elections were decided by those tenants in chief who were on the list of freeholders and there was much excitement each year when the roll was made up, and it was here that clan loyalties came into play. With Seaforth in eclipse there was a fairly happy arrangement by which the Rosses represented the county and the Munros the burghs. Sir Robert Munro of Foulis was member of parliament for more than 30 years but in 1721 he thought it necessary to kidnap and detain three councillors of Dingwall and when they escaped the Munros forcibly took over the election meeting to ensure the result. Again in 1740 he abducted ten of his opponents and in dispersing the riot that followed Munro supporters fired on the crowd and the wife of a Mackenzie town councillor was killed and others injured.

In 1745 the clans once more took the field in what was to be the last of the Jacobite risings. On this occasion Seaforth did not call out his exhausted clan but Cromartie rallied the Mackenzie Jacobites. It was to him that Prince Charles Edward wrote soon after landing in Scotland: 'I have some reasons not to make any application to the Earl of Seaforth without your advice. . .' Cromartie was slow to raise his Mackenzies and joined the Jacobite army while the Prince was still in England but with 400-500 of his clan he was at the battle of Falkirk in January 1746. The allegiance of the Rosses was divided during the rising — Lord Ross and his son raised, rather slowly, one independent company for the government but Malcolm Ross, son of Pitcalnie, abandoned his commission in Loudon's Highlanders and brought some of his clansmen to join the Jacobites. The Munros, many of whom were already in the regular army, fought on the government side in their own units and in newly raised independent companies rather than as a clan — one regiment (37th Foot) was commanded by Sir Robert Munro of Foulis, formerly lieutenant-colonel of the Black Watch, and as was then the custom it was called Munro's Regiment, though few if any of his clansmen served in it with him. Sir Robert's son and heir Harry, serving as a captain in Loudon's was captured with other officers by the Jacobites at the battle of Prestonpans and was a prisoner on parole in the lowlands when his father and uncle Dr Duncan Munro were killed at Falkirk. Another of Sir Robert's brothers, George Munro of Culcairn, a veteran of the '15 and the '19, brought 200 volunteers to enroll in Inverness to act as scouts. He commanded them through the rising but was shot, probably in mistake for another officer, near Loch Arkaig in the summer of 1746 in the course of the grim mopping up operations after Culloden.

During the early months of 1746 there was considerable activity around the Dornoch Firth although no battle was fought in Ross. On their return north after Falkirk the Jacobites took over Inverness, and Loudon with the government troops crossed to the Black Isle and made for Balnagown and Sutherland. There were said to be more than 2,000 Jacobites scattered around Easter Ross in March 1746. An attack by Cromartie on Loudon was made by sea unobserved during a thick fog but Loudon himself escaped to Skye while Sutherland crossed the Moray Firth to join Cumberland. The Jacobite success was short-lived but they did much damage and spread consternation around Tain. Cromartie marched north into Caithness but failed to raise more men and was surprised and captured in Sutherland on 15 April, the day before the fatal battle of Culloden. His life was spared, and that of his son, but they were exiled and their estates forfeited.

Penal legislation hastened the end of the traditional ties between chief and clan and a new era broke the pattern of relationships between the Rosses, Munros and Mackenzies which had played such an important part in the affairs of Ross since the days of the old earldom.

Chapter eight

THE KIRK SINCE THE REFORMATION

Rev. Alec MacAlpine

For the long pre-Reformation centuries documents are all too scarce but important work has been done by a wide variety of scholars. Anyone who does not know where to start will find a wealth of information in "An Historical Atlas of Scotland c400-c1600;" in addition to maps there are authoritative notes and bibliographies.

The urgent need for reformation throughout the whole Church had long been recognised. The Council of Trent was itself proof of that awareness; the length of its deliberations indicated the complexity of the problems. In the local scene the dilapidated condition of small parish churches and the appropriation of their endowments by individuals, clerical or lay, have been documented. In this District the comparative wealth of the cathedral at Rosemarkie and of the collegiate church at Tain must have meant the near poverty of their neighbours. A remarkable example of pluralism was John Thornton who drew his income from his office as subdean of Ross, Chantor of Moray and parson of eight parishes in the Borders, Perth, and of Tain and Edderton!!

Two men from Easter Ross attended the Parliament of 1560 in Edinburgh, taken as the official start of the Reformation in Scotland; they were Robert Munro of Foulis in the parish of Kiltearn and Nicholas Ross, Provost of the Church of Tain, a layman and a cleric. That Parliament passed acts prohibiting the celebration of Mass according to the Roman rite and approving the Scots Confession; a statement in 25 short chapters of the reformed belief.

Chapter XVI "Of the Kirk" states, "We most earnestly believe that from the beginning there has been, now is and to the end of the world shall be a Church . . . which Kirk is catholic, that is universal, out of which Kirk there is neither life nor eternal felicity ". These reformers had no thought of setting up some new organisation. Their aim as they saw it was to restore "the reverend face" of the Apostolic Church as seen in its original documents, the Scriptures.

In the same year approval was given to the First Book of Discipline, i.e. of structure and polity. After a statement on the Scriptures and the Sacraments come regulations for Ministers and Readers, the care of the poor and provision for teachers in universities and schools. Of particular interest for the subject of this chapter are plans for ten Superintendents for the whole of Scotland. (The term was taken from a Lutheran source as alternative to Bishop). The Superintendent of Ross was to have for his diocese "Ross, Sutherland, Moray with the North Isles of Skye and the Lewis with their adjacents, his residence in the Chanonry of Ross". There is no proof that any appointment was made for so vast an area.

The Book of Common Order appeared, popularly known as Knox's Liturgy, "received by the Church of Scotland in 1564". It is a substantial volume opening with the Confession of Faith "used in the Englishe Congregation at Geneva" and ending with "A Forme of Prayers to be used in Private Houses everie Morning and Evening", such as to be said "of the Childe before he studie his Lesson" and "before a Man begin his Worke". It was translated into Gaelic in 1567.

A real problem for the Reformers was to find men qualified to be accepted as ministers. Many priests in this District conformed and were continued in their charges, if judged suitable after public examination of "their gifts, utterance and knowledge". In the event of a division between a man nominated by the Council of the Kirk and one proposed by the people, care was to be exercised. "It must be altogether avoided that any man be violently intruscd or thrust in upon any congregation". Had such caution been heeded in the following centuries, how much strife would have been avoided!

Where ministers could not be found, readers were to be appointed. They were to be such as can "distinctly read the Common Prayers and the Scriptures." They were to be endowed with gravity, wit and discretion, lest by their lightness the Prayers or Scriptures read be of less price and estimation".

If these plans are tested in Ross and Cromarty, we see the progress and the problems. Taking Avoch, the first parish mentioned in the Fasti of the Church of Scotland, it appears that Alexander Pedder, vicar at and presumably before the Reformation, continued in his charge until his death nine years later. He was followed by Andrew Mylne, styled Exhorter, a step above Reader. At Cromarty John Anderson was vicar; though he did not conform, he was allowed to keep two thirds of the stipend; a Reader appeared in 1569. Fortrose had a Reader that same year, followed by a Minister, John Robertson, who held a variety of posts. Donald Fraser, Archdeacon of Ross accepted the reformed doctrine and is reckoned as minister of Killearnan; a man of courage, he is reported to have held the Bishop's residence against a band of armed men but was killed in 1572. Enough to show the uneven process over the County, especially in the west.

Twenty one years after the official date of the Reformation the General Assembly set out a system of Presbyteries for the whole of Scotland. Ross and Cromarty was to have four such courts, viz. Chanonry, Dingwall, Tain and Lochcarron. Tain was at work by 1588, Chanonry by 1598; the earliest reference to Dingwall occurs in 1638, though it may have started earlier. When travel by sea was easier than by land, Lochcarron in the west was connected with the Synod of Argyll. It was not established until 1724, when it went under the name of Gairloch.

An unexpected upset for the plans of the first reformers came when King James VI began to show his understanding of monarchy. "No Bishop, no King" has become so familiar a saying that it has lost its force. In effect it meant a choice between episcopacy on the one hand or republicanism on the other; the second being incredible, the King had his way and bishops were duly consecrated.

Another part of the royal plan for the Kirk was to have "constant Moderators" in Presbyteries, (a scheme which, when put forward recently as a step towards re-union, sounded to most ministers more like constant punishment). King James' idea took shape for some time: George Munro of Fortrose, William Pape of Nigg and John Ross of Logie Easter carried such titles. Outwardly the plans looked possible but, as at the Reformation, there were too many unsolved problems, which later events would uncover. Already the lines were being drawn for increasing conflict between Kirk and King, as within the Kirk itself.

A word should be said about the treatment of buildings. The removal of obvious signs of what were regarded as unscriptural forms of worship would proceed. That work was by no means confined to the "rascal multitude". The disposal of the relics attributed to St. Duthac was carefully arranged by the ecclesiastical Provost himself. Local lairds took possession of church buildings at Tain and were compelled to restore them only after the Presbytery carried the matter to the Privy Council. It was by royal order that at least some of the lead from the roof of Fortrose Cathedral was removed; part at least of the building was continued as the parish church, until the English army next century is said to have taken much of the stone to build Inverness Castle. The collegiate church of Tain was in regular use until the beginning of the 19th century, when the crowds attending made a new place of worship essential. Fearn

Abbey, after many repairs and renovations, is still in regular use. Wholesale demolition was in nobody's interest.

Outstanding events in the troubled 17th century can be mentioned in only a few paragraphs. The General Assembly of 1607 continued its deliberations in Aberdeen after the royal dismissal; John Munro of Tain, on a short leet as Moderator, was arrested and banished. The "Five Articles of Perth", passed by a reluctant Assembly there in 1618, look rather harmless at this distance but in their setting, as at the Synod of Whitby some thousand years earlier, people must have asked, "What comes next?". The sudden introduction of what is called "Laud's Liturgy' sparked off something like rebellion. The National Covenant became a symbol of belief. It was read aloud at least in Rosemarkie church and signed; "every honest man in the town that could subscribe did so". (A copy was given in 1728 to the Bodleian Library by Gen. Charles Ross of Balnagowan, Kilmuir Easter).

The shorter Solemn League and Covenant of 1642 tried to ensure a uniformity of religion on broadly presbyterian lines in the United Kingdom. The result, however, sharpened division; open warfare broke out. James Graham, the Marquis of Montrose, took up the royal cause, as he saw it, but after early victories had to flee to the continent. The execution of Charles I in 1649 brought him back but he was defeated at Carbisdale in Sutherland and was hanged in Edinburgh a year later. Seaforth's "Humble Remonstrance", corresponding to Hamilton's "Engagement" farther south, drew many into the civil war. David Munro, son of the minister of Suddie, and Kenneth Mackenzie from the manse of Dingwall were both killed at Worcester.

The records of the Presbytery of Dingwall 1649 to 1688 as printed by the Scottish History Society abound in references to both national and local history. Thanksgivings are reported for the victory at Balvenie (Dufftown), where a "royalist" rising had ended. The Covenant was to be inserted in Presbytery and Session books. Mr. John Macrae was "ordained to be more painful (careful) to reform the evil manners of Dingwall". Mr. Farquhar McLennan (of Fodderty) was "to forbear his oft repair to the hielands" (the western parishes with their own political and ecclesiastical outlooks). It is reported that the minister of Kiltearn does not meddle in civil affairs and that the minister of Urquhart lives "ministeriallie . . . Kirk is to be helped, the pulpit repaired, a new table for the Communion to be provyded and all other things necessarie for the decencie of the same". Evil doers are "to mak repentance in sacco".

Reference is made to pagan customs. "Margaret Dow summoned for sorcerie by burieing a lamb under the threshold, acknowledged the fact, affirming she did it only in simplicitie by the information of a poor

woman as a preventative against the death of her bestiall". Margaret
Munro of Culcraggie "delated for charming . . acknowledged the turning of the seive and sheir". All the way from Fodderty to the west there
are reports of sacrificing bulls at Loch Mourie (Maree), "approaches and
circulateing of ruinous chapels" and trying to put heads through a "holl
of a round stone". Curses, false accusations and threats of death were
seriously regarded and rigorously prosecuted.

Vivid examples of conditions in the western parishes are seen in the
visitations of 1649. When the deputies went to Kintail they found no
elders or people "except some few that were not considerable . . no gleib
or manse . . no pulpit, no collectiones for the poor, no desks". Instructions were issued that "the Kirk be repaired, a pulpit made, a suitable
stool for repentance erected, the Kirk floor pavemented, the beams of
the couples filed, no burials to be within the Kirk, the Kirk Zaird dycks
to be bigged, the windowes to be brodded and glasend, the Kirk to be
plenissed with desks".

A more desolate situation appeared at Lochalsh. "No elders in
capacity (office). Nothing found in this Kirk but the bare walls . . . there
is neither gleeb nor manse designed . . . John Buy, Kirk officer, declared
by the Minister faithfull and painfull. Referres to Session and Minister
that the Minister raise letres of horning and charge the parochiners to
roofe and thech the Kirk", followed by the same instructions as to
Kintail.

Lochcarron could hardly be more bleak. "No elders in capacitie by
reason of Malignancie (opposition to the Covenants) . . . A formall stool
of repentance found but neither pulpit nor desks. The late (former)
Elders being present declares that the minister did urge the subscription
of the League and Covenant first and last bot that they refused the same
both the tymes for fear of their Superiors . . No collections for the
poore and no kirk box".

Considering the difficulty of travelling and the many problems of
communication it is remarkable that meetings of Presbytery were held
fortnightly and that records were so fully kept. A recurring problem is
the search for teachers.

A small chapter of history can be studied in Prof. Terry's volume in
the First Series of the Scottish History Society under the title *The
Cromwellian Union*. After breaking the military power of the nation, the
Protector made plans for international settlements. Deputies from counties and burghs were invited to Dalkeith and Edinburgh to hear the
terms. The first article looked attractive to those who hoped for what
they understood by "the advance of true religion" but a closer reading
showed no mention of the Covenants and appeared to open the door to

"a vast and boundless toleration of all sorts of errors and heresies". It must suffice to note here that the Ross-shire burgh of Tain "accepted the tender" and sent deputies; Dingwall pled poverty and kept out of the scheme. In the event nothing came of the plan; the restoration of monarchy and of episcopacy set the old problems before the nation in more acute forms.

"Covenanter" is a wide term covering a range of belief and policy; Charles II and the Marquis of Montrose with many others had signed the National Covenant for varying reasons. Increasingly, however, the name was kept for those who held to the idea of a "covenanted nation" and disowned all who appeared to go back on their signature. Most of the ministers and people in Ross and Cromarty accepted the new regime, though there were too many changes after 1660 to be explained as co-incident. Four names stand out as convinced opponents: Thomas Hogg of Kiltearn, John McKillican of Fodderty, both of whom endured spells of imprisonment on the Bass Rock, Thomas Ross of Kincardine and Hugh Anderson of Cromarty. Bishop Paterson of Ross advocated " the regulation of Church government by the Civil Authority", which echoed the extreme claim of the King to have "the supream authority and supremacy over all persons and in all cases ecclesiastical within this kingdom". Absolutism could not go much further. Reports of the treatment of Covenanters in the south-west and of Huguenots in France would lose nothing in the telling in Ross and Cromarty.

A gap of five years in the Dingwall Presbytery minutes shows the difficulty in making a new start after the Restoration. The closing pages of the previous volume have been scored by a later hand; marginal notes like "shameless lying", "the spirit of lieing and malice" and "Maister Johne Macgillican was clerk to thir lying records" convey something of the temper of the times. The ministers of Kiltearn and Alness having been deposed, arrangements were made for Services on alternate Sundays. The minister of Dingwall complained that he could not get the town's men to build the kirk yard "dyk"; the Baillies, when at last they compeared, found ways of delaying for seventeen years any real plan for repairing "the ruinous fabrick" of the Church. Similar complaints were made by other clergy: that they had no manses and that part of their stipends were detained. These and other problems were referred to the Bishop and the Synod but they were long-standing difficulties and there is little evidence that much was done until the next turn of government.

When that turn came with the arrival of King William of Orange and Queen Mary, Presbyterianism once again became the official form of the church. Once again the transition was complicated by the scarcity of approved ministers. The episcopal clergy had been divided into three groups — the nonjurors (who refused to take the oath of allegiance to the new king), those not deposed for other reasons and those who accepted the Presbyterian system, as provided by the Act "For Settling the Quiet and Peace of the Church". A joint Presbytery, variously called "Ross" or "Ross and Sutherland" was at work intermittently for several years, meeting at Golspie, Fearn, Alness, Rosemarkie, Tain and Cromartie, for ordinations and inductions.

At the end of 1706 the Presbytery of Tain was re-established, though Nigg was attached to Chanonry, presumably with the help of the ferry. Edderton, Logie Easter and Rosskeen continued for some time to be served by "curates". The Scottish Parliament, soon itself to vanish, had abolished "all superiority of office in the Church above Presbyters". Lay patronage was ended. "Heritors and Elders" were empowered to make choice of a minister and propose him to the Congregation for approval or disapproval. The Confession of Faith was ratified but no mention was made of the Covenants.

The "rabbling", of which much has been made, came from both sides of the church, as might be expected of violent times. It needed no small courage to face hostile mobs and a loaded pistol, when William Ross of Kiltearn tried to conduct a Service in Dingwall. In the same way there has been misunderstanding on the exercise by a Presbytery of its power, the jus devolutum, when heritors and elders did not choose to use their rights of nomination; such cases show rather the physical danger of the work in some parishes or, more generally, the unwillingness of a generation, which had forgotten how to go about the never easy task of choosing a minister.

Colin Macnaughton's *Church Life in Ross and Sutherland* gives an abstract of the Presbytery of Tain's minutes up to the year 1910. An early entry appears unjust until followed to its end. A Catechist from the parish of Tarbat was brought before the Presbytery on the charge that he not only taught the words of the catechism but explained their meaning, which sounded natural enough. It later emerged that he upset public worship by singing another tune from that begun by the precentor; there was therefore more in the matter than first met the ear. The same caution might apply to any opinion of the act "anent promiscuous dancing . . . discharging that disorder" — especially when at "lykewakes" (funerals).

In 1696 an Act of Parliament made the building and endowment of a school in every parish an obligation of the heritors. The chief problem was to find and to pay teachers. In 1701 a "few private gentlemen" in Edinburgh began a movement which led to the formation of the Society in Scotland for Propagating Christian Knowledge. This is another subject for scholarly study. It must be enough to note here that in the

Presbytery of Tain's report of 1707 it was stated that "in the remote skirts of the parishes of Fearn and Tarbat, which were very populous and the people generally poor, it would be necessary to plant a school . . . and that the Inver of Lochslin (nowadays simply Inver) is the most convenient place". The present Meeting House is said to be the original school.

The Scots Parliament disappeared in 1707 on its union with the English House. Seven years later an act restoring lay patronage was hurried through in record time. Assuming its legality, there can be little doubt about its divisive effects. Long disputes between rival patrons and family intrigues, as at Killearnan in the Black Isle, were almost inevitable results. Much has been made of the reluctance of patrons to exert their new powers but almost immediately the Earl of Cromartie asserted that he would insist on his rights as patron, if steps were taken to instal Daniel Mackilliken as minister of Alness. A similar warning was given by the patron of Avoch in 1712.

Without waiting for the Act of Patronage, the Laird of Coul opposed the induction of Rev. John Morrison to Gairloch, kept him and his servant prisoners for several days and declared that "no Presbyterian should be settled in any place where his influence extended, unless H.M.'s forces did it by the strong hand". The result was a vacancy of almost ten years. A more notorious case, with less physical violence but more legal proceedings, followed in the middle of the century at Nigg in Easter Ross. With a royal presentation Patrick Grant was finally admitted by an unwilling Presbytery, whereupon the entire congregation registered its protest by seceding to form the charge of Nigg Chapelhill. Fortunately most presentations were prosecuted with a care for all the parties involved, but the right of the people became the focus of other and wider problems real or exaggerated.

Opinions about the '15, the '19 and the '45 Risings or Rebellions are so firmly fixed in popular imagination that appeals to reason and re-appraisal of the evidence are almost useless. Religion and politics, national and regional, being so interwoven, it was not easy to maintain old loyalties, especially when calculations of commercial gain were uncertain. It may suffice to say that Easter Ross was mainly for the Hanoverian succession, while the west tended to support the Stewart cause. It is generally agreed that the "1715" was the most serious threat to the Government and that the '45 with the battle at Culloden the next year was a needless disaster, due to the ambition of the main actor.

In the ebb and flow of advancing and retreating armies the ordinary people must have suffered to a degree not easily imagined nor fully reported. Beyond the "rabbling" at and after 1689 came the most violent attacks of political and ecclesiastical foes. The manse of Alness was wrecked and the Presbytery library carried off. Similar troubles came to Killearnan. John Porteous of Kilmuir Easter found it safer to hide in the Strath of Kildonan in Sutherland during the '45. On the other side Rev. John Stewart, Episcopal incumbent of Tain, reported "my meeting house was burnt to ashes in the month of May 1746 and my dwelling house plundered of all that was not put out of the way before the plundering party came . . . Mr. Grant's house at Fortrose was burnt, the other was only shut up and Mr. Urquhart's two meeting houses were both shut up". Both branches of the church had their wounds and their fruits.

It must have been more than war-weariness which opened the next stage in history of the Kirk. Theological interest was constantly stirred by fresh study of the Covenants. Social changes went with changes in agriculture and trade; emigration, voluntary or enforced, altered the balance of thought and the perspective of outlook. The usual terms "evangelical" and "moderate" are too sharp to allow for the wide variety of personality and of influence as the 18th gave place to the 19th century. In the fullest use of the term evangelical, the area could best be described by that word.

A welcome change from the usual run of controversy is to be found in the "Northern Missionary Society". Its formation owed much to the general widening of the church's concern and in particular to the visit to the north by Dr. Alexander Duff, one of the earliest advocates of Christian mission to India. In 1800 the Society was founded after a meeting in Tain, which issued "an affectionate Address to all Christians in the north of Scotland, who are anxious for the success and propagation of the Gospel". It was signed by representatives from almost every parish in Easter Ross and from "as far as Nairn and Inverness to Lochcarron and Kintail in the west". Roderick Mackenzie of Scotsburn was the first Praeses and Dr. Angus Mackintosh the first secretary. The work went on for more than forty years, when it merged in the Free Church of Scotland.

Payments were made to a wide variety of objects. A link with the Clearances is found in the entry, *To Rev. R. Williamson for a Missionary to itinerate in Prince Edward's Island, Canada.* This was the minister of Croick, who went with some of his people, who had been driven from Strathcarron and Glencalvie. Another connection with the wider world appears in the Society's work between the Black Sea and the Caucasus, ended only by the intervention of the Russian Orthodox Church.

Church collections are usually assumed to be for the local poor. Other entries are noted in the Presbytery minutes: "The brethren ar ordained to use diligence in the contributione for the distressed people off Glasgowe"; "the Moderator presented a supplicatione in behalf of the distrest men of Portpatrick, some whereof were captives with the Turks"; "contribution for the bulwarks off Peterhead and Stonhyve" (Stonehaven); "for the Scots Congregaton in New York, America"; "towards the ransome of Alexander Stewart, Shipmaster in Inverness and his crew, who are slaves in a galley"; "a supplication given in by the burgh of Dingwall for putting up of their brigg . . . by the parisheners of Alness for upputting the bridge of Alness". Such notices would raise talk in the churches; it would be of interest to know if they raised much money!

Visitors from the south must be puzzled by the number of churches all making claim to be of the Church of Scotland; even a rural parish like Fearn has four such notice-boards. Part of the explanation is in the great Disruption of 1843, when the "Ten Years Conflict" gave way to open separation. Though usually reduced to the issue of lay patronage, the causes were many, social as well as ecclesiastical. The problem of patronage had been with the Church since the Middle Ages; the factors in 19th century Scotland were briefly the Reform Act of 1832; (if the franchise was extended in parliamentary elections, why not in the church?), the deepening divide between Moderate and Evangelical parties, the increasing tension over Acts passed by the General Assembly of the kirk but overturned by the civil courts, not least the long suppressed resentment over the Clearances.

Whatever the causes, the result was the division of the established church; in every parish there now appeared not a free church but "The Free Church of Scotland", claiming the right to set its own house in order. Feeling ran very high through the whole nation, not least in Easter Ross; 28 of the 45 ministers in the former county "came out" of the established church. The people who took the step now had to pay stipends and provide churches, manses and glebes, which they did. A vast amount of writing appeared on the subject and is still being studied. The best known and most lively book from the seceding side is *The Annals of the Disruption*. Outstanding figures in the area are John Macdonald of Ferintosh, "the Apostle of the North", Gustavus Aird of Croick and Creich, John Macdonald of Kishorn and Killearnan and his son of the same name of Dingwall, Angus Mackintosh of Tain and Donald Sage of Resolis, to mention only a few.

Debate on "Declaratory Articles" of the church's sub-ordinate standards so disturbed some that in 1893 the ministers of Raasay and Shieldaig withdrew to form the nucleus of the Free Presbyterian Church. A full statement of their beliefs and of their work at home and abroad may be found in *History of the Free Presbyterian Church of Scotland 1893-1970.*

In 1900 after long preparation came the fusion of the two main non-established parts of presbyterianism to be called The United Free Church of Scotland. A considerable number of ministers and people in the north did not agree and, after taking the issue through the civil courts as far as the House of Lords, secured the right to the name "The Free Church of Scotland" and to its property. A commission later gave powers of adjustment to votes at congregational level. Attempts at union between these two smaller groups have so far been unsuccessful, though in form of worship and in belief there would seem to be little difference, perhaps rather in emphasis and ethos.

Another union in 1929 between the established Church of Scotland and the United Free Church was approved throughout Ross and Cromarty with only one exception. According to the position taken, the last 150 years will be seen either as a series of unions, large and small, or as the emergence of other branches. The paradox may be traced to the perfervid genius of the nation in religion and politics, where anything like compromise is held to be a betrayal of principles, or to an awareness of the faith underlying all the diversities. In a living church there must be room for growth, sometimes in unexpected directions, as there must be at least some understanding of those who still fear "a vast and boundless toleration" as a threat to truth. There is now only one presbytery for the District, with the exception of some western parishes which go with Skye.

Lack of space allows only the briefest mention of other branches of the Church. The Episcopal Church of Scotland with its wide diocese of Moray, Ross and Caithness has its clergy and people distributed throughout the District. Though perhaps increasingly influenced by the "Oxford Movement" and in full communion with the Church of England, it lays stress on the word Scotland in its title. The Roman Catholic Church has shown marked gains with new buildings in Invergordon and Alness, where there have been increases in population; there is reciprocal use of places of worship with the Episcopal Church. Baptist and other denominations are active especially in the east of the District and the Congregational Church in Avoch approaches its second century.

The present debate is on the substance of the faith, on what is fundamental and what is of lesser importance.

At least the Kirk is not static and it always insists that it is part of the catholic or universal church.

A postscript may be added on books which have come from the manses of Ross and Cromarty. At first sight it is disappointing that so few writings of note have been produced; part of the explanation is that the emphasis, especially in the earlier times, was on the spoken word. This would be particularly obvious in Gaelic speaking areas. Ministers made their own translations of portions of Scripture until the whole Gaelic Bible was available; some turned Bible passages into verse set to familiar tunes.

The earliest extant writing attributable to Ross and Cromarty, though not printed until long after his death, may be Donald Munro's *Description of the Western Isles*. Archdeacon of the Isles, he conformed at the Reformation and is reckoned the first minister of Kiltearn. John Lesley, the last of the Roman Catholic Bishops of Ross, produced his *History of Scotland* in 1578.

Of outstanding interest are the Journals of Rt. Rev. Robert Forbes of 1762 and 1770. In response to an appeal from "the Remotes" in their troubles after the '45 he made his visitations mainly to the Black Isle and surrounding country. Roderick Mackenzie, who had a call to Lochbroom in 1743 had two intriguing titles. *Reading No Preaching* and *The Consequence of the Present Pulpit Language*. Thomas Ross of the same parish, born in 1768, was a celebrated Gaelic poet and had a hand in the second edition of the Gaelic Bible.

Glenelg, though in Inverness-shire, is in the Presbytery of Loch-carron and may claim two authors in Donald Macleod and Alexander Beith, later of Stirling, whose *Highland Tour with Dr. Candlish* makes fresh and pleasant reading. John Beaton of Rosskeen, a Fellow of the Royal Society, wrote philosophical dissertations in two volumes. Lewis Rose of Nigg and later of Tain composed *A Humble Attempt to Put an End to the Present Divisions*, a solid, to the point of heavy, work; he tried without success to save Macleod Campbell from deposition in his trial for heresy. *Lash to the Old Seceder* suggests a different approach by John Downie of Urray. *The Days of the Fathers of Ross-shire* by John Kennedy of Dingwall went through several editions. *The Clan Donald* in three volumes came from the joint labours of Angus Macdonald of Killearnan and of his neighbour Archibald Macdonald.

In a class by itself is the work with the rather daunting title *Memorabilia Domestica* by Donald Sage, minister of Resolis from 1822 to 1869. Covering more than a century of everyday life, it records in fine detail the changing patterns of home, church and society as recalled by a grave and shrewd man. Perhaps it would be best read aloud by a grave and shrewd man not lacking a dry sense of humour.

Mention should be made of a group of scholars who came to international fame in this century. Donald and John Baillie were born in the manse of Gairloch, Hugh Ross Mackintosh was brought up at Edderton, John A. Mackay and John Murray just over the borders of the District. They were all scholars of the first rank and came to positions of academic distinction in Scottish and American universities.

Chapter nine

AGRARIAN CHANGE, MODERNISATION AND THE CLEARANCES

Eric Richards

The clearances, of which Ross and Cromarty had its full share, were the most dramatic and most socially disruptive variant of a more broadly based, and less sensational, series of agrarian changes which caused the reconstruction of Highland society during the 18th and 19th centuries. The intensity and the form of these changes shifted from decade to decade and from district to district. But the outcome showed certain general features: these included a more efficient agriculture, a redistributed population, and a radically altered social and economic structure. There was, too, an embittered memory of social conflict in many places, generated during those years of transformation. The clearances, in Ross and Cromarty, as elsewhere, are best seen against the larger sweep of economic and social change.

There were several origins of these great changes, but one of the catalysts was the famine of 1782-3. It remained vivid in the folk memory in Ross and Cromarty for decades to come. The famine, caused by a run of poor weather and associated crop failures, was nothing new to the Highlands; it was one of those recurrent crises of the pre-industrial age which produced sharp peaks in the parochial mortality records. The emergency, known as *"the Black Year"* was harsh but did not compare with that of 1740-1 when "Many were . . . found dead on the highways and in the fields; and others, through long fasting, expired as soon as they tasted food".[1] Yet there could be no doubting the severity of the great scarcity of 1782-3 which destroyed crops and caused high mortality in cattle, which then bankrupted many farmers who were thereby forced to quit their farms. Cereal crops failed and there was public begging: there was "a real want of bread for the use of man", and people from the high country flocked into the lower parishes: "a pitiable case it was, to see persons young and otherwise vigorous, in this condition, having hunger and distress of mind painted in their countenances". In fact death from starvation was avoided and credit was given to local proprietors and the government who acted with sufficient dispatch to secure cargoes of meal and pease from the south. "But for these supplies, disorder and rapine would have prevailed, and the poor rendered desperate by famine like so many wolves, have broke loose, and laid their hands on whatever they could find".

It was recognised generally that the relief measures had been remarkably efficient and had prevented an appalling catastrophe. Some districts recovered quickly from the crisis, and arrears were paid off swiftly; in other parts, however, there were permanent consequences: farmers were reduced to the status of day labourers and domestic servants, others in employment were dismissed and migrated to Glasgow and the low country; Highlanders who had scoured Easter Ross for food during the height of the emergency stayed on, often as mealers; new varieties of seed and cereals were introduced to broaden the basis of agriculture, and the potato rose to greater prominence in the common diet. The famine, indeed, had been a warning to the community, powerful evidence of the elemental vulnerability of the population. It accelerated the mobility of the people but, most of all, it gave urgency and immediacy to the messages of improvement in agriculture and local industry.[2]

I

The 1790s were the hinge of the great changes which transformed not only the agriculture but also the society of the northern and western Highlands. In Ross and Cromarty it was the decade of some of the most explosive sheep clearances. It was also a time when, under the prodding of Sir John Sinclair, the ministers summarised the condition of the people, society and religion of each parish. Their reports expressed tellingly the tension and ambivalence they felt about the agricultural change already manifest in most parts of the county. Vestiges of feudalism, and acute economic and social dependency, were juxtaposed against the growing pressures of inflation, population growth and modernisation. The responses were most advanced in the easterly parishes, but even there the success of 'improvement' remained halting and uncertain.

Most surprising in the world of the 1790s was the mobility of the people. This was a shifting society with large numbers of people both entering and leaving their parishes. The disruptive effect of the new sheepfarming was already visible, but it was not yet the most potent force at work. In Urray, for example, general agricultural improvement had emerged in a relatively quiet and gradual way. But the population shifts in Urray had been both radical and complicated. For, though the total population had apparently fallen almost 25% since Dr Webster's count of 1755, there had been a rapid increase in the last twenty years. The recent growth was attributed to the settlement of cottagers or mealers on improvable moorland. This was a form of internal colonisation adopted widely across the Highlands in these years. It was a technique which increased arable acreage at minimal cost to the landlord and, simultaneously, provided opportunities for the rising population to gain or retain a foothold on the land. It also provided a refuge for small tenants who had been displaced by larger agricultural changes. The minister of Urray described the process thus:

> these people . . . build huts on barren ground and improve spots around them, for which they pay nothing for a stipulated number of years. The proprietor frequently indulges them with tools and seed for the first season. After the first period is expired, these crofts are rented from 3s. to 40s. a year. Every year produces one or more of these new settlers.

In this way a new crofting district was carved from previously unutilised land. Often the cottagers became part-day labourers, part-fishermen, and part-farmers. They became a semi-proletarian fringe which helped service the new large-scale agriculture, most notably in Easter Ross.

There was contemporary controversy about the status and welfare of the emergent crofter class. As displaced landholders their circumstances seemed to be worsened. At Rosskeen, however, it was claimed that the cottagers-cum-day-labourers were actually more prosperous than the old-style small farmers: "it is observed, that from their labour, and the industry and their wives and children, they live more comfortably, than those in a supposed superior class, and enjoy perfect independence". But such betterment depended on the availability of local employment, the want of which was re-echoed through many parishes.

At Urray the settlers were local people augmented also by the people migrating from the Highlands and even the Hebrides, displaced not by sheep but by "a severe season" which "destroyed their cattle". Yet, concurrently, while Urray proved hospitable to newcomers, many others departed, "by the annual emigrations to the South country in harvest, and by the great numbers enlisted into the Highland regiments, at the commencement of the last two wars".[3] Emigration to America was also a recurrent anxiety. In 1772, for instance, Gilbert Robertson in his disquiet remarked that emigration was "a hurtful practice that ought to be discouraged by every lover of his country. What is a country without inhabitants, what are lands without people, what is . . . a minister's charge without parishioners?" Even then, however, some Ross-shire opinion,

General Alexander Mackay's for one, held that emigration might be both inevitable and beneficial.[4] There was, therefore, much movement of humanity into and out of Ross-shire parishes. It pre-dated the clearances, but the clearances would undoubtedly accelerate the process.

There were many local variations on the theme of mobility. At Urquhart there had been a dramatic fall of population in the late 1780s when many departed in search of employment when the special exemption from spirits duty ("the Ferintosh privilege") was withdrawn from the heritor, Forbes of Culloden. Yet, within a couple of years numbers were recovering because poor people there had been induced "to settle in the moor grounds on the skirts of the parish, rather than seek for subsistence by emigration, and because the proprietors are beginning to see . . . the good policy of giving them all due encouragement in their little improvements".[5] At this time the displacement effect of agrarian change was more pronounced in the eastern arable districts than from the incursions of sheep farmers. The rise of commercial, large scale, export-oriented, cereal production was emerging in many places. At Tarbat corn production far exceeded local requirements and, as well as exports, the parish also fed Highland cattle en route for southern markets. But its population had fallen: "One cause of the decrease of the numbers of inhabitants is uniting farms into one, a practice undoubtedly inimical to population". Yet, the people seem to have been suggestible already: "what chiefly contributes to the decrease of the inhabitants is the yearly emigration to the south of young people who never return".[6]

Enclosure, of course, was simply one component of "agricultural improvement" (which also affected rotations, crop varieties, animal breeding, tenures, rents, services, use of labour) and was commonly encouraged by the example of landowners on their home farms. They also introduced southern specialists, granted leases, raised rents and increased the scale of operations. It required capital, enterprise and skill, but in an age of inflation its results were generally lucrative. There were periods of accelerated progress, but there was a longer continuity too — remnants of the old system lingered late in the 19th century (such as rents in kind on the Balnagown estate in 1877).[7] In part, the entire programme of improvement was perceived as the final eradication of the evils of feudalism, and the achievement of the blueprint outlined by Adam Smith and his Highland advocates. Enclosure, however, was its most controversial and disturbing characteristic. At Nigg, where the minister complained of a general lack of progressive agriculture, the number of sheep was in decline because of the expansion of cattle and cultivation — nevertheless, "the population is rather on the decrease, owing to the union of farms, and several places where cottages once stood, [are] now being enclosed and planted".[8] The same was true at Logie Easter where dairying had been substituted for small-scale sheep pasture: meanwhile displaced small tenants (as well as some Highland refugees from the famine 1782-3) were hard at work converting wasteland into arable crofts.

Improvement was a double-edged weapon for the small tenants. The "monopoly of farms" caused them to resettle on moorland and to become increasingly dependent on the ubiquitous potato. (It was 50% of subsistence at Kintail and Logie Easter, 66% at Applecross, "the principal food" in Kilmuir Easter and, with herrings, the staff of life almost everywhere). At the same time there was widespread liberation from anachronistic exactions, most significantly from labour services. At Logie Easter the minister was vehemently enthusiastic for the change:

> The servitudes which disgraced human nature, by rendering tenants almost slaves, are, in this parish, done away; and I hope the day is fast approaching, when proprietors will find it proper to have their rents paid in victual and money only.[9]

These changes were preliminary to the wholesale rationalisation of the Highland and Lowland economies for greater productivity and wealth.

The transition was, doubtless, often disruptive. At Kiltearn in the 1790s the re-definition of society was in full train; there was no sheep-farming but the new agriculture had divided the community into two classes — the gentlemen's farms "all . . . managed either by natives from the south of Scotland, or by persons bred to farming there", and the mealers or cottars, augmented by an immigration of labourers who, presumably, found employment on the recently enclosed farms of the district.[10] In Kilmuir Easter improvement continued to be inhibited by the smallness of farms, the backward prejudices of the people, the lack of leases.[11] Meanwhile the parish of Fearn produced far more food than its people could consume, but its population had declined, partly by the annual emigration to the south (including northern England), but also from the familiar "monopoly of farms" by which a single farmer might possess land which was "formerly possessed by 4, 6, 8 and 10 tenants".[12]

The spread of improvement farming generated communal anxiety, even alarm. At Contin the people were reported "averse to enclosures, as they wish to have all lands of pasture in common", and there was a fear that the population would decline because "the gentlemen are encouraging shepherds to come and settle on their properties, which must necessarily remove the present inhabitants, and force them to go in quest of bread to other countries, as there are no manufactures established here to employ them".[13] On the east coast, at Avoch, despite the development of some commercial fishing and muir settlement schemes,

many of the new generation had little, or only a tenuous, hold on the
land; many worked as day labourers or travelled to the southern harvests
each year.[14] In the west, at Applecross, the only agricultural change worthy of note had been the expansion of potato production — the roads remained abysmal, the fishing produced no saleable surplus, and though
servitudes were being abolished, there was little division of labour.
Nevertheless, population had more than doubled in forty years and this
alone had wrought a profound change in social relations:

> The increasing population of the country, at large, is favourable to the in-
> terested views of the proprietors. For every farm, a multitude of candidates is
> ready to appear, and the culture of the ground, being the sole occupation of
> the inhabitants, the disappointed have no other option but either to emigrate
> or beg.[15]

The balance of economic and demographic forces had tilted towards the
landowning class.

The pressures and opportunities generated in agriculture by the
1790s clearly derived from several sources, and it would be mistaken to
compress the process into the unsatisfactory phrase "the clearances".
Technical changes in usage, new directions in local and national
movements, as well as demographic shifts, all contributed to a re-
alignment of the factors of production and to a reconstruction of social
and economic relations. The consequences of agrarian and demographic
changes depended on the options available in each locality, and on the
speed and timing of improvement. Some landlords, while they revolutionised land tenure, were conspicuously solicitous for the welfare of the
small tenants they so dislocated. At Alness, for instance, people removed
from old lands were resettled by their own landords;[16] in other places proprietors welcomed displaced tenants from other estates, incorporating
them in their own programmes of new development, particularly where
there was promise of fat profits.

The most favoured option for a growing population, for refugees
from enclosures, and for the generally underemployed, was the encouragement of local industry. There were many advocates of manufacturing industry but the omens were not favourable. True, there was spinning and weaving for home consumption in many places, and pockets of
hemp manufacture on the pattern of the domestic system. At Cromarty
there was a hempen cloth factory in operation which employed as many
as 200 people, and some of the poor of the county had been absorbed into similar enterprise in the town of Inverness. Flax spinning in Kilmuir
Easter had attracted immigrants from Highland parishes, and women
especially benefited from such opportunities for employment.[17] But most
parishes needed far more manufacturing if they were to accommodate

the unemployed and the rapidly rising local populations already identified by the ministers in the 1790s. Moreover, the problem was exacerbated by the apparent decline in demand for domestically-produced tex-
tiles from the impact of competition of the dazzlingly fashionable products of southern industry. Thus in Cromarty it was reported:

> English clothes, and those of Scottish manufacture, are now worn by all
> ranks, and printed cottons have become a very general dress among
> housemaids and others, who were wont to be clothed with coarse woollen
> stuffs of home manufacture.[18]

The decline of "country-made apparel", especially visible in the east was
a spreading problem throughout the Highlands during the coming half-
century, and it seriously aggravated the difficulties of labour surplus in
the local economy. In Lochcarron the minister remarked forlornly, "If
there were a woollen manufacture established here, it would employ a
great number of idle hands, and might prevent emigration".[19] To make
things worse, one of the most lucrative Highland industries, distilling,
was to be governed by regulations which probably reduced the extent of
employment and revenue. The distilleries consumed a significant part of
the grain surplus, such as that of Killearnan:

> Distilling is almost the only method of converting our victual into cash for
> the payment of rent and servants, and whiskey may in fact be called our
> staple commodity.[20]

Distilling caused much moral contortion for the ministers of the
church, but its regulation and concentration further weakened the ability
of the small tenantry to compete with the inflated rents offered by large
farmers at the turn of the century.

Fishing, combined with crofting, notably in Easter Ross, eventually
helped to absorb a considerable proportion of the population of the interior. But in the 1790s the development of commercial fishing was
relatively modest. All coastal parishes had fishermen, and fish supplied
part of the diet of the potato-eaters. Fishing was relatively labour-
intensive with strong backward and forward employment linkages, and it
promised well for a more balanced growth of the local economy. Avoch
and Tarbat both witnessed the rise of fisher-towns each drawing upon
widely dispersed fishing grounds, and providing fish for export as well as
for home consumption. Fish was regularly hawked inland in prodigious
quantities on the backs of the womenfolk. Though there was complaint
of the lack of curing facilities, the eastern centres had already attracted
enterprise from Northumberland and London. Distinctive fishing communities emerged, subcultures somewhat apart from the more
exclusively agricultural societies about then. On the west coast there was
great optimism for the planned British Fishery Society village at Ullapool
where a colony of settlers and merchants had been created, reinforced by

the development of curing houses (by London, Stornoway and Skye capitalists) at Isle Martin and Isle Tanera. The fishing was "precarious", but in 1792 the minister of Lochbroom felt able to anticipate cumulative development. By 1798 there were reported to be 1000 permanent settlers at Ullapool and there was talk of the promotion of ancilliary manufacturing enterprise. In the long run, however, the shift of the herring to the east coast decisively undermined locations such as Ullapool. Even in 1803 the curing sheds at Ristol near Ullapool were being used as byres, and the long run-down of the installations and employment had begun. The facilities were finally sold off in 1848. But the east coast villages grew continuously and provided important refuge for the growing population of the interior which, palpably, could not be accommodated in the transformed agriculture of the early 19th century.[21]

Population growth was probably the greatest single determinant of social and economic change, creating pressure on resources, land, food supply, employment and prices. The reasons for the unprecendented growth in the late 18th century remain unfathomed, and the exact scale and timing of the demographic change is obscured by internal and external migration; it is made the more mystifying by the apparently greater growth in the remote west than in the east. In Lochbroom, for instance, population grew from 2,211 in 1755 to 3,500 in 1792; it more than doubled in Lochalsh and Applecross; smaller increases, and a few declines, were registered in the eastern parishes (though Kilmuir Wester showed a trebling of its numbers), but all their ministers realised that population growth was in train, a conclusion amply confirmed by the first censuses. The reasons for population growth offered by contemporaries were diverse: almost all commentators mentioned the impact of potatoes — "for prior to the introduction of this useful root, a general scarcity pervaded the Highlands".[22] The abolition of servitudes was also regarded as favourable, as was the settlement of muirland by mealers. The introduction of inoculation against smallpox had been remarkably successful, but its incidence did not coincide exactly with the growth of population.

While several factors, notably the rapid increase of productivity from the potato and from fishing, were highly favourable to the growth of population, there was already rising anxiety about underemployment and, more immediately, the impact of sheep clearances upon the ability of the local economy to cope with the increased numbers. Improved arable agriculture in the rapidly commercialising east had not prevented a substantial exodus of people. The approach of large sheep farming threatened far greater problems.

II

Sheepfarming in Ross and Cromarty was part of the increasing specialisation of function in agriculture. In some parishes the transformation of agriculture required a diminution of sheepfarming in favour of arable or dairying or cattle fattening, Sheep numbers fell in Logie Easter and Nigg. Elsewhere, however, the rapid advance in the price of wool and the consequent inflation of rents for pastoral land, was already in the 1790s causing the conversion from black cattle, the mainstay of the old small-tenant system, to sheep farms in the hands of pastoralists with large capital. The movement northwards of commercial sheep farming had begun in the 1750s from Argyll and Stirlingshire. In Ross and Cromarty the invasion was much anticipated. The higher parts of Rosskeen, it was said in 1792, were "fit for no other purpose, than the summer pasturage of a few black cattle, which, perhaps might be converted with much advantage, into sheep walks". In Urray sheep farming was already held responsible for raising the cost of grazing for low country cattle; there had been experiments, but no more, in Kirkmichael; there was no mention of sheep in Gairloch, Urquhart, Lochalsh and Applecross; in Lochcarron the main concern was overstocking caused by the high price of cattle. But at Fodderty cattle had already made way for sheep and at Contin the sheep were expected at any moment.[23]

The fear of the imminent sheep was represented in Glensheil where, in 1786, the heights of the parish attracted an offer of triple rent from sheepfarmers. The proprietor had responded with an absolute refusal: "declaring that he would *never prefer sheep to men*, at the same time he set the lands to the old inhabitants (who are not over fond of sheep) and their paying a pretty moderate augmentation". But at Kilmuir Easter, sheepfarmers had already taken over the higher lands, causing the black cattle farmers to pay more for grazing and to reduce stock. A direct conflict of interest was plain to for all to see. At Kincardine too, border sheep farmers had taken over land and had demonstrated the possibilities of lucrative returns to landlords and tenants alike, and the local minister predicted a reduction of population. The minister of Lochbroom declaimed against the oppression of the landholders who, he said, caused people to emigrate. Sheepfarming had just been introduced and was decidedly "unfriendly to population" — in Lochbroom it had "proved the occasion of reducing to hardship several honest families who lived tolerably happy on the fruits of their industry and frugality". He opined that "whoever would wish to see the population of this country flourishing, should do all in their power to put a stop to the sheep traffic, and to introduce manufactures among the people". Already depopulation had made a desert of whole districts: "no human faces are now to be met with, except a shepherd attended by his dog".[24]

The first *Statistical Account* was written at the very time when opposition to sheepfarms reached a moment of social explosion, the so-called "tumults of 1792" (discussed below). The violence of that year was an interruption of the continuing debate about the benefits of agrarian change which, everywhere, had profound effects on the social order. The transformation had undoubtedly been most thoroughgoing in the favoured eastern lowlands — parts of Easter Ross and the Black Isle eventually became the vanguard of the revolution in agricultural productivity. Large heavily capitalised farms, a new technology, modern buildings and a clear distinction between the day-labour force, the tenant farmers and the proprietors — these were the marks of the new society. Sir George Steuart Mackenzie, a proud enemy of outmoded forms of agriculture, stated categorically that "our great want is south country tenants of skill and real capital" who, like the Middleton family, would carry the torch of improvement into the country. Mackenzie quoted instances in which landowners (as a prerequisite for the import of a new tenantry) had been "under the necessity of removing the old inhabitants by degrees" though, he said, these folk usually found resettlement in the same district. Mackenzie could see nothing but good in the changes:

> The present race of Highland tenants will find themselves much happier, and more comfortable, in the capacity of servants, to substantial tenants, than in their previous situation.[25]

The perceived loss of status involved in this change, less acceptable to the people dislodged than to their masters, appears to have been widespread throughout the east of the region. Moreover the relatively labour-intensive system required in the new arable agriculture may have absorbed more people than before. Mackenzie indeed claimed that it reduced the propensity to emigrate as well as the seasonal drain of labour to the southern harvests. There appears to have been some concentration of population into villages and a growing specialisation of function in the more successful fishing centres. The intensive settlement of marginal muir lands (some of which were subsequently absorbed into larger commercial farms) further enhanced the capacity of the eastern districts to accommodate part of the movement of population growth.

Sheep farming was positively unfriendly to people and exacerbated the problems of a growing and ostensibly redundant native population. Even its more fervent admirers conceded the point:

> We know for certain, that no other stock could yield half the rent which sheep can well produce. The great objection which has been stated against this mode of occupying our mountains is, that it depopulates the country.

27. Lonbain Thatched Cottage, Wester Ross   (R.C.A.H.M.S.)

28. Applecross Mains: heather-thatched Barn   (R.C.A.H.M.S.)

29. General Sir Hector Macdonald   *(Dingwall Museum)*

30. Cromarty Fishmarket, probably about 1900

31. Tarbat Old Church, Portmahomack   *(R.C.A.H.M.S.)*

32. H.M.S. Mars in dry dock at Invergordon, 1st World War
(R.C.A.H.M.S.)

33. Crofting Township of Letters and Logie on Loch Broom
(J. Smith)

34. Avoch, Black Isle   *(J. Smith)*

35. Clipping Sheep in Wester Ross   *(L. MacNally)*

That it does so, may be allowed, though there are instances where more people are to be found in districts occupied by sheep, than before these animals were introduced; but, in almost every case, the original occupiers have been removed.[26]

Landlords and their spokesmen, naturally enough, tended to minimise the dislocation and opposition engendered by the introduction of sheepfarming. Sir George Mackenzie claimed "we have heard but a few feeble voices exclaim against the necessity of removing the former possessors, to make way for shepherds".[27] This was misleading (even Mackenzie's own account contradicts the claim): sheepfarming, in its nature, caused a crude and rarely moderated conflict of interest between landowner and people.

The origins in Ross and Cromarty are fairly clear. Credit is attributed to Sir John Lockhart Ross of Balnagown, a retired military man who devoted his energies to estate improvement. Observing the success of blackfaced sheep in Perthshire, he overcame local scepticism to try them in his native county in the early 1770s. As early as 1763 an English farm manager, John Baldrey, had been brought to Balnagown, and Ross began importing southern shepherds who soon faced the enmity of the local people. The latter were treated as unwanted aliens and "every art [was used] to discourage them", and to "render their lives miserable", including depredations on their sheep stock. Until 1781-2 Ross's initiatives were purely experimental (directed particularly to the problem of wintering), and restricted by unexpired leases which tied up his estate. At the first opportunity he rented lands to Geddes, a Perthshire sheepfarmer attracted north by promises of virgin grazing lands. Geddes soon faced substantial but sporadic resistance from the people — "wicked and flagrant depredations" upon his flocks — "numbers were shot, and droves were collected, surrounded, and forced into lakes and drowned". Neverthless, Geddes and his son persevered and prospered as the first great sheepfarmers in the northern Highlands.[28]

The current of sheepfarming ran faster in the 1780s: sheepfarmers took leases at Culcairn and also on the west coast where a man from Ayrshire leased sheep runs from Davidson of Tulloch; Macleod of Geanies conducted his own sheep trials in Lochbroom from 1790-1. In essence these several experiments between 1780 and 1792 demonstrated conclusively the potential of sheepfarming in even the most exposed parts of the northern and western Highlands. It also put pressure on the black cattle economy, driving up the price of grazing. It struck fear into the minds of the existing occupiers of potential sheep country. "Strong symptoms of opposition to sheepfarming began to appear about this time."[29] Indeed, in 1792 conditions had become inflammatory, especially in those districts sufficiently densely populated as to suggest that resistance was feasible. In the marches between the Easter Ross communities and the new sheep lands there seemed a chance of concerted opposition.

III

Clearances for sheep in Ross and Cromarty, as elsewhere, were dominated by a few inflamed episodes — the "year of the sheep" 1792, Culrain 1820, Glencalvie 1845, Coigach 1852-3, and Greenyards in 1855 — and for these there are relatively copious accounts. Yet it would be a serious distortion of the record if these events were taken as representative of the transformation of the pastoral economy of Ross and Cromarty. Most of this great change was executed quietly, without commotion, resistance or publicity. The dimensions of the story are best indicated by the sheer numbers of sheep — from a few thousand in 1780 they grew to 252,000 in 1854 and to 391,000 in 1869.[30] Typically, in the spread of the sheep empire, a lease came to a close and the landlord would advertise its availability in northern and southern newspapers — a contract would be drawn up with a new sheepfarmer, and the previous smallholders given notices to quit. The more mindful of the landlords allowed twelve months notice of his intention, offered some small compensation for buildings and crops, and, occasionally, provided alternative crofting accommodation. But there was no stopping, nor even much delay of the spread of the sheep.

The so-called "insurrection of 1792" was one of the best-known episodes of modern Highland history and needs only brief recapitulation.[31] The confrontation of the common people and the proprietory of Easter Ross had wide significance because it was the moment at which the northward advance of commercial sheep farming reached the Great Glen. For a month or so, it seemed possible that the invasion might be thrown back. It was also a local climax of popular feeling against sheepfarming which had previously expressed itself in sporadic attacks on the sheep and general abuse of the shepherds and their masters. All this was disturbing enough for the keepers of civil peace and private property, but now physical resistance to the sheep threatened to create a local alliance of forces some of which were suspected of Jacobinical radicalism; even worse it threatened to expose the paltry basis of the forces of the law in the north of Scotland. It set the local landed oligarchy into a high state of panic.

The actual "insurrection" was provoked not by a direct act of eviction, but by events connected with the untidy aftermath of a previous clearance. The trouble began at Kildermorie near Strathrusdale in Easter Ross — the location was significant since it was close to heavily settled villages, increasingly committed to fishing, and populated by many who had been dislodged from the interior Highlands. Their proximity, and their reputation for social solidarity, may have encouraged ideas of resistance. At Kildermorie, on the estate of Munro of Novar, a considerable clearance had been effected in 1791: but it was only a partial removal because the resident people were resettled, with their black cattle, on ground, presumably inferior, adjacent to the newly-created sheep farm. The contiguity and ill-feeling of the displaced tenants quickly gave rise to a series of petty disputes, the poinding of animals, and threatened legal proceedings from the sheepmasters, namely the Cameron brothers, who came from Lochaber. In July 1792 the hostility broke into open violence when the people, in the act of liberating their poinded cattle, set upon the Camerons and assaulted them. An attempted precognition was similarly thwarted by the obstruction of witnesses and on 25 July 1792, in the euphoria of their apparent triumph, the people of Kildermorie devised a much more grandiose plan to remove all sheepfarmers not only from the immediate district but also from all the neighbouring parishes. In short, they hatched a scheme to mobilise popular opposition to landlord policy and literally to drive the detested sheep out of the northern Highlands. Notices to six parishes (two in Sutherland) were dispatched instructing the dissidents to muster at Strathoykel on the last day of July in preparation for the expulsion of the sheep. On the appointed day 200 people gathered and sheep — some said as many as 10,000 — were rounded up and driven to Strathrusdale on 4th August. There was alarmist talk among the landowners that the rebels were radical insurrectionists, inspired by the works of Tom Paine, and armed with firearms and gunpowder, but there was negligible evidence for these allegations.[32]

During the period in which the sheep were rounded up, the local proprietors gathered their own forces, alerted Edinburgh and London, obtained military support, and planned their counter-offensive. The Sheriff Depute, Donald Macleod of Geanies, at his wit's end, believed that the uprising was reaching such appalling proportions that only a very large force of troops could extinguish it. In the upshot, in the early morning of August 5th, the local proprietor's posse was able to surprise the rebels and, in a short and un-violent debackle, set the whole lot to flight. The sheep were rescued and the rebellion snuffed out within a few hours. Eight prisoners were taken, and the rest of the people dispersed rapidly. A subsequent trial at Inverness imposed a sentence of transportation on two of the rebels, but they quickly escaped and were never retaken. The event passed into legend and, though the rebels were plainly vanquished, the episode lived on as an inspiration for defiance in future years.

In reality the insurrection of 1792 was a defeat for the people and signalled the rapid extension of sheep and clearances into the northern Highlands. The opposition of the rebels had been ill-co-ordinated, poorly led and lacked resolution and physical force. In retrospect it appeared an isolated and somewhat naive expression of popular revulsion from the new sheep economy. Nevertheless, in a lesser sense, it was a moral victory: public sympathy, even among the landowning class, it was virtually universal. Ministers, newspapers, and especially southern opinion, had been outraged that the rights of private property had been employed to cause the wholesale eviction of a peasantry, in favour of sheep. Yet it was sympathy which did them little good: it had no impact on the spread of the sheep. The suppression of the rising left its mark on the collective memory, and kept the community simmering with inchoate outrage.

It was another thirty years before physical resistance was raised against a clearing landlord in Ross-shire. Most clearances passed quietly, in a process of attrition, by stealthy dislodgement. The Lovat estate, not much renowned for evictions, was in 1808 in the midst of widespread "removings";[33] there were recurrent displacements on the Cromartie estate and on Lewis: sometimes these re-arrangements were connected with sheepfarming, sometimes they were routine exercises of estate management.

The riots at Culrain in spring 1820 were precipitated by an act of eviction more aggravated than those of 1792, and yielded a more directly violent response. The estate of Munro of Novar was again the centre of the disturbance which at one stage, threatened to co-ordinate into a system of resistance with the disaffected small tenantry of Sutherland (where a simultaneous bout of clearance was in progress). There was also proprietorial fear of a parliamentary enquiry. Novar had embarked upon a scheme to evict a tenantry of about 600 people, many of whom were said to be aged or bedridden. It was claimed that they were willing and able to pay the new rent set on their lands. Novar provided no re-settlement facilities: The evicted were simply set adrift. This action prompted a substantial spasm of resistance in the traditional form and it was alleged (again an echo of 1792) that there was a radical root to the rebellion. In reality these events lacked any kind of political sophistication. According to a report published in the *Scotsman*

> On notice being given to these poor people to remove, they remonstrated, and stated unequivocally, that as they neither had money to transport them to America, nor the prospect of another situation to retire to, they neither could nor would remove, and that if force was to be used, *they would rather die on the spot that gave them birth than elsewhere.*

Resistance to the legal eviction party was vigorous and even a party of military sustained injuries from the staves aimed by "a body of illiterate people, unable to state their own case"; the womenfolk were notably violent and abusive. The military had opened fire in their own defence, and before the violence was renewed the minister effectively interceded and defused the situation. The revolt did little more than delay the clearance, but it again demonstrated the popular disgust at the entire idea of sheepfarming.[34]

Violence erupted in the same district in the following year, at Gruids. A further attempt to serve notices by a sheriff's party was frustrated by the repeated obstruction of the local people. And once more it was the women who stood at the front of the rebels, and they who systematically humiliated the officers who were stripped naked but not otherwise harmed. There was talk of combinations of resistance which would defeat all landlord authority, but when troops were introduced in April 1821 the opposition (which had broken out in three separate places in the eastern Highlands) dissolved and the clearances were then executed without further ado. In Ross-shire, as elsewhere, native opposition to the evictions was sporadic and, until the 1880s, of little avail except to express the revulsion of the common people against the clearance system.

The case of the Redcastle Estate, in Killearnan Parish, provided a parallel but contrasting case of forcible internal readjustment. Here the resident small tenantry were removed to create great arable farms for six tacksmen, equipped with capital and the latest techniques. Sheep appear to have been relatively unimportant in this case, but soon there were "many scores of acres yielding wheat and green crops, which were then [i.e. previously] useless, without any other cover than short heath and broom". The destination of the people evicted was well documented — they were received by Colin Mackenzie of Kilcoy in the same parish, one of several estates which provided asylum for the victims of clearance. The population of Fodderty, for instance, had been much augmented by the influx of refugees from the heights, accommodated in the villages of Maryburgh and Keithtown. At Kilcoy the Highlanders were settled on commonty land, on zones where eventually they might expect "to keep a horse, a cow, a fallower, and a few sheep." The net consequence was that the total population of the parish was little affected, though its agriculture and distribution had been fully revolutionised.[35]

Clearances in Ross and Cromarty attracted little attention until 1845 when the miserable plight of the people evicted at Glencalvie was widely publicised by a reporter of *The Times*. Glencalvie was only a part of a much larger and little known series of clearances in the county — it was said that 2000 people in Ross-shire were shifted in that single year. In May 1845 eighteen families were cleared from the straths of Amanatua, Greenyards and Glencalvie. In their subsequent desperation, and with the help of Free Church ministers, they made a public appeal for asylum and resettlement. They had tried in vain to find alternative accommodation and employment in the north, and they had been reduced to living in tents in Glencalvie churchyard. There was no direct criticism of the landlord, Robertson of Kindeace, but the factor, though he had given legal notice, was singled out for public opprobrium. *The Times* reporter wrote vividly: the people he said, "did not know where to go to, and what to do to live". He regarded the people as the pathetic victims of the abuse of landlord authority, who had been dissuaded from resistance by the pacifying intercession of ministers of religion. Despite the flood of unfavourable publicity, the clearance was finalised and the sheepfarmer took possession of the lands. Significantly, however, Robertson thereafter adopted a policy to remove no more than two families each year: gradual clearance, as was well known across the Highlands, caused less likelihood of either resistance or publicity than the wholesale eviction of entire communities.[36]

In the same decade the Balfour estate in Strathconon was also completing its re-organisation for sheepfarming. In total and over several years something of the order of 500 people were displaced — dispersed to adjoining estates, or to arable lands on the Black Isle. For the most part these clearances passed in silence, but in 1849-50 the last acts were given full description in the *Inverness Courier*. The reports illustrated the frustration as well as the methods of landlords repeatedly delayed in their efforts to extract an economic return from their capital; equally it illustrated the distress and pathos of an unwanted peasantry forced into a wider world. Leases were terminated, houses demolished, and the people told to go elsewhere. Many found refuge at Kirkhill, Knockfarril and Beauly. It was not a particularly sudden, large or cruel eviction — rather another act in the continuing readjustment of the economy to demographic and economic upheaval. Strathconon lost most of its people and the Balfours provided relatively generous conditions to the residual population. Twentyfive years later the estate was described as chiefly a deer forest, with a dozen great sheepfarms, a few crofts and a home farm. Of the original population all that was left was "about a dozen crofters ... and these eke out the produce of their small holdings by employment received from Mr Balfour and by cartage.''[37]

The Cromartie Estate for many years enjoyed a humanitarian reputation for receiving refugees of clearances in other parts of the country. At Strathpeffer the new settlement lots at Auchterneed and Knockfarril were partly populated by such cast-offs from Strathconon, Redcastle and elsewhere. Nevertheless for over half a century Cromartie itself had introduced sheep and displaced small tenants, most notably in the far west, in the Barony of Coigach.[38] But it was not until 1852-3 that such re-arrangements engendered repeated popular resistance, which then brought Cromartie to the eye of the newspapers. The Coigach episode was unusual in that the landlord repeatedly attempted to push through the clearance and was on each occasion successfully repulsed by the collective will of the rebellious tenantry. The point was reached eventually when the landlord desisted and came to the view that the clamour and opprobrium were simply too much to stomach. Coigach therefore was one of the few unequivocal victories for the people over the landlords: many factors in the north regarded the entire event as a spineless capitulation which threatened all rights of property.[39]

The most sensational clearance in Ross and Cromarty, at Greenyards in 1854, was also the last great confrontation between the forces of inertia and change. The recent Coigach events served as an inspiration to the people, and as a goad to retribution among the police. Greenyards, effectively, was the finale of the history of the Highland clearances. The scene was set near Bonar Bridge, in the same general district which had witnessed social protest, not only in early clearances, but also in the food riots of 1847. The existence of a large fishing population nearby may have steeled the people to resist their landlord, Robertson of Kindeace (responsible for the Glencalvie evictions ten years before). It produced a classic confrontation between a sheriff's party (about 35 men) from Tain and a crowd of about 300 peasants, mostly women. In the early morning the two forces met head on and, from various accounts, engaged in a skirmish which left several of the women in a seriously injured condition. It seems likely that the police were eager for battle, and had resolved not to repeat the debacle enacted at Coigach. In their enthusiasm for the task they had moved vigorously to subdue the provocative resistance of the womenfolk in particular. The people of Greenyards had been reinforced by common people from a radius of fifteen miles. Lurid accounts of the battle were given wide circulation, but the people were entirely defeated. One year later the clearance was completed and the people set to flight.

There was an interesting and revealing footnote to the Greenyards eviction. Among the prisoners taken in the aftermath of the battle, was a youth, Peter Ross, who was subsequently sentenced to 18 months imprisonment at Perth Gaol. He belonged to a family evicted at that time. The Reverend Gustavus Aird, prominent in the publicity which surrounded the episode, interceded on behalf of Ross, and maintained that he had not been at the scene of the riot, and that "his sentence was not only severe but unrighteous". Ross was a model prisoner and his sentence was eventually reduced by six months. Meanwhile his family had fled to Langwell, and his brother and sister emigrated to Melbourne, Australia, by way of Liverpool. Aird used the network of the Free Church to minister to Ross's needs, to pay his fare back to Ardross, and to make sure that he had employment on his return from gaol.[40]

After Greenyards the drama of the clearances was over. For the rest it was mainly a matter of gradually reducing the population; the crofting communities had little alternative but to subsist quietly on the fringes of the great estates. Small scale removals, it is true, recurred at various times until the Crofters Commission in 1883. For instance, in 1875, William Munro sold the Swordale estate to Major Jackson, a Dundee jute-spinner. Jackson, as a condition of his purchase, required that all the tenants be removed — and consequently twenty families received notices to quit from the Clare district.[41] There was no rekindling of the spirit of resistance until the 1880s and the Crofters' Revolt in which Ross and Cromarty, east and west, played a prominent part.

IV

By the time of the second *Statistical Account of Scotland,* in the late 1830s the process of economic change had run most of its course. In agriculture almost all the quasi-feudal excrescents had been removed, though the farther west the less complete was the change. The commercial production of cereals and stock for the great southern markets favoured the continued growth of large and heavily capitalised farms, and a greater specialisation of output. In 1835 it was said that the district of Easter Ross and the vicinity of Inverness and Beauly exported annually more than 30,000 quarters (381 tonnes) of wheat alone;[42] practically everyone, even cottars, produced wheat for markets and were now much assisted by better port facilities (such as those of Invergordon).[43] In the mid-century this region achieved high distinction in its agricultural productivity — a later commentator spoke of "the long-sustained and united exertions of an intelligent, enterprising, liberal class of landlords, and of a painstaking energetic race of tenants, [who] have made that part of the county a formidable rival to the Lothians and to the plains of Morayshire". Rents began to match those of the south.[44]

An agricultural labour force had now emerged to service the great tenant farmers, sometimes as a full-time proletariat, sometimes in part employment as crofters or fishermen. In the west the population had continued to grow alarmingly and, without the benefit of a rising modern sector to its economy, the congestion of people had created great pressure on the resources of the crofting community. This, in many places, was compounded by the decline of household industry and the eclipse of the herring fishery on the western shores. While the seasonal emigration to the eastern fisheries helped to sustain the crofting villages,[45] permanent outmigration remained too slight to relieve much of the demographic problem on the west. Consequently the contrast between the east and the west of the county was heightened by the combined forces of economic and demographic change.

The parish of Cromarty demonstrated the essence of the transformation. The minister reported that "the breaking of the small farm system" had scattered many of the people into the low country where they became labourers, fishermen or mechanics. Cromarty had received sufficient migrants from the Highlands to warrant the erection of a Gaelic church, early in the century. In thirty years the population had grown from 2413 to 2900, helped by "the continual influx of strangers who settle in the outer skirts of the parish", and who often became dependent on local poor relief. During the 1830s "every farmer in the parish had reared and exported wheat". But the influence of low prices and overproduction had dimmed the enthusiasm of agriculturalists, and many of the fishermen had fallen into abject poverty. The denudation of local industry was the most severe loss to the parish. The minister summarised

> the influence of those changes, which, within the last fifty years, have remodelled the domestic economy of the country. The steam looms of Glasgow and Paisley have stripped the village weaver of his employment; the manufacturers of Sheffield and Birmingham have discharged its smith; the taste for fashionable furniture, to which the improved dwellings of our agriculturists naturally led, has shut up the workshop of its carpenter; and the love of dress, so universally diffused in the present age, has levelled the domicile of its tailor, and the stall of its maker of Highland shoes.

Yet, for all his candour, the minister of Cromarty was full of contradiction. Poverty was abject, ignorance widespread and morals deteriorated; but "the people of Cromarty in general eat and dress better in the present day"; they worked harder, were less superstitious and better "acquainted with the principles of agriculture and of trade". They were more literate and read the Bible more earnestly than before; the coming of newspapers had caused "a noiseless revolution".[46] Such indeed was the ambiguity of improvement in the north.

Contemporaries experienced the greatest difficulty in their comprehension of the moral and economic force of the changes that had upturned the foundations of life about them. The ministers, who appear to have been little constrained by the fear of landlordly rebuke, were loudly critical of the large farm system, but conceded the benefits even to the common people. At Nigg, "many families were driven from their homes, a few strangers were introduced in their room, and poverty succeeded in the train of almost all the actors and sufferers in the scene"; the old weavers had had to give up their trade; the population was in flux, many leaving, many strangers entering; in the 1830s there was a general improvement in the comfort of housing, dress and in morals.[47] Where population was static or falling, it was common to blame enclosures — as at Kirkmichael,[48] and at Logie Easter where dispossessed tenants removed to neighbouring farms, to America, or cultivated waste moors, as "best they can". Meanwhile the agriculture of the parish was thoroughly modernised and exported very superior wheat.[49] At Kilmuir a scheme for moorland improvement helped prevent emigration;[50] in Kintail, dispossession and eviction had left many in penury, and their poverty was the only impediment to their emigration.[51] At Dingwall there was a familiar story of influx and outflow (to Canada and the lowlands), but a substantial net growth of population.[52] Rosskeen registered a rapid growth of numbers between 1801 and 1831, but this masked a great deal of internal demographic turmoil — here sheep clearances had caused depopulation in the Highland parts of the parish, and while some sought refuge in Glasgow, most flooded into the villages of the parish itself. According to the minister there had been an unfavourable qualitative consequence:

> There is no longer an independent peasantry. The morals of the people are deteriorated by the loss of independence, and their spirits embittered by what they deem oppression. The ties which united master and tenant are severed; and when the time comes, to which we look forward with fearful anticipation, it will, we fear, be found, that an error has been committed, by grasping too much, at the risk of sooner or later losing all.[53]

Almost identical were the reports from Kilmuir Easter, where the population had fallen in the decades since 1795. Arable land was "in the possession of a few" who had increased productivity impressively — but it was "certainly ... not calculated to improve the state of the population. In consequence of this, many of the people are always on the wing shifting from one parish to another, in quest of a better place or one of more congenial employment".[54] It was the great age of social and geographical mobility. Moreover the gulf between the classes in eastern agriculture was vividly exposed in the food riots of early 1847 when hundreds of the common people acted collectively to prevent exports of wheat at a time when prices rose to levels associated with famine. There were great fears of starvation in the midst of plenty; the poor at Evanton were reduced to living on turnips and there was a large rise in the number of dependent poor. But in reality the region was a great producer of agricultural surplus.[55]

The peasantry had become day labourers,[56] crofters or fishermen and had swollen the populations of the eastern villages; sheepwalks monopolised the interiors and emigrants poured out of many parishes. As the minister of Kiltearn put it, they were "thus deprived of all means of subsistence, and driven to seek in a foreign land for the shelter and protection which were denied them in their own." He added coolly, "The rights of landlords ... to manage their properties to their own pleasure, no one will pretend to doubt".[57] The choice at Alness was similarly that of emigration or village settlement, neither of which was incompatible with an improvement of living standards. Sheep clearances in Kincardine had caused emigration of "the finest of our peasantry to a foreign shore", and the same effect had resulted from arable enclosures in Urquhart and Avoch.[58]

Few of the eastern parishes retained much of their manufacturing activity. At Urquhart it was reported that the competition of southern machinery had superseded the spinster and the country weaver; domestic linen manufacture had ceased, and the gaudy and less substantial fabrics of Glasgow and Manchester were ubiquitous.[59] Tarbat kept more of the old crafts, but local producers were being out-competed by imports.[60]

Yet, despite the all-conquering vigour of southern competition, and its principles of political economy, the contrast between east and west in Ross and Cromarty, remained as great as ever. In the 1830s much of the west remained remarkably insulated from the inflowing influences. Demographic expansion continued within a social and economic structure hardly yet much transformed. It created growing superabundance of numbers and anxiety. Lewis, (formerly part of Ross and Cromarty) itself not free from clearances, was in common with much of the western littoral, threatened repeatedly by crop failure throughout the 19th century. Seaforth, in the severe year of 1817, owned that "thousands of people have been saved from starving in this island" by government assistance and grain imports. Again in 1837 the proprietor told Sir John Russell that 16,000 people in Lewis were in danger of starvation unless prompt imports were arranged: the entire future of the people was bleak, especially since the collapse of the kelp industry and the poor performance of the local fishing. His people were too poor to emigrate, and were "harrassed with anxiety and tortured by ... gloomy anticipation".[61] Sir James Matheson had bought the island in 1844 and invested large capital in its development: but it brought little joy, despite some growth of fishing. An agricultural journalist remarked

> In 1884 the condition of Lewis was primitive in the extreme, and even after thirty years of great activity and heavy expenditure of money, the island is hundreds of years behind the social standard of the nineteenth century.[62]

Failure of the potato and the fishing, and woeful standards of social welfare, continued most notably in 1847-48 to mark the west coast and islands throughout the century.

On the western mainland, in the late 1830s, Lochcarron had witnessed little improvement in its agriculture; its population had grown on a regime of subdivision, on a diet of potatoes, herring and oatmeal gruel, and with little prospect of material betterment.[63] At Applecross the population had increased by a thousand in four decades and there were few signs of outright evictions; but a combination of high rents, low cattle prices and a failure of the fishing had caused much poverty.[64] At Glenshiel sheep clearances were said to have swept away " the valuable and respectable class of substantial tenants" — they went to America, or else sank to the status of cottars, "poorly fed, scantily dressed, and miserably lodged; theirs is a life of penury and toil"; they lived in "continual fear of impending want, and [were] uncheered by any prospect of amendment in their conditions,"[65] At Gairloch, by contrast, population increased from 1437 in 1801 to 4,445 in 1831, which was attributed to early marriage and subdivision — there was no reference to clearances, "but the population is by much too dense for the means of support which they enjoy". Here the community was partly sustained by the income brought in from the Caithness fishing.[66] From Lochs, Barvas and Uig it was the same story — slow agricultural change, rising population and slow emigration, though the growth and centripetal influence of Stornoway helped to give greater stability in the local fishing industry.[67] Despite seasonal migration on the western coasts, the dominant feature of the community was its relative immobility, and the consequence was the continuation, indeed exacerbation, of the problems connected with unrelieved population growth.

Footnotes

1. *The Statistical Account of Scotland* edited by Sir John Sinclair, 1791-9, 1981 edition Vol. XVII (hereafter cited as *O.S.A.*), pp. 649 fn, 541, 529; see also the oral testimony of John Wallace, cited by James Macdonald, 'On the agriculture of the counties of Ross and Cromarty', *Royal Highland and Agricultural Society of Scotland,* Journal, volume 9, 4th series, 1877, pp. 88-9. For contemporary description see W. Macgill, *Old Ross-shire and Scotland* (2 vols., Inverness, 1909-11), p. 173 and Ian R. M. Mowat, *Easter Ross 1750-1850* (John Donald, Edinburgh, 1981), p.97.

2. *O.S.A.*, pp. 323, 334, 511, 509, 529, 537fn, 582, 614-5, 630, 649-50fn.
3. *O.S.A.*, pp. 619, 677.
4. Macgill, op.cit., pp. 47, 50, 158.
5. *O.S.A.*, pp. 658-61.
6. *O.S.A.*, pp. 639-45.
7. See James Macdonald, op.cit., p.187, and *Lewis A History of the Island,* Donald Macdonald (Edinburgh, 1978), pp. 63-88.
8. *O.S.A.*, pp. 590-2.
9. *O.S.A.*, p. 582.
10. *O.S.A.*, p. 480.
11. *O.S.A.*, p. 404.
12. *O.S.A.*, pp. 390-1.
13. *O.S.A.*, pp. 331-4.
14. *O.S.A.*, p. 312.
15. *O.S.A.*, p. 292.
16. *O.S.A.*, p. 432.
17. *O.S.A.*, p. 438; see also Mowat, op.cit., Chap. 3 pp. 53-6.
18. *O.S.A.*, p. 351.
19. *O.S.A.*, pp. 332, 391, 521, 616, 650-1, 675.
20. *O.S.A.*, pp. 332, 362, 428.
21. *O.S.A.*, pp. 287, 313-4, 556-8, 567; Scottish Record Office, B.F.S. Papers GD/9/1 Report to Duke of Argyll by Lachlan Mactavish, 12 September 1787; E.D. Hyde, 'The British Fisheries Society: its Settlements and the Scottish Fisheries 1750-1850', unpublished Ph.D. thesis, Strathclyde University 1973. For a comprehensive account see Malcolm Gray, *The Fishing Industries of Scotland* (O.U.P., Aberdeen, 1978).
22. *O.S.A.*, p. 291.
23. *O.S.A.*, pp. 483, 590, 618, 676, 331.
24. *O.S.A.*, pp. 408, 444, 509-10, 562-3.
25. George Steuart Mackenzie, *General Views of the Agriculture of the Counties of Ross and Cromarty* (1813), pp. 74, 86-7, 107; J.A. Symon, *Scottish Farming, Past and Present* (Edinburgh, 1959), pp. 146, 171; see also Mowat, op.cit., pp. 28ff.
26. G.S. Mackenzie, op.cit., p. 125.
27. Ibid., p. 126.
28. S.R.O. Balnagowan Castle MS, GD 129/7/11 Ross to his factor, 15 April 1778, 10 May 1779; Macgill, op.cit., p. 175; J. Macdonald, op.cit., p. 108; G.S. Mackenzie, op.cit., passim.
29. Mackenzie, op.cit.
30. James Macdonald, op.cit., p. 193.
31. A recent consideration of the evidence is in Eric Richards, *A History of the Highland Clearances 1746-1886* (London, Croom Helm, 1982), Chapter 9.
32. See for instance Henry W. Meikle, *Scotland and the French Revolution* (Glasgow, 1912), p. 83.
33. S.R.O. Fraser Mackintosh Papers, GD 128/32/2.
34. *Scotsman,* 11 March 1820, 1 May 1820.

35. N.S.A., p. 256, 67.

36. See Richards, op.cit., pp. 369-77.

37. *Inverness Courier,* 15 August 1850, 5 September 1850; James MacDonald, op.cit., pp. 122-3.

38. Part of Coigach was advertised as sheepfarms in the *Inverness Journal,* 1 January 1813.

39. A good description of one of the bouts of confrontation is in *Scotsman,* 2 April, 1853.

40. Aird to Patterson, 4 September 1855, a letter preserved in the Tain Museum, for which my thanks are due to Mrs R. Mackenzie. See also P.A. Macnab, *The Church at Croik,* and Alexander Macrae, *The Life of Gustavus Aird.*

41. Information kindly provided by Mr William Munro, Clashnabuic, Evanton, by the courtesy of Mrs Jane Durham.

42. *N.S.A..,* Vol. XVI, p. 24; Vol. XIV, p. 294.

43. Ibid., pp. 275, 295.

44. James Macdonald, op.cit., pp. 74, 80, 92, 95, 99.

45. See Gray, op.cit., pp. 104-8.

46. *N.S.A.,* Vol. XIV, pp. 1-8.

47. Ibid., pp. 28-33.

48. Ibid., p. 48.

49. Ibid., p. 54.

50. Ibid., p. 63.

51. Ibid., p. 177.

52. Ibid., p. 222.

53. Ibid., p. 279.

54. Ibid., p. 312.

55. See Eric Richards, *The Last Scottish Food Riots* (The Past and Present Society, London, 1982); Mowat, op.cit., p. 110.

56. Their importance as a pool for arable agriculture was noted in Macdonald, op.cit., pp. 173-4, 207-8.

57. *N.S.A.,* p. 322.

58. Ibid., pp. 344, 321.

59. Ibid., p. 377.

60. Ibid., pp. 326, 48, 33, 15.

61. S.R.O. GD 46/13/178 Lewis Destitution Papers. Mary Stewart Mackenzie, 27 August 1817; J.A. Stewart Mackenzie to Russell, 22 February 1837, 2 March 1837.

62. James Macdonald, op.cit., pp. 155-6, and on crofting generally, pp. 164-5.

63. *N.S.A.,* op.cit., pp. 111-2.

64. Ibid., p. 198.

65. Ibid., pp. 102-6.

66. Ibid., p. 96.

67. Ibid., p. 166.

Chapter ten

MODERN TIMES
John S. Smith

The marked contrasts in primary resources between Easter, Mid and Wester Ross which were evident during the historical period have tended to sharpen in the last twenty years as a result of contrasting levels of gross capital investment and differing population trends. Writing in 1795, Sir John Sinclair, the noted Caithness improver eulogised over the fatlands of Easter Ross as 'a countryside possessed of many natural and artificial beauties, being situated on the borders of the beautiful Firth of Cromarty, adorned by the seats of many opulent and respectable proprietors by whose exertions the lower parts of the district have been considerably improved, and the upper covered in plantations'. The fruits of laird initiative and the hard work of the tenants is paramount in the present landscape, both in terms of a farming economy which in terms of productivity and advanced agricultural technology compares favourably with the Scottish Lothians, and in the sheer attractiveness of the rural environment with its woodland copses and trim cottages and steadings. Wheat and seed potatoes are commonplace crops on the sandstone-derived soils of the Black Isle and Easter Ross, while beyond, on the hill edge, reseeding programmes have been successfully carried out leading to substantial increases in the stocking rate of cattle and sheep on the hill farms. The farming structure in terms of unit size is varied with the mainly owner-occupied farms of the low ground margined by groups of Department of Agriculture smallholdings dating from the early 20th century, while higher up, or occupying patches of poorer land within the larger farms are smaller units justly termed crofts, varying in size from 2 to 15 hectares (4.9 to 37 acres) and reflecting in their distribution a former association with mid-19th century estate reclamation policy, on occasion coupled with the need to resettle a population displaced from inland straths during the sheep clearances. Easter Ross and the Black Isle combined, with about 32% of the land area of Ross, account for nearly 90% of the tillage, 75% of the crops and grass, and a high proportion of the cattle stock.

By contrast the land potential of Mid- and Wester Ross is much more limited with the population grouped in scattered crofting settlements chiefly occupying bayhead and valley bottom sites, the majority of them within sight of the coast. The primary and service sectors of the economy are predominant here with the agricultural economy dominated by pastoral activities, chiefly the production of breeding stock destined for fattening either on the eastern side of the District or beyond. With the exception of Gairloch, Ullapool and Loch Carron, no permanent nucleated settlement exceeds a population level of 100 persons. In the Mid-Ross area, more extensive land uses are dominant, including seasonal pastoral activities, forestry and sporting land uses, mainly deer forest. In both Wester Ross and Mid-Ross, the scarcity and dispersed distribution of ground which can support crops or rotation grasses places severe limitations on the carrying capacity of the enterprises for stock, particularly in terms of the provision of winter keep for the animals. In the crofting areas the supplementary employment generated by the Forestry Commission, the roads and bed and breakfast revenues are vital to the viability of the economy. Equally important have been the investments made by the Highlands and Islands Development Board in terms of direct job creation through grant and loan to small enterprises, particularly fish farming and hotel provision, and by the Highland Region through road improvements and the identification and servicing of sites for small advance factories. The seaboard area has also benefitted through financial support via the Common Market as a less favoured remote and sparsely populated area. Highland Board aid per head of population is significantly higher in Wester Ross than that in Easter Ross, although the latter area has enjoyed a significant number of large employment-generating industries since the mid-sixties.

POPULATION CHANGE

TABLE 5   POPULATION TRENDS FOR SELECTED PARISHES WITHIN ROSS

Parish	Year of Maximum Population	Maximum Population	1981 Population	1971 Population	% 1981 Population of Maximum
Applecross	1851	2709	612	551	23%
Gairloch	1861	5449	1828	1792	34%
Loch Broom	1861	4862	1714	1562	35%
Loch Carron	1871	1629	822	582	50%
Alness	1981	3750	3750	1257	100%
Cromarty	1911	5637*	789	861	—
Dingwall	1981	5099	5099	4331	100%
Contin	1801	1944	1037	1076	53%

* Cromarty's 1911 population included 3,999 men of the Royal Navy.

The population of mainland Ross (Ross and Cromarty District) in 1981 was 46,137, representing about 24% of the total population of the Highland Region. An increase of 33% has been recorded in Ross since 1971. For the purposes of comparison, the Highland Region experienced a growth of 13% over the same period. Table 5 reveals that in Ross the increase has been heavily concentrated in Easter Ross (the parishes of Alness and Dingwall, for example), although significant increases have also taken place in Wester Ross (Applecross, Gairloch, Loch Broom and Loch Carron parishes). The hill edge parish of Contin occupies an intermediate position and may be regarded as typical of the Mid-Ross area. In Easter Ross, much of the growth attested by the figures in Table 5 has been by in-migration, and is thus mainly in the younger age groups. For example, population in the Alness-Evanton area increased by nearly 4000 in the period 1971-6, chiefly as a result of the location there of a housing expansion to cater for the employment opportunities offered by the British Aluminium Smelter sited in nearby Invergordon. Population increases have also been recorded in many other parts of Easter Ross which now falls within a well-developed commuter belt. In Wester Ross, the increases between 1971 and 1981 are more modest, but are in part associated with job opportunities and economic spin-off associated with the Howard Doris Rig Fabrication Yard at Kishorn which was established in 1975. In fact this trend is rather longer established, and dates from the 1961 Census when for the first time since the year of the maximum population census, the falling population trend was reversed. Within these Wester Ross and Mid-Ross parish figures however, the totals mask a continuing depopulation of the landward areas, and since 1961, the parish population structure increasingly reveals a gap in the 15-25 year age groups, and a bulge in the over 65 and beyond cohorts, suggesting a selective outmigration in the search for job opportunities and immigration for retirement purposes. Thus although Ross has overall a relatively high proportion of its population in the 0-15 age groups and a lower proportion in the retired group than the average in the Highlands and Islands as a whole, there are significant variations in the pattern between the west and east of the District.

As a result of in-migration over the last 15 years in Easter Ross and the loss of 890 jobs with the demise of the Invergordon Smelter, there is at present a major imbalance between the population of working age and the number of jobs available. The situation varies considerably from month to month as a result of the fluctuating jobs available at the Nigg Fabrication Yard (Plate 48) which exceptionally (January 1984) reached a total of 4000, but has on occasion fallen to around 1000. In the absence of major constructional activities with the completion of the major A9 road alignment across the Black Isle and the arrival of downstream petrochemical activities around the Cromarty Firth, unemployment levels periodically reach levels in excess of 20% in the Dingwall-Invergordon area (August 1982). The equivalent figure for Wester Ross at the same period stood at around 9%.

EASTER ROSS AND THE BLACK ISLE

The twin peninsulas of Easter Ross and the Black Isle are by far the most favoured parts of Ross, and indeed, within the Seven Crofting Counties encompassed by the Highlands and Islands Develpment Board. The average population density of 36 persons per square kilometre (0.4 per square mile) compares with a figure of 0.2 persons per square kilometre for Wester Ross. In Easter Ross, nearly 50% of the population live in towns and villages, all of which operate in varying levels of provision as service centres. The total infrastructural package of roads, schools and services, and the distance required to reach such services, is much superior to any other part of Ross, and the farm structure is favourable in terms of scale and productivity. These clear advantages coupled with an urge by both national regional government bodies to provide an industrial component to the local economy have led to its recognition as the best industrial growth point in the North of Scotland. Its infrastructural advantages are complemented by the considerable natural asset of the deep sheltered waters of the Cromarty Firth, a resource first utilised on a large scale by the Royal Navy during both the First and Second World Wars (see figures for Cromarty — Table 5). The promotion of this industrial potential has been an important element in the development policy of the former Ross and Cromarty County Council, the regional development body of the Highlands and Islands Development Board and Highland Region. The nearness of the Cromarty Firth coastlands to the administrative and commercial capital of Inverness can be viewed as an additional bonus, recently enhanced by the re-routing and upgrading of the A9 trunk road over much of its length north of Perth, and the creation of a fast dual carriageway linking Inverness with Invergordon, completed by the Kessock Bridge in August 1982.

In 1960 a very large whisky grain distillery (then Europe's largest) was established at Invergordon, based on local initiative and labour availability. At that time it was the largest single industrial enterprise north of Inverness. From its by-products arose the concept of the potential locational advantages in Easter Ross for petrochemical industries, and the beginnings of the serious promotion of the deepwater assets of the Cromarty Firth. The concept was strongly supported by the

Highlands and Islands Development Board and aroused the interest of Occidental, an American company who financed a feasibility study which proved favourable, although subsequently it withdrew its interest. A physical planning study by the Jack Holmes Planning Group: *The Moray Firth — a plan for growth,* Inverness, 1968 which was commissioned by the Highlands and Islands Development Board claimed that the coastal plain from Nairn to Tain could accommodate a population of 250,000 (ten times the existing level) without detriment to the environment, and suggested the establishment of a series of small new towns scattered along the old 'head of the firth' alignment of the A9. As some of the settlement and industrial sites were to be located on quality agricultural ground, there was opposition from sections of the agricultural community. The publicity associated with this 'linear city' and indeed, the opposition it engendered from sections of the local community, only increased the unconscious promotion of the potential of the area in the national arena. In late 1967 and early 1968, the Government took steps to encourage the expansion of aluminium smelting capacity in the United Kingdom, and it was announced that British Aluminium intended to construct an aluminium smelter at Invergordon. The site identified at Ord Farm occupied high quality agricultural land including areas of man-made plaggen soils, and the rezoning of this land for industrial purposes was only permitted after a public inquiry following objections to the rezoning proposals. The 101,605 tonne (100,000 ton) smelter built at a cost of £40 million commenced production in 1971 and eventually employed a labour force of 890. The bauxite was imported via a new pier constructed at Saltburn and the alumina ingots were exported by rail using a specially constructed British Railway siding adjacent to the smelter. The population increases associated with the construction and production phases of the smelter led to the re-opening of Muir of Ord and Alness railway stations for passenger traffic. Although closely monitored, the emission of hydrogen fluoride from the smelter chimneys in both gaseous and particulate form and its condensation into sodium fluoride on grasslands in the environs of the smelter led nearby farmers to manipulate their farming enterprises, and in several cases led to decreased farming opportunity. Although compensation for damage was generous, it was unfortunate that such restrictions were placed on the potential range of farming possibilities, particularly the breeding of cattle if it involved lengthy residence on grassland within the affected zone. The eventual demise of the aluminium smelter in December, 1981 resulted from the costs of power supply by comparison with its rivals both in the United Kingdom and abroad, the general world recession, and an over-capacity in world production of alumina. At the time of closure, there was a disputed debt between the company and its power supplier which totalled £47 million.

During the period of smelter establishment in 1968, the petro-chemical bandwagon was taken up by Grampian Petrochemicals who proposed a £55 million complex using feedstock imported by sea to be sited mainly on agricultural land north-east of Invergordon, with the storage depot planned for Nigg on the coast of the northern entrance to the Cromarty Firth. The farm of Delny of around 152 hectares (376 acres) arable was purchased in 1955 for £30,000, but was sold to the company for £350,000 and its re-zoning for industry subjected to a lengthy public inquiry during which questions including viability, environmental hazard and the loss of good agricultural land were debated. Alternative sites for the petro-chemical complex involving the reclamation of land in nearby Nigg Bay were strenuously opposed by conservationists on the grounds that the intertidal sandflats of the Bay supported a wintering wildfowl population of international importance. During the inquiry it emerged that while virtually all parties agreed on the desirability of at-tracting industry to the Cromarty Firth, there were differing opinions as to the 'bestfit' location. Eventually the Secretary of State for Scotland permitted the rezoning of around 405 hectares (1000 acres) of land bordering the Firth, a decision described by a spokesman of the Highlands and Islands Development Board as 'unlocking the future of the Cromarty Firth'. A contemporary planning document envisaged the Firth as 'the Clyde of the twenty-first century'. Although Grampian Petrochemicals scheme collapsed in 1970, before the planning permission elapsed in 1972, the land was purchased by the American company Planet Oil for a sum alleged to be around £1 million.

In late 1971, Brown and Root established a rig fabrication yard prin-cipally on reclaimed dune and saltings at Nigg. The company, later re-named Highlands Fabricators, specialises in the fabrication of steel production platforms for the North Sea Oil and Gas Industry, and to date have completed a total of nine steel jackets in their immense dry-dock, together with a variety of smaller modules. The labour force is drawn from a wide hinterland, including East Sutherland, and as with the smelter, the wages offered attracted job mobility from the agricultural and service sector. The company's latest completed contract was the 40,000 tonne (39,368 ton) Magnus platform, constructed at a cost of £105 million, which was floated out from the flooded drydock to the B.P. Magnus Field sited 200 kilometres (125 miles) north-east of Shetland, in 1982. At the time of writing (February, 1984), the yard is employing an exceptionally large labour force of 4000 in an attempt to meet the summer deadline for the Conoco Hutton Field tension leg platform, but have little further contract work to follow. It is clear that despite Government reduction in Oil Company taxation levels, development of known fields (as opposed to exploration which still remains at a high level of activity) is currently in a trough, and competition for the limited number of potential platform contracts likely to emerge in the next few years is extremely keen, both at home and abroad, principally in Norway and France. Thus the potentially large employer of Highlands Fabricators and the smaller establishment of M.K. Shand near Invergordon, which specialises in oil and gas pipe coating, are directly tied to the peaks and troughs of North Sea Oil and Gas production activity, and the correspondingly fluctuating job opportunities.

During the fat years of steel jacket fabrication, the search for the elusive petro-chemical catch continued. The land assets (now without planning permission which had elapsed) changed hands yet again, first to the Cromarty Firth Development Company, and subsequently to Cromarty Petroleum Ltd., in the latter case for a sum of around £2 million. Cromarty Petroleum had the intention of establishing an oil refinery, and in 1974 lodged a fresh planning application for a £180 million oil refinery to be sited just east of the established fabrication yard at Nigg. A £1 million planning inquiry was upheld by the Scottish Office despite the fact that United Kingdom refineries were at that time only working to about 65% of their refining capacity. Subsequently Cromarty Petroleum linked themselves with the American petro-chemical giant Dow Chemicals, and they jointly in 1980 lodged a further planning application on the same ground for a petro-chemical plant. Two other companies with petro-chemical aspirations — Highlands Hydrocarbons and British Gas — were also interested in a similar development at Nigg — a situation rather similar to the interest shown in the smelter site by several companies in the late sixties — and perhaps emphasising the physical attributes of the Firth for industrial development. All three companies were looking for their feedstock from the £2700 million gas gathering pipeline system planned for the North Sea, then actively under discussion between the producing companies and the Government. Preliminary proposals envisaged a primary landfall on the Aberdeenshire coast at St. Fergus, and a dispersing land pipeline network, of which one branch might lead to Nigg. Although the North Sea Gas Gathering System is at the time of writing in abeyance, it is worth remembering that the feedstock from such a network were it constructed would be strongly competed for by the existing petro-chemical establishments at Grangemouth and Moss Morran. Since 1981, Highlands Hydrocarbons have increasingly shifted their emphasis towards a chemical plant producing MTBE — the substitute for lead in petrol — and claim to have a working agreement with Total Oil Marine and the B.N.O.C. for the critical supplies of butane and methanol, both to be supplied to the Cromarty Firth by tanker. The amount of interest expressed, planning applications lodged and the money involved in successive land purchases in the area adjacent to the Cromarty Firth all highlight the widely agreed suitability of the area as the site for any new petro-chemical activity in the United Kingdom, but to date the long-mooted downstream petro-chemical activity remains elusive.

However, the deepwater resource offered by the Firth which at-tracted the Royal Navy there in the early years of the 20th century has, since 1974, been controlled and promoted by the Cromarty Firth Port Authority, whose wide remit includes powers of land reclamation. Paradoxically their spatial sphere of influence virtually coincides with the Nature Conservancy Council's Site of Special Scientific Interest, again emphasising the problem of melding industrial development with environmental conservation. In the last few years, the Firth has attracted oil rigs to it for servicing and maintenance. Eleven such rigs were serviced during 1983. The release of Admiralty shore space at Invergordon per-mitted the development of a servicing facility, which in turn has recently been taken over by a consortium headed by the Wood Group, Aberdeen and the Port Authority. With the assistance of a grant of £¾ million from the Scottish Development Agency, the base is being expanded for both maintenance and conversion of rigs, utilising the facility, unique to Peterhead and Invergordon on the east coast, of sufficiently deep water for rigs to moor alongside the quay.

Despite this promising investment, and the declaration of the Invergordon-Alness Enterprise Zone, the uncertain future of the fabrica-tion yard industry and the closure of the smelter casts a shadow on the short term future of the industrial base of Easter Ross. The relatively high proportion, by Highland standards, of the population in the younger age groups, including present school attenders, inevitably means an increasing shortfall between job opportunities and job seekers in the near future. Clearly the implementation of the Gas Gathering Pipeline System is a major key to the unlocking of the petro-chemical future of the Firth as it would provide a construction surge, potential contracts to the pipe-coating and fabrication enterprises, and an ultimate modern establishment with a high value product. On the other hand, to be strictly realistic, while the oil terminal for the Mesa Field at Nigg and the im-plementation of a petro-chemical works in the future would provide fulltime jobs, the number involved is small by comparison with the number currently provided by the fabrication yard, suggesting at best a remaining shortfall in relation to local demand.

The developments described above have had, and continue to have, a considerable impact on the agricultural and service sectors of the Easter Ross economy. Indeed, in terms of journey to work, the effects do extend beyond the bounds of Ross into East Sutherland, but not westwards beyond the hill edge zone bordering Mid-Ross. The benefits of increased spending power are thus confined to the relatively narrow coastal plain and peninsulas. A new academy was built at Alness, and other expanded settlements have required new or expanded primary schools. The range of shops and services offered has increased in Alness (plate 37) and Invergordon. Both Evanton and Invergordon have A9 bypasses which reduce the heavy traffic movement through the settlements although in turn, they decrease potential passing trade for shopkeepers and hotels. The higher wages and overtime offered by the new industries, and often by the construction phases associated with them, resulted in considerable labour mobility from agriculture in terms of farm workers, and from services like the electric and plumbing trades where young people were serving their apprenticeships. These difficulties were particularly marked during the early seventies but have now disappeared by a process of natural adjustment. Although the large acreages envisaged by the Jack Holmes Study were not rezoned, the prospect of further industrial developments and associated housing requirements led to a degree of farming blight, with farmers being reluctant to invest in sustained yield policy, and cropping for short term gain in areas which seemed likely to be lost to agriculture. In the late seventies which marked the apogee of likely petro-chemical developments, some 1860 hectares (4600 acres) of land in Agricultural Land Classes 1, 2 and 3 (basically land capable of producing commercially acceptable grain yields) were at risk to rezoning for non-agricultural purposes — some 80% of it sited in Easter Ross, the remainder around the city of Inverness. In the event around 263 hectares (650 acres) of class 1 and 2 land were taken for development which may be considered a small price to pay for the scale of development achieved, or alternatively a failure to seriously seek alternative sites on lower quality ground. The dual carriageway re-routing of the A9 linking Inverness and the Cromarty Firth coastlands across the Black Isle has halved the journey time from Invergordon to Inverness but on the other hand the land loss including cuttings and verges averaged about 0.4 hectares (1 acre) every 150 m (490 ft) of road length. In addition, farms have been severed by the road and field shapes distorted by road alignment.

On balance, however, the very considerable injection of capital into the Easter Ross area within the last fifteen years has provided a much improved infrastructure, but the nature of the incoming industries, despite their large scale, has not provided a secure long term employment foundation. As a result, the current rate of unemployment in Easter Ross is more than twice that of the mid-seventies, and the future remains very uncertain, and linked to decisions over which the Highland Region has but little control.

THE SETTLEMENT PATTERN

In the still predominantly rural peninsulas of Tarbat Ness and the Black Isle, the pattern of settlements which had been established by the 19th century, and in some cases, several centuries previously, remains, although several like Fortrose, Balintore and Culbokie have expanded considerably as a result of the commuting possibilities offered by improved communications and the demand for housing engendered by the improved employment prospects. Virtually all the parishes of the Black Isle show modest increases in the intercensal period 1971-81, and the degree of change reflects settlement planning strategy and distance from the main centres of employment. Generally, planning policy has been to discourage housing construction in the immediate vicinity of the new A9 to protect agricultural interests, and to direct housing demand to identified settlements. Although in terms of raison d'etre, villages like Avoch (Plate 34), Portmahomack and Cromarty were primarily fishing settlements and thus still retain the architectural aura of their origins, only the former retains a commercial interest in that industry, and Avoch's fishermen are mainly suitcase fishers, operating from other bases according to season. Cromarty, apart from its white-washed Fishertown, contains a number of more substantial former merchant houses, reflecting its site on the Cromarty Firth roadstead, and the agricultural richness of its former hinterland. Its range of Scottish vernacular architecture is particularly rich and complete (Plate 30).

Planned agricultural villages created by improving 18th century estate lairds to provide employment for displaced agricultural tenantry following agricultural rationalisation of land holding include Charlestown, Maryburgh and Jemimaville, the first greatly expanded from its original core as seen from the Kessock Bridge, the last scarcely expanded since its creation by a young Munro, and named after his Dutch wife. The royal burghs of Tain, Dingwall, Fortrose (and for a period, Cromarty) can claim more ancient origins, the last, despite its modest size, having the quiet dignity that befits a cathedral town with Chanonry and market cross, while Tain services a prosperous agricultural hinterland which overlooks the vast sandflats and dunefields of the southern shore of the Dornoch Firth, whose sedimentation was partly responsible for the demise of its historical entrepot trade. Dingwall, a town with authentic Norse origins and formerly the county town retains its very important stock market and agricultural services, although certain of its administrative and service functions inevitably deserted to Inverness following the Wheatley reorganisation of Local Government Boundaries in 1975. The old established villages of Beauly, Muir of Ord and Conon-Bridge have recently been effectively bypassed by the crossing of the two Firths at Kessock and Ardullie, leading to a decrease in traffic volume estimated recently at 60%. This may be expected to have effects on hotels and shops as far as passing trade is concerned, although all three have established a loyal local patronage. Work is now progressing on the land acquisition programme prior to the construction of the Maryburgh-Brahan-Contin section of the improved A832 (T) to the West, following the completion of which there will be increased pressure for the Dornoch Firth crossing, which would complete the concept of the Crossing of the Three Firths first proposed in the late sixties.

The Victorian spa of Strathpeffer (Plate 39), then advertising itself as 'the Harrogate of the North' still displays the substantial mansions and hotels which were then filled with families and house-parties from the south, travelling by train along the former branchline from Dingwall to the splendidly restored Strathpeffer Station Buildings to take the waters, now serves as a touring centre from which to explore the Northern Highlands. There are also ambitious plans to develop Alpine-style access from there to the winter ski-slope potential of nearby Ben Wyvis by rack and pinion narrow gauge railway. On the outer coastline of the Easter Ross peninsulas, villages like Rosemarkie and Balintore are popular summer holiday resorts boasting a range of coastal habitats including cliffs and sandy beaches within easy walking distance, and experiencing a warm, dry climate which competes with Nairn as the driest in Scotland. The four major secondary schools are sited at Alness (a new Academy responding to the needs of the incoming population), Tain, Fortrose and Dingwall, the last named providing hostel accommodation for secondary pupils resident in Wester Ross. Other smaller nucleations of varied origins have experienced very little growth in the 20th century, although their residents have modernised houses while jealously guarding their amenities. These include the cliff-ledge village of Rockfield on the Tarbat Ness peninsula, the splendidly picturesque village of Kilmuir on the Black Isle and the former fishing village of Inver on the shores of the military bombing range of the Morrich More, Dornoch Firth.

Inland of these narrow coastal plains, and across the hilledge which is constantly visible from most parts of the Easter Ross peninsulas, the land uses and population densities dramatically change. The land uses become increasingly extensive in nature, and involve a dominance of grazing, forestry and sporting interests. This rather intangible region of Mid-Ross is characterised by broad interfluves, with narrow eastward trending straths which finger into the moors and mountains. Many such straths, like the Bran and the Blackwater pass westwards by cols below 330m (1000 ft) to the shorter, more sharply graded valleys which feed the sealochs of Wester Ross, as at Loch Carron, Loch Maree (almost a sea loch!) and Loch Broom. Extremely small population clusters occur at valley junctions as at Contin, or railheads such as at Garve, with people employed by the railway, the Forestry Commission and the Hydro-Board forming important proportions of their total population. Other clusterings occur around shooting lodges or in small agricultural townships, but Mid-Ross is very much an area characterised by scattered and sparse population, and one where a retreat from the 19th century frontier of agricultural settlement has freed ground for extensive, seasonal and on occasion, multi-purpose land uses.

HYDRO-ELECTRICITY

Amongst the more extensive land uses characteristic of the Mid-Ross area, hydro-electricity generation is perhaps one of the more obvious as demonstrated by reservoirs and generating stations. Although the potential for power generation had been recognised from the pre and inter-war period, a succession of Private Parliamentary Bills to develop water resources in Ross promoted during that period foundered either at the Parliamentary Committee or House of Commons level. In 1943, however, the Hydro-Electric Development (Scotland) Act established the North of Scotland Hydro-Electric Board which combined its remit to provide national power supplies with a strong social commitment to supply domestic electricity to the glens. In the fifteen years post-dating the Second World War, in advance of the construction of the very large thermal power stations in the Central Lowlands of Scotland, a series of conventional hydro-electric projects and associated works including roads, were implemented in the Conon catchment. These hydro-schemes provided welcome employment prospects in the post-war period. The scale of public works was to be broadly comparable to the employment associated with the construction of the Caledonian Canal in the first three decades of the 19th century.

In Ross, a small-scale local tapping of water power potential was developed at Glenskiach and then at the Falls of Conon below Loch Luichart since 1903 when Colonel Mackenzie pioneered a power supply for Strathpeffer spa. The completed Board development of the Conon and its tributaries involved the construction of seven power stations with a total annual output of 440 million units, approximately 12% of the total output in the North of Scotland Hydro-Board's area.

THE CONON HYDRO-ELECTRIC SCHEME

Initial developments took place in the Loch Fannich catchment with water from the natural loch (whose capacity was to be subsequently enlarged by a rockfill dam) carried by tunnel to the Grudie Bridge power station on the Garve-Achnasheen road. A second phase development involved the creation of reservoirs in Strath Vaich (water surface 254m (833 ft) above sea level), Loch Droma and Loch Glascarnoch — all near the Garve-Ullapool road. From the main collecting Glascarnoch reservoir, an 8 kilometre (5 mile) tunnel carries the water in turn through the turbines of generating stations at Mossford, Luichart and Torr Achility. Water from Loch Meig is fed into the enlarged Loch Luichart and power generated at a station situated just above the junction between the Meig and Conon rivers. In Strath Bran, to the west of Loch Luichart, a barrage with sluice gates across the outlet of Loch a' Chuilinn regulates the outflow of the Bran, and provides water to drive the turbines of the Achanalt power station. The third stage of the Conon development involved the harnessing of the water resources of the Orrin valley. Dam construction created the 7 kilometre (4.4 mile) long Orrin Reservoir, from which water is led by tunnel and pipe to a power station on the southern shores of Loch Achonochie, the reservoir formed by the Torr Achilty dam where the control centre for the total Conon development is sited.

Apart from the natural catchments of the reservoirs, small aqueducts and pipes collect additional supplies from more distant streams to augment water volume and assist in the annual management of the water resource which heavily relies on spring snowmelt for its volume. For example water collected by such means from streams which would naturally flow westwards into the Corrieshalloch Gorge and thence into Loch Broom, travels to Loch Droma. Although the hydro-electric construction period pre-dated the strong environmental pressures which today face any major development, considerable efforts were made to minimise effects on the amenity of the Conon catchment. Many of the power stations are faced with Moray Firth sandstones with its sympathetic weathering qualities. The Torr Achilty station is faced with Black Isle Tarradale sandstone, while others in the chain use Hopeman sandstones from Moray. The lower dams in the sequence are equipped with Borlund fish lifts which through the daily flooding of an internal chamber within the dam structure during the appropriate season permit salmon to ascend the obstruction naturally. The fish are monitored by electric counter, the system having the additional benefit that the general public can, when convenient, view the fish passing.

While the development of water resources for power provided a very welcome boost to employment in the post-war period, the flooding of valley bottoms for reservoirs as in Orrin and Glascarnoch involved the loss of valuable deer wintering ground, and on occasion required modifications to estate management of cattle and sheep stock. In some cases road alignments had to be changed, and in one case — Luichart — a railway line. The control of runoff, particularly on these upland catchments with thin soils underlain by relatively impermeable rocks, should theoretically benefit downstream land uses on floodplains although experience shows that the rapid rises in reservoir levels which can result from rapid melt of lying snow coupled with heavy rair.fall and the management policy of maintaining full reservoirs during the prime winter and spring water gathering periods is incompatible with the prevention of occasional severe flooding. Such flooding with damage to crops, banks and fences took place in December, 1966 and again in January, 1984 in lower Cononside. As part of its remit, the Hydro-Board collaborates with District Salmon Fishery Boards, notably in the stripping of fish to obtain eggs for their hatchery at Contin and in the distribution of fry in those tributaries which lie beyond reservoirs not equipped with a fish lift. The Orrin Reservoir is equipped with several fish lifts to cater for the wide range in reservoir level encountered from year to year. As a complement to these extensive hydro-schemes on the easterly flowing catchments of Mid-Ross, the Hydro-Board developed very small water power stations in Wester Ross to supply the scattered populations of the west coast. These are sited at the Kerry Falls near Gairloch and at Loch Dubh north of Ullapool. Although these were originally designed to serve all local needs, recent population increases in Wester Ross have resulted in these small local stations requiring to be augmented by linking them with the main grid system.

Although potential remains for further conventional water power developments in Ross, notably in the Fada Loch area north of Loch Maree, the current economics favour the development of large pumped-storage schemes where energy generated by large thermal or gas-fired stations located furth of the Highlands is used at low peak demand times to pump water from a low to a high reservoir where water can be stored, and 'run' to generate electricity at times of peak demand, as in the Foyers scheme on Loch Ness. However, the Board is at present considering developing small 'run of river' schemes in Wester Ross in sites where effects on scenic quality and angling interests can be minimised.

AFFORESTATION

Afforestation was envisaged in the sixties as a major provider of rural employment in sparsely-populated Highland areas (see also chapter 5). In comparison with other parts of the Scottish Highlands, the planting programme in Ross is relatively modest, and is mainly concentrated in Easter Ross and the hilledge zone of Mid-Ross. The low planting programme in the west reflects the limited areas of plantable ground, the competing established land uses, and difficulties in land acquisition. The main substantial Commission holdings arc Ardross (recently increased in area by the acquisitions on the Struie), Torrachilty and Black Isle. In all three plantations, the woodland is old-established with mature timber now being marketed, and replanting taking place. On the western side of the watershed, smaller plantations occur at Achnashellach and Lael. The Woodland Dedication Scheme has also encouraged private landowners to invest in commercial forestry in part as a taxation device to delay payment of death duties. A notable estate in Easter Ross with long established commitment to forestry is the Novar Estate near Evanton. On private estates, most of which have a forestry enterprise, the woodland rotation is only now beginning to adjust to the major fellings during the Second World War. Nonetheless their policy woodlands, shelter belts and game coverts are an important element in the total estate economy as well as providing habitat diversity and environmental quality to the rural environment. In addition to these established private and Commission interests, private forestry groups are now beginning to extend their operations into the Highlands, increasing the competition for plantable land. Woodland resources, apart from the marketable crop, should be viewed as an important recreational resource, and the Forestry Commission have increasingly developed car parks, picnic areas, forest walks and gardens, notably at Torrachilty near Contin and at Lael on Strath Broom. The favourable oceanic environment for conifers is demonstrated at Lael by the superb mature trees along the main Ullapool road. The plantation of stands of conifers of non-native provenance even with the 10% broad-leaved species which is now standard Commission practice, creates a substantial change in the texture and general characteristics of the moorland landscape. However, considerable effort and ingenuity is put into landscaping and improvement of habitat in afforestated areas, as can be displayed on the newly planted Struie Hill between Strathrory and Aultnamain Inn on the Evanton-Bonar Bridge road, where planting will ultimately produce a more productive and attractive environment.

Since the early days of public sector afforestation in the 1920's and

1930's when both the competing land uses of sheep grazing and agriculture were both in a relatively depressed state, subsequent Government and Common Market support to the hill farming industry has notably strengthened the position of sheep grazings, while agricultural interests have been safeguarded by the necessity of obtaining the agreement of the Department of Agriculture prior to the afforestation of land in use for farming. Thus the modern pattern of public commercial forestry is set within rather smaller forest blocks, set within the financial constraints engendered by the high costs of deer fencing, leading to a more realistic attempt to integrate the forestry enterprise with adjacent land users. Re-seeding enterprises of hill grazings sited downwind of forestry plantations thus may benefit from shelter derived from the forest, and on occasion, from improved vehicular access to the hill for the modern mechanised shepherd. The blanket afforestation of valley sides as between Garve and Inchbae on the Ullapool road which effectively separates the valley bottom wintering ground from the summer pastures beyond the economic planting limit would now be regarded as poor land use practice. However, overall, the competition for upland ground has markedly increased over the last fifteen years, meaning that often foresters are competing for land which was little if ever used for agricultural purposes, but may be valuable for sporting land uses. The lower tree growth rates which follow from the planting of this inherently poor ground is partly compensated for by improvements in tree establishment and fertilising techniques. The choice of species relates primarily to the physical and climatic environment with the native conifer Scots Pine important in Easter Ross, especially on the Black Isle, while as rainfall increases westwards, the high yielding Sitka Spruces are dominant. On peaty ground, Lodgepole Pine is planted but growth rates are slow by comparison with the spruces.

In evaluating these more extensive land uses of forestry and water power generation in Mid-Ross, it is important to stress that in both, social considerations have been major factors influencing investment and policy decisions, and that the modern support for hill farming, the main competitor for land which might be planted, is perhaps more stimulated by social considerations than by the production of wool, mutton and breeding stock. Much of the ground (apart from improved and fenced in-bye or re-seeded ground) currently under hill farming land uses also doubles up as deer forest, although on the highest and poorest ground, the latter is the sole stock land use. The valley bottoms like Strath Vaich, particularly if they support unfenced birch or pinewood, are vital attributes to the deer forest economy for wintering. The relatively buoyant level of sporting lets and the rising price of venison at present are likely to guarantee that the upper parts of the valleys like the Dirie More, which cut through the main watershed at levels below 350m (1150 ft) will remain under the present land uses rather than be released for afforestation. The integration of commercial forestry with deer forest land uses requires careful planning of the siting of forest blocks to avoid major interference with established patterns of deer migration related to season and weather. In the absence of this, red deer will extend their pre-existing range and maraud the lower agricultural ground.

The large private estates within Mid-Ross all suffer from an imbalance between large areas of predominantly barren ground at high levels which at best is only available for summer grazing, and very limited low ground which must provide winter keep and land for stock wintering — replicating on a somewhat larger scale, the situation in Wester Ross. Even the line of smaller estates on the eastern hill edge of Mid-Ross suffer from a similar imbalance, and several had to adjust their management practices following the loss of valley floor land consequent on reservoir construction in the 1960's.

Fiscal problems of capital taxation, high interest rates and rising costs (including labour) when coupled with the urgent need to invest in modern machinery and buildings have inevitably led to the gradual disintegration through sale of portions of land or fishings on formerly larger viable estates, thereby reducing the possibility of integration of a variety of land uses which the relatively severe physical and resource geography of the Mid-Ross environment is best suited to in terms of optimum management. Inevitably such processes of estate adjustment further increases the rate of depopulation in these relatively remote areas.

WESTER ROSS

In contrast to the eastern coastal plain, Wester Ross has a much more restricted land use potential with its population scattered mainly in coastal crofting townships or in the limited valley floors near to the coast. There are few nucleated settlements and none exceeds a resident population of one thousand. The main centres are Ullapool, Gairloch and Loch Carron, all of whom combine service functions with tourist-related activities. The Wester Ross economy is heavily dependent on the primary sector (fishing, farming and forestry) although there are small Defence Establishments at Loch Ewe and Applecross. Since 1975, Howard Doris have established a successful concrete production platform yard at Loch Kishorn, recently diversified to make it possible for steel jackets to be fabricated. The prime locational factor attracting the company here was the presence of nearshore deep water which permits the mating of the concrete structure with its deck modules by progressive submergence. The yard has employed up to 1000 personnel in this remote and highly scenic area. At least 10% of these jobs have been filled by the local labour pool, and a further 70% of the workers reside within the Highland Region. It is estimated that the yard annually injects around £2.5 million into the local economy. The Wester Ross parishes have recorded modest increases in population since the 1961 census, and these have continued through to the 1981 census with a 12% increase overall recorded in the Applecross, Gairloch (Plate 40) and Loch Carron districts. These averaged figures however conceal a gradual concentration of the resident population into the villages, and a withdrawal from the more remote areas. The increase also mirrors a significant retired population returning to the area, particularly in Gairloch and Loch Carron. A significant percentage of the housing stock, perhaps 20%, can be classed as second or holiday homes.

AGRICULTURE

On the coastal bayheads, and particularly where blown sand machair exists, formerly cultivated croft inbye land is now given over to pastoral activities. Almost without exception the crofting townships scattered around the shores of Loch Gairloch, Loch Ewe and Gruinard Bay display this pattern. The Morefield township just north-west of Ullapool and clearly visible from the Ullapool-Stornoway ferry reveals in its broad clearance walls and heaps the immense human effort required in this rather less favourable stony environment to create agricultural land during the period of maximum population in the early 19th century. Today crofting interests are centred on livestock breeding for the lowland farm fattening market, and the old cultivated lands now form inbye grazing for wintering the breeding ewe stock, while behind, the ground on the hill takes the form of common grazings, traditionally managed in common, although increasingly fenced with individual apportionment to active crofters. In the more remote crofting areas like the Applecross peninsula, there have been recent major improvements in road communication, notably the Applecross-Shieldaig coastal road, in rural electrification provision, and also in improvement to township roads. Croft amalgamation and the communal marketing of stock have also progressed over the last ten years. Nonetheless crofting remains almost exclusively a part-time occupation, and its limited income is supplemented by road, forestry or transport service employment. Supplementary income is also derived from bed and breakfast trade during the summer season, and the letting of caravan stances. The present policy of the Regional Council

36. Scots Pine, Black Isle   *(F. Macrae)*

37. Alness and Fyrish Hill   *(J. Campbell)*

38. Dingwall, at the head of the Cromarty Firth, and Ben Wyvis
(J. Campbell)

39. Strathpeffer, formerly a famous Victorian Spa   *(J. Campbell)*

40. Gairloch, Wester Ross   (J. Campbell)

11. Inverewe Gardens (founded by Osgood Mackenzie in 1865) and Poolewe   (J. Campbell)

42. Looking across Loch Ewe to Aultbea, with Mellon Charles on the far left. *(J. Campbell)*

43. Fish Farming at Ardmair, near Ullapool *(J. Campbell)*

limits the number of lets to three per croft. In some machairs, as at
Mellon Udrigle and Opinan on the southern shores of Gruinard Bay,
over-grazing and recreational pressures have severely deflated the scarce
machair resource, although fencing and replanting of natural grasses
have recently improved the situation. The continuing programme of road
improvements coupled with the scenic quality of Wester Ross encourages
the touring caravan but the current policy is to encourage the provision
of permanent holiday accommodation rather than mobile homes,
although the buildings 'shall be subservient in size, colour and form, and
not outstanding in contrast with the landscape which must be
predominant'. Rather more extensive although still based on livestock
production are the hill farms generally encompassed within the pattern
of sporting estates. As with the crofting holdings, these suffer from
limited supplies of inbye ground, while re-seeding programmes on higher
ground which are essential to the increase in stocking rate, require expen-
sive deer fencing to obtain the improvement grant. Livestock is
predominantly breeding ewes although occasionally store cattle are kept.
The economy of these hill farms is closely tied to grant and subsidy aid,
particularly for fencing and liming, both of which are essential inputs to
maintaining stocking rates.

FISHING

Commercial fishing is heavily localised at the two landing ports of
Gairloch and Ullapool. Although Ullapool was developed in the late 18th
century by the philanthropic British Fisheries Society to stimulate the
local fishery, the herring and mackerel catches achieved by the hundred
or so boats operating from Loch Broom in the late summer, autumn and
early spring are landed almost exclusively by East Coast fishermen who
commute home to the Moray Firth coastlands at weekends. A high proportion of the landings are purchased by East European klondykers who
remain anchored in Loch Broom during the season and process the fish
onboard. The remaining 30% of the landings are transported by road to
the processing centres in Eastern Scotland, notably Aberdeen. In contrast, the shellfish and white fish landings at Gairloch involve chiefly
locally registered boats, and landings in 1981 were valued at £1 million.
Within the last fifteen years, stimulated by grant and loan schemes and
research investments provided by the Highlands and Islands Development Board, fish farming has developed off the western seaboard of
Ross. These enterprises are sited either in relatively sheltered locations in
the inner sea lochs or on specially prepared land sites and involve the production of salmon, trout and shellfish. There are at present seven fish

farms in Wester Ross, while the Department of Agriculture and Fisheries operates a salmon research station in the area.

FORESTRY

Although the percentage of land carrying commercial woodland at 2.5% is low by Highland standards, the jobs created remain locally significant. It seems unlikely that there will be further significant afforestation in the foreseeable future as not only are there problems in acquisition related to the values of sporting land on the market, but also in this remote area there are extraction and marketing difficulties because of weight restrictions on access roads. In addition, much of the plantable land is closely tied to existing agricultural interests. It might also be observed that the wilderness character of Wester Ross which is a major selling point in terms of its tourist industry might be perceived to have diminished as a result of extensive plantation. On the other hand the splendid stands of conifers at Lael on Strath Broom and at Slattadale on Loch Maree testify to the mildness of the western seaboard climate.

THE WESTER ROSS ECONOMY

Since 1975, the establishment of the Howard Doris yard at Kishorn has generated new job prospects on a scale which bears comparison with equivalent development in Easter Ross. There has been a corresponding investment in housing, school accommodation and road improvement. With a work force of over a thousand on site, the local service sector has clearly benefited from the increased spending power and expansion of local contracting facilities. However, competition in the rig construction business is extremely keen and competitive, and the Ross yards are competing for a limited number of contracts with other equivalent enterprises in Britain, France, Spain and Norway. The recent diversification of the Kishorn yard to cater for steel fabrication thus adds a welcome edge to its sharpness in the contract market. In the long term, the key employment opportunities seem to remain constructional and transport services, particularly road maintenance and improvement, the latter in its turn increasing the possibility of new forestry investment, increased tourist revenues and the establishment of small businesses. With the vogue for self-catering holidays now perhaps overtaking traditional hotel-based holidays, there is a clear scope for providing more thematic car and walking trails, and visitor centres. The National Trust for Scotland runs visitor centres at Torridon and Inverewe. The centre and gardens at Inverewe attract over 100,000 visitors per year. Tourist revenue thus remains a very vital part of the local economy not least at the level of the crofter offering bed and breakfast.

The splendid scenery which is the area's main attraction for visitors is founded on a very varied and internationally recognised environmental base. As a result, large areas of Wester Ross have been designated by a variety of Government bodies including the Countryside Commission for Scotland, the Nature Conservancy Council and the Regional Planning Authorities. In addition certain lands, notably in Torridon, are the property of the National Trust for Scotland whose aims are broadly the management of the ground for the benefit of the nation. Designation on nature conservation grounds or as areas of 'Scenic Heritage' while they represent a guarantee of the maintenance of wilderness, scenic and biological quality for the future, also on occasion curtail, restrict or even prohibit developments which might, in the short term, be viewed as beneficial to the residents of Wester Ross. Within the Scenic Heritage Areas as scheduled by the Countryside Commission for Scotland, there are restrictions on the construction of vehicle tracks above an altitude of 300m (984 ft) above sea level, and on large agricultural or forestry structures. While a recognition of wilderness and scenic quality attributes has existed in this area since the inter-war period, and was largely responsible for the restriction of water power development at that time, it is perhaps important to consider the conservation of such qualities with the need to provide the local population with a livelihood. It was perhaps with apparently conflicting aims in mind that the Highland Regional Council in its Structure Plan published in 1978 adopted the principle that 'the best use of land is that which provides jobs for the people.'

Part three

GENERAL

Chapter eleven

LOCAL BUILDING TRADITIONS

Geoffrey Stell and Elizabeth Beaton

Not surprisingly, in view of its vast size and varied character, Ross and Cromarty exhibits many different building traditions, some of which are now largely a matter of historical record. To the architectural historian and the casual visitor alike, however, the most marked contrast in patterns and styles of building are between those of the western and eastern coastal districts.

In Wester Ross the prevailing building-type is the single-storeyed or 1½-storeyed cottage and croft-house, many of them modernised, harled or brightly whitewashed. Dotted around the irregular indented coastline, they occur in loosely grouped clusters or are spread over wide areas as in the dispersed crofting townships around Gairloch and Loch Ewe. The abiding impression is of small-scale building, dwarfed even more in areas of spectacular and rugged mountain scenery; the buildings are memorable and significant mainly by reason of their setting and grouping.

The most memorable and distinctive group of them all is of course the planned fishing village of Ullapool (1788) on Lochbroom, seen to such clear and impressive effect from the hill to the east. Ullapool is the exception rather than the rule, however, for the buildings here have always been mainly of two or more storeys, were built strictly in line in accordance with the regulations, and were set out on a formal grid-pattern with wide spacious streets. The original layout was mainly the work of David Aitken, a surveyor from Tain, but there were strong controlling influences from outside the county; Robert Mylne (1733-1811), the well-known architect, was consulted by the British Fisheries Society on the designs of the earliest public buildings, and Thomas Telford (1757-1834) became closely involved in efforts to develop the site after 1790. The first building-contractor was an East Lothian man, and on his second inspection in 1788 the Society's adviser was 'sorry . . . to observe that these buildings were meant to be covered with tiles, a kind of roof that will not suit the variable and tempestuous climate'. Indigenous building practices were more truly represented by the 'black hut' squatters, described in a report of 1796 as the 'forty other inhabitants of houses, for the most part thatched huts or little better, who have not property to build houses and become regular settlers but who are nevertheless useful labourers, fishermen and traders'.

Sizeable houses on the west coast are comparatively few in number and generally plain in style. They are not, however, without their local peculiarities. The double-pile block which forms the early 18th century nucleus of Applecross House has its original main entrance set unusually at the rear of the building and the staircase is placed against the centre front, hence the dropped levels of the central windows lighting the stair landings. The smaller laird's house at Udrigle (1745) is of a similar disposition and layout with a rear stone-built porch dated 1756; it retains much of its original panelled interior with doors, chimney-pieces and balustraded scale-and-platt staircase to match, all of which would certainly not have been out of place in a Lowlands laird's house of the second quarter of the 18th century. The panelling and associated details are similar to those which still survive in the parlour of the larger Flowerdale House, built by the MacKenzies of Gairloch in 1738 and restored and extended in 1904. Apart from Udrigle, most of these 18th century west coast houses appear proportionately tall and long, a characteristic well exemplified by Applecross House and by Dundonnell House (1767) in Lochbroom Parish.

The large farmsteads of the west coast from Kintail to Gairloch also have one special distinguishing feature: their barns are of a distinctive type with wattle-panelled or louvred walls and lofty cruck-framed roofs, sensibly adapting older building traditions for the purposes of improved farming in the 18th century and later. The heavy rainfall in the west meant that space was needed to dry, as well as simply to store the hay and grain. The wattle or louvred panels are thus designed to maximise ventilation, and the barns are usually aligned to take greatest advantage of the prevailing westerly winds. At Applecross Mains a pair of low hip-roofed barns (Plate 28) — built on stone piers rather like the drying shed of a brickworks — are set in line on top of a knoll above the farmstead, rendering them even more exposed. The Reverend Aeneas Sage passed the night in such a barn before his induction as minister of Carron in 1726; the inflammable nature of the wattling meant that an unwelcoming parishioner had no difficulty in setting the building on fire but the new minister was not to be so easily deterred from his calling. Detailed examination of the wattle still surviving in one panel at Applecross Mains showed that it was of hazel; that in a barn at Balmacara in Lochalsh, formerly Ross-shire, was made up of heather and yew intertwined.

Wattle or wickerwork shows up well in some of the older photographs of buildings in Wester Ross like the well-known view of the settlement on the shores of Loch Duich (now Skye and Lochalsh District). As a walling material it has a considerable ancestry in these parts, for houses as well as barns. 'Creel houses', as they were known, usually had an outer turf cladding, and this form of construction as it applied to the farmhouses of Lochcarron and Lochbroom parishes was described in detail in a report of 1754: 'The side walls are made of stakes stuck into the ground, which are wattled with branches of trees and other small wood. The roof . . . is supported with coupled trees fixed in the ground, and these are also wattled like the side wall with small [wood]. On the outside of the wattling there is built a wall of turf or, other ways [otherwise] there are pinned on it thin divots after the manner of slate. The roof is covered with divot thatch ed over with stubble, straw or ferns. This is the manner is which most of the houses in the county are built. The only houses we saw built with stone were those on the lands of Inverlayle and Lochmill at Lochbroom. The side walls of the houses are repaired every year and the roof of thatch every three years and if thus taken care of they will last from eight to twenty years'.

Surviving evidence of wattle panels has also been found among the smaller barns of the crofting townships in the Applecross peninsula. Prior to the completion of the Shieldaig-Applecross coastal road in 1976 the northern end of this peninsula was a remote area, each of the townships having access to the sea and linked to each other by a narrow overland track. Traditional building features of various kinds have thus persisted here into modern times, although the croft-houses and steadings in which they have been found are all of post-1800 date. Even the small trabeated clam and clapper footbridges associated with the track linking the township (and found also at Aultbea) are of a type known to British prehistory.

One of only two thatched cottages in the District that remain habitable at the time of writing is at Lonbain (Plate 27) on the west coast of the Applecross peninsula; the other, which is at 27 Big Sand by Gairloch, has the distinction of possessing the only surviving box lum or cowl around which the rush thatching has been gathered. The Lonbain cottage is believed by its occupant to have been built, like others in this one-time linear fishing village, in the 1820s by a mason from Kalnakill just up the coast. The thatch, in this case straw, is laid on turf divots and secured by wire netting and anchor-stones. Elsewhere in the Applecross district heather seems to have been the most common thatching material, latterly at any rate. According to local information, the heather used for thatching at Kalnakill had been brought across the Sound from Raasay, and in the course of a survey carried out in 1973 a deserted building at Fearnbeg was found to contain two bales of heather ready for thatching. Another of the heather-thatched buildings at Fearnbeg had a rounded verge at the gable fairly bristling with thatching pins to prevent lifting by the wind. Many of the pins were shaped in the form of an elongated staple, each made either from one bent piece of wood or two single barbed pins linked by a holed leather tab. At Fearnmore and Kalnakill thatch of rushes and ferns was also found, usually in combination.

One of the gablets of the cottage at Lonbain is of pegged turf construction, a technique also seen in one of the barns at Fearnmore. As already noted, turf was once common as a building medium throughout Wester Ross. The last all-turf house in Gairloch parish is said to have been at Moss Bank, Poolewe, and at one time there was even a temporary turf-built church in Tollie Bay.

The vast majority of the ruinous buildings in the Applecross townships show evidence of cruck framing or 'Highland couples' for the support of their roofs. The technique has probably been widespread throughout the western mainland, and, although no systematic search has been made, examples have been noted at random from places and contexts as different and as far apart as the large improved barns in the Lochcarron area and small croft-buildings in the township of Mellon Charles. The large barns have well carpentered jointed crucks of substantial scantling; the crucks in the smaller buildings are of a correspondingly slighter section. Most are scarf-or lap-jointed at the wall-head, but a few surviving examples consist of pairs of single blades. They are generally cross-lapped and pegged at the apex, carrying a ridge-purlin in the cradle thus formed; some have a short high collar supporting a purlin at each side thus creating a broad ridge profile. Some of the cruck-framed dwellings and most of the surviving barns and byres are, or have been hip-roofed, not gable-ended, but the hipped ends are formed with conventional hip-rafters at the angles, not end-crucks. The houses usually preserve evidence of two pairs or crucks forming three bays, but five-bay byres and seven-bay barns have been encountered among the small steadings in the Applecross area. Internal clear spans vary between about 2.9m (9ft 6in) and 3.6m (11ft 10in). Bay lengths, depending on the weight of the roof and the quality of the timbers, could be anything from about 2.1m (6ft 10in) upwards; a typical three-bay house would be between 9.9m (32ft 6in) and about 10.7m (35ft 1in) in overall length. The crucks themselves appear to have been wrought from various kinds of wood; fir, oak, ash and birch have all been identified, with branch-rafters of birch or larch.

The surviving house interiors in the Applecross area are mainly of a simple tripartite plan with central closet and flanking rooms. Byre-dwellings were recorded by Sir Arthur Mitchell in the 19th century, and a plan of a specimen in Applecross was published by Captain Thomas in his article of 1866-8. At the time John Dixon was writing in 1886 'many of the crofters [in Gairloch] still have their byres under the same roof; still have no chimney in the living room, whence the smoke from the peat fire escapes only by a hole in the roof'. Fifty years earlier Sir Francis MacKenzie in his *Hints for the Use of Highland Tenants and Cottagers* (1838) was driven to 'protest against human beings and cattle entering together in your present fashion at the same doorway . . . I will not raise a laugh at your expense by describing your present smoky dens, and the hole in the roof with sometimes an old creel stuck on it in imitation of a chimney. The smoke you now live in not only dirties and destroys your clothes and furniture, but soon reduces the prettiest rosy faces in the world to premature wrinkles and deformities'.

Several houses in the Applecross townships preserve traces of timber canopied lums set above simple hearths or stone hob-grates; the evidence is often confined to the tell-tale vent at the gable apex where the chimney flue broke back into the stone wall, or to the sockets for the 'dooks' or brackets that supported the flanks of the boarded chimney-hood. Among the surviving domestic fittings mention should also be made of sliding wooden door-latches, and of pairs of small window-shutters, the size of a single pane, hung on leather hinges.

Most townships possessed at least one corn-drying kiln and kiln-barn, usually placed in a sheltered spot some distance from the main groups of dwelling-houses. That at Cuaig is below a cliff-face, while, remarkably, that at Lonbain is on the foreshore built hard against one of the larger rock outcrops. The grain for the kilns was produced locally, but surface stones and boulders had to be removed from the ground where it was to be cultivated. Stone clearance heaps are a conspicuous feature of the associated arable enclosures at Lonbain, and there is a particularly good cairnfield of this kind on the flat ground to the west of the township at Toscaig.

Map evidence suggest that shielings are quite numerous in parts of Wester Ross, and it is possible that here and there the practice of transhumance may have continued into the crofting era. On high ground at about 150m (492ft) altitude and within sight of Lonbain 1.6km (1 mile) to the west, for example, there is a well-preserved shieling which may have been associated with that township and its predecessor. The shieling comprises some eighteen huts disposed on either side of the Allt na Moine which flows through the centre of the site; there are largish oblong huts and small circular ones but none has traces of mounded foundations (which usually means re-use of earlier building-stances).

It would, however, be a serious mistake to characterise Wester Ross wholly as a remote architectural backwater where old traditions died hard and some building fashions never penetrated at all. In its setting and layout Ullapool is one of the most outstanding planned villages in Scotland. The barn near Flowerdale House must be the earliest dated barn (1730) in northern Scotland and is of a stylish east coast design, modified for use in the damper conditions of the west. On the industrial front, Wester Ross can also boast the remains of what is likely to be the earliest charcoal blast furnace in Scotland at Red Smiddy, one of three ironworking sites near Loch Maree exploited by Sir George Hay, 1st Earl of Kinnoull, in the early 17th century.

It is indeed a remarkable fact that there is not a single castle or fortified house within the western half of the District. But it is merely an accident of modern administrative history that the Ross-shire castles of Strome and Eilean Donan are excluded from this survey. Of these, Eilean Donan on Loch Alsh, ancestral home of the MacKenzies and their MacRae constables, even though much rebuilt, is arguably the oldest and most important stone castle in the whole of the old county. To many, it is the most picturesque and romantic in the whole of Scotland. And, although there are no physical remains to testify to the fact, Wester Ross (then known as North Argyll) was also the original power-base of the line of native earls of Ross established some time after 1225 by Ferquhard (Macintagart), representative of the lay abbots of Applecross.

With these few reservations, however, the contrast with the fertile and accessible lowlands of the eastern seaboard is as clear in architecture and building traditions as it is in terms of physical geography and land use. The sheer density, variety, quality and, to a lesser extent, antiquity of the buildings in Easter Ross bear closer comparison with those of the well-favoured lands on the southern shores of the Moray Firth. Regular sea traffic and ferries maintained strong links with Moray and Nairn, probably a much greater contact than with the west coast which was reached by rugged overland routes. For all these reasons top-grade building by the richer landholders in Easter Ross has often been astonishingly up to the minute in fashion and occasionally exotic, so much so that these characteristics can be regarded as a proper part of its architectural traditions.

For the medieval period the quality and elegance of the surviving aisle (Plate 21) of the cathedral church of Ross at Chanonry (Fortrose) has few equals in the Highlands, bespeaking generous funding from the late medieval earls of Ross. Even the erstwhile bishop's house nearby was described by one of its occupants as being inferior to few others in beauty and magnificence. After the Reformation it was the ubiquitous MacKenzies who set and sustained the pace and standard of building, and it was Sir George MacKenzie (1630-1714), Viscount Tarbat and (after 1702) 1st Earl of Cromartie, who excelled them all with the building of his great mansion of Milntoun of New Tarbat. Here he introduced the sash-window into the Scottish Highlands within about a decade of its very first appearance in Britain, and here he commissioned work by the exceptionally renowned plasterer, George Dunsterfield, fresh from his superb achievements at Holyroodhouse. The gardens were equally outstanding, but unfortunately none of this now survives. In the 18th century the influence, if not the actual documented activity of the celebrated Adam brothers is detectable in some of the very handsome classical mansions of Easter Ross, most notably Cromarty House (1772) and Foulis (1754-), an influence that permeated down to fine classic Georgian houses of the middle size such as Allangrange (1760) in the Black Isle, buildings that would be a credit to any part of Scotland, Lowlands and Highlands alike.

Parts of Easter Ross acquired an even more cosmopolitan and exotic character in the 19th century. Aided latterly by the railway, villa development expanded in the unique spa settlement of Strathpeffer (Plate 39) Scotland's answer to the Bavarian watering place. Here there is everything from simple symmetrical houses to elaborate confections decorated with ornate verandahs, bargeboards and cast-iron finials. The sumptuous excesses of Victorian Britain were also well represented by mansions such as Rosehaugh which was considerably enlarged and remodelled after 1864 by the Fletcher family, natives of nearby Avoch who had made a fortune in Liverpool. The house was demolished in 1959, but was survived by a number of interesting estate buildings dating from about 1900, the most outstanding of which is the dairy. They are all of an English Vernacular Revival idiom, almost certainly designed by the talented Scottish-born architect, William Flockhart (1850-1915). About a decade earlier, in 1889, a pastiche of English West Midlands timber framing made its appearance in Ross-shire when a local architect, Andrew Maitland of Tain (see below), produced a new gate lodge for Tarbat House at Kildary using dummy timber-framing jettied on tooled ashlar members. His patron was the Sutherland-born lady Cromartie, no doubt familiar with the traditional forms of building on the vast Sutherland estates in Staffordshire. Wyvis Lodge, on the other hand, is of a southern English Home Counties style, somewhat unexpected in its remote setting at the head of Loch Glass; meticulously detailed outside and in, the shooting lodge was built in 1886 to suit William Shoolbred, member of a London cabinet-making firm.

The fashionable, the exotic and the alien thus form a significant element in the architectural traditions of Easter Ross. But beneath this rich veneer the area has also managed to preserve some equally distinctive and more humble building traditions that relate rather more closely to the everyday life of the majority of its inhabitants. From North Kessock in the Black Isle right round to Inver on the Dornoch Firth the coastline is punctuated with a number of fishing villages full of character, most notably Avoch and Cromarty 'Fishertown' in the Black Isle, and Shandwick, Balintore, Hilton of Cadboll and Portmahomack in the Tarbat peninsula. The villages are of various shapes and size, but their layouts generally include terraced rows of cottages, often with gables facing seawards, public community buildings, sheds and open spaces, all of which have essential functions in seafaring communities. A few of the older unmodernised cottages at Inver have internal cross-passages and short baffle partitions or 'hallans' screening the kitchen fireplaces, a distinctive plan-form that has so far not been encountered elsewhere in the country. At Inver and Shandwick the kitchen fireplaces are known to be of canopied timber construction like those of the west coast, a design that would certainly have facilitated fish curing. The walls of many of the cottages here and inland are built of clay and rubble stone mixed with chopped straw or bent grass; in some cases the stone is laid in even courses like the 'clay and bool (boulders)' construction of Moray. A few cottages have party walls and gablets of 'caber and mott' construction, that is, closely spaced vertical poles covered with a smooth clay surface. Clay floors were at one time quite common, being easy to keep clean and practical for such jobs as baiting. Nor was clay building confined to the villages and the cottages of the countryside. In September 1789 a mud mason was offered and accepted a contract to erect two houses in one 60ft (18.29m) long block in Geanies Street, Tain, 'to be built of what is called solid mud except the corners, door and window skimshions [scontions], lintols and soles, chimneys and chimney heads, sque [skew] and wall tabeling, all of which is to be of the best quarry stones neatly hewed . . .'. Turf-built gablets have been found in at least one cottage at Lechanich in Edderton parish, but how far these clay and turf wall-building practices in the east were associated with cruck framing like those of the west is difficult to say. Surviving evidence of cruck construction has so far been recorded only from Culeave in Strathcarron, Kincardine parish (now Sutherland District), and from North Kessock, respectively on the northern and southern extremities of Easter Ross; these isolated examples also seem to relate more closely to building practices in adjacent cultural zones, the crucks of the North Kessock building being closely akin to Inverness-shire types.

Girnals are another distinctive and waterside feature of Easter Ross, especially around the shores of the Cromarty Firth. These are large storehouses designed to receive and store the grain crops produced in abundance on the estates of the fertile coastal districts, as payment in kind for agricultural rents. The grain — mainly bere barley and oats — was then re-issued either as wages for farmworkers and others, or as cash sales for export by sea. The buildings were thus best sited by the shore where boats could land and load easily; they also needed a spacious yard or assembly area on the landward side where the grain was gathered in. There are at least seven identifiable storehouses of this kind at six different locations on the coast from Foulis Ferry (Plate 26) round to Port mahomack, the densest known concentration of surviving girnals in Scotland. Among these, the 'Old Rent House' at Foulis Ferry is a fine and conspicuous specimen situated on the northern shore of the Cromarty Firth; it was built in about 1740 for the Foulis estate, and acquired some local notoriety during food shortages in 1796 when it was marched upon by a meal mob from Dingwall. At Portmahomack there are two girnals which stand in line close to the harbour: the smaller and older one to the south was built by Viscount Tarbat in the late 17th century and still retains its original double collar-rafter oak roof; the larger seven-bay structure is dated 1779.

As might be expected, Easter Ross possesses some fine threshing-barns of convential kinds, usually equipped with opposed winnowing doors in the side-walls and aligned with the long axis set athwart the direction of the prevailing winds. The large two-storeyed barn at Balnagown Mains has crowstepped gables and a steeply pitched roof-structure, probably of early 18th century origin. Although now somewhat disfigured in its outward appearance, the smaller Townlands Barn at Cromarty has a similar roof profile and structure and is probably of about the same date. It has a much worn carved armorial above one of the winnowing-doors, and there are paired quatrefoil vents within the base-angles of the crowstepped gables.

Among other ancillary estate buildings it is noticeable that dovecots are an exclusively east coast phenomenon. They are to be found mainly integrated within farm buildings and courts of offices, and there appear to be no more than two free-standing examples altogether, one at Cadboll and the other at Conan Mains. The Cadboll dovecot, a crowstepped lectern type, is the earlier of the two, probably mid 18th century, with a silhouette weathervane in the form of a country gentleman in breeches, boots and black hat, carrying a gun, said to be a likeness of Crawford Ross, tacksman of Cadboll for fifty years until his death there in 1862.

A conspicuous feature among 19th century gentry houses and farm-houses in Easter Ross is the projecting segmental bowed bay. This fashion made its way down the social and architectural scale from mansions such as Conan House and Geanies *via* early 19th century villas like Mountgerald and Knockbreck, where paired bowed bays form part of the original design, to numerous lesser houses and manses. In these latter cases single bowed extensions providing ground-floor dining-and first-floor drawing-rooms were added, usually to the fronts of the houses, when the owners prospered through commerce, farming or inheritance. The two-storeyed bowed wing lit by fashionable tripartite windows at Meikle Tarrel (Plate 25) is a good case in point, being the most prominent of the additions made to this house by 'Farmer George' MacKenzie after he had taken over the farm in 1800.

The burgh architecture of Ross and Cromarty, non-existent in the west, also has some distinguishing hallmarks. The civic functions of Tain, Dingwall and Cromarty were served by town-houses of very different styles, making up a most interesting heterogeneous group. At Tain the tolbooth with its strong-looking turreted tower was built mainly between 1706 and 1708 to replace its storm-damaged predecessor; it follows traditional tower house lines and is a late, not an early example of its kind as has sometimes been claimed. Dingwall Tolbooth, which dates substantially from a remodelling of 1730, is of a more symmetrical outward appearance with a central tower and, formerly, a forestair, while Cromarty has its elegant little town-house of a more homogenous classical design dating from 1782.

Urban housing in these towns and in Fortrose and Rosemarkie generally follows the pattern of the larger villages of the east and west coasts. They usually comprise terraced rows of fairly plain single- and two-storeyed dwellings, some in Dingwall being gable-fronted to the High Street. The modern world has tended to by-pass the once-thriving seaport of Cromarty with the result that parts of the town preserve in near-perfect measure the buildings and *ambiance* of a small maritime burgh of the 18th century. Individually, however, few of its two-storeyed three-bay houses, many formerly thatched, would have looked out of place in rural surroundings. The somewhat over-restored Hugh Miller's cottage (Plate 24) with its gable fronting Church Street is dated 1711, but the oldest identifiable house is a fine L-plan building in The Causeway. It is a domesticated tower house derivative, ascribable to about 1700; in its time the building has served as a manse for Cromarty East Church and as a gardener's residence for Cromarty House.

Tain, on the other hand, has very few houses dating from before 1800; the single most memorable characteristic of its urban architecture is the high quality of the stonework which has been taken from the excellent sandstone quarries in the area. In colour, texture and treatment the masonry conveys an impression of handsome solidity throughout the town, but these qualities are particularly well displayed in the walling and dressings of 10 Knockbreck Street (c.1830-40) and of the former Secession Church of 1839 in King Street.

The splendid masonry traditions of Easter Ross are also embodied in many of its earlier castles and churches, and not just in showpieces like Fortrose Cathedral either. Even in its decayed and ruinous state the 16th century tower of Ballone or Easter Tarbat shows excellent detailing, particularly in its angle-turrets or bartizans. The general composition of Castle Leod (Plate 22), the first eastern home of Sir Rorie MacKenzie of Coigach and his descendants, is also reminiscent of the styles of some of the elaborate contemporary towers of late 16th and early 17th century Aberdeenshire. Church belfries, too, give a decorative and an idiosyncratic touch to the exteriors of many a Post-Reformation kirk. That added to Cromarty East Church in 1799 is of simple classical style with stumpy corner pinnacles, one of a local type also represented at Nigg, Alness and Edderton. The Munro burial-aisle and circular belfry at Kilmuir Easter — possibly used as a sea-mark for the narrows of the Cromarty Firth — is topped with a conical stone-roofed 'pepper pot'. It has lucarnes and belfry-openings with carved heads, and although bearing a Munro datestone of 1616, the tower bears a strong resemblance to the early 18th century upperworks of Tain Tolbooth, and indeed to the turreted belfry of Kirkhill Church near Inverness which has lucarnes dated 1722. However, there is nothing else in the Highlands, or even perhaps in Scotland as a whole, quite like the delightful and exotic domed belfry — another in this early 18th century group — that sits atop the western gable of Tarbat Old Parish Church at Portmahomack (Plate 31).

Sculptural traditions have manifested themselves in churchyard memorials and architectural sculpture, especially in the production of some elaborate fireplace lintels in the 17th century. The surviving fragments of strapwork decoration from Castle Brahan are testimony to the quality of this work, as also is the fine decorated hall fireplace of 1679 in Kilcoy Castle, commissioned by another branch of the MacKenzies. The two most noteworthy carvings, however, are associated with the Urquharts of Cromarty: one slab which dates possibly from about 1633 and is preserved in Cromarty House, bears a hunting scene with various supporting decorative motifs; the other, which is now in the National Museum of Antiquities of Scotland, has in the words of Hugh Miller 'perhaps more of character impressed upon it than any other piece of sandstone in the Kingdom'. It is an heraldic slab, still retaining traces of colour, carved for the remarkable and eccentric Sir Thomas Urquhart of Cromarty; it is dated by the *Anno Christi* 1651 and the *Anno Mundi* of Sir Thomas's calculations, 5612. The slab bears the names and armorials of some of the very remote ancestors from whom Sir Thomas claimed descent in his entertaining and outrageous pedigree tract 'Pantoxronoxanon'. Pride of place in the centre of the slab is thus given to Esormon, Prince of Achaia, allegedly sixteenth in order from Adam, the first to be called Urquhart (in Greek!) and with a record of a coat-of-arms in 2139 B.C.!

Whether this fanciful piece and other architectural sculpture was carved locally or by mason-sculptors from Moray — which is generally credited with a monopoly of this talent in the lands around the Moray Firth — is simply not known. But with so much freestone of excellent quality abounding in Easter Ross it is not difficult to believe that the area has always had its own body of craftsmen with the necessary skills. However, Hugh Miller, the most celebrated mason from these parts — and indeed the most renowned mason in Scottish history — is best known for his geological and literary talents, not for any special proficiency as a craftsman. Just for the record, however, the building work at the steading at Conan Mains (1822) was the scene of one of his apprenticeship jobs graphically described in *My Schools and Schoolmasters* (chapters 9 and 10), while a rather undistinguished tombstone of 1829 in Nigg churchyard is attributed to him. A group of local masons who emerge from the shadows of anonymity in the 17th and 18th centuries are those of the family of Stronach who are known to have carried out commissions for Viscount Tarbat and the Cromartie family, for Tain burgh and possibly for other families in the neighbourhood. The earlier meal girnal at Portmahomack and the rebuilt Tain Tolbooth were works of Alexander Stronach, and some of the turrets and belfries mentioned above may bear the Stronach imprint.

And, finally, whilst Easter Ross was not the cradle of any architects of national importance, the firm of Andrew Maitland and Sons in Tain was a notable local practice which made the very best use of the patronage, materials and craftsmanship at its disposal. With fine Victorian buildings in Tain like the Royal Hotel (1872), the Town Hall (1874) and the Parish (former Free) Church (1891-2) to its credit, Maitlands was a firm of architects of whom Tain and Ross-shire in general can be justifiably proud. The earlier members of the Maitland family were masons, and, as craftsmen turned architects, they epitomised all that was good in the stone building traditions of Ross and Cromarty.

Chapter twelve

THE PLACE-NAMES OF ROSS AND CROMARTY

Ian Fraser

Little has been written on the place-names of the area since the late W. J. Watson published his *Place-Names of Ross and Cromarty* in 1904. Apart from the same author's treatment of Celtic names in his later volume, *The History of the Celtic Place-Names of Scotland,* and occasional references in later articles and books, the subject has remained largely dormant, at least as far as publication is concerned. However, that is not to say that research has remained static — quite the contrary. Since its inception in 1951 the Place Name Survey of the School of Scottish Studies in the University of Edinburgh has collected much material in Ross-shire, largely from oral tradition, and consisting mostly of minor place-names which do not appear on the Ordnance Survey 6" map. This has largely applied to the west, where Gaelic-speaking informants have been able to supply the information.

Mainland Ross and Cromarty has been subjected to a number of linguistic influences. The earliest settlement names are Pictish, and contain the Pictish element *pit-,* 'share', 'portion'. These are almost all in the east, and are confined to the more productive land. The majority of these names relate to farms of no great size, yet they are important evidence of a Pictish presence in the area.

Other Pictish elements in Ross-shire place-names include *aber,* 'confluence', (as in Applecross, formerly Abercrosan), and *carden,* 'thicket', 'wood', as in Urquhart. The fact that these are relatively rare, however, should in no way distract us from the idea that much of Ross was extensively settled by Pictish folk. The replacement of Pictish names by those of Gaelic, and to a lesser extent Norse, origin was a natural development. The *pit*-names themselves contain elements which are clearly Gaelic. *Pitfuir* in Avoch contains *pòr,* a Gaelic term for 'pasture'; *Pitnellies* in Tain is thought to be from *ianlaith* 'birds', and *Pitcalzean* in Nigg is probably 'stead of the little wood' from *coillean.* Few of the early

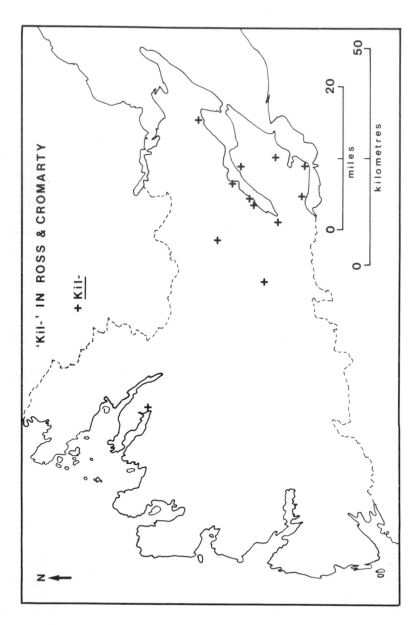

Figure 13 — "Kil" in Ross and Cromarty.

forms for these names suggest much of a breakdown in a Pictish-Gaelic continuum. The likelihood is of gradual change, with incoming Gaelic-speakers adopting *pit-* as an acceptable term in place-names, although the occasional change of *pit-* to a Gealic element did occur, especially in a vernacular form, such as *Pitglassie* in Dingwall being referred to as *Bad a' Ghlasaich* by Gaelic speakers. (Watson 1904, 94.)

The advent of Gaelic speech in Ross resulted in a large number of place-names which display the standard Gaelic elements to be found in other parts of Gaelic Scotland. The influence of the early Celtic church, for example, can be seen in the widespread use of the term *cill,* 'church', in such names as *Kildonan,* 'St. Donan's church' in Lochbroom on the west coast and *Kilmichael,* 'Michael's church' in Resolis. The term *annaid* or *annait* from the Irish *unnóid,* 'a church containing the relic of its founder' is found on six occasions in Ross, usually in a simplex form such as *Annat* in Kildonan, Lochbroom, *Annat* near Torridon, *Annat* and *Loch na h-Annaid* in Nigg, and *Annat* in Contin.

One name which is of particular interest is that of the Applecross peninsula, still known in Gaelic as 'a' Chomraich', It is stated in the Annals of Tighernach for 673 that *Maelruba fundavit ecclesiam Aporcrosan,* thus beginning an important ecclesiastical foundation which has left us a number of useful indicators of the wide influence of this individual. The peninsula was referred to as *Comraich Maolruibh* 'Maelrubha's sanctuary'. The island on Loch Maree (formerly Loch Ewe) which was used as a cemetery, and which has a holy well was *Eilean Ma-Ruibhe.* It was a place of pilgrimage for many generations, and was resorted to within living memory, since the well was reputed to cure insanity and other disorders. The loch itself was referred to as late as 1654 (on the Blaeu map) as 'Loch Ew', but clearly the association with Maelrubha was so strong that the loch was re-named probably some time in the late 17th century. The village at the southern end of the loch, however, recalls the original name — *Kinlochewe* 'Ceann Loch Iù'.

The other major sanctuary in Ross was connected with the church of St. Duthac at Tain. The only remaining place-name associated with this lies on the road between Tain and Scotsburn, *Clais na Comraich,* 'the ravine of the sanctuary'. (Watson 1904, lxvi.)

Various other onomastic terms commemorate other important ecclesiastical establishments, such as *manachainn* 'monastery' in *Manachainn 'ic Shiomidh* 'the monastery of the Frasers', for Beauly, and Fearn parish was originally *Sgìr na Manachainn* 'the parish of the monastery'. Similarly the Gaelic name for Fortrose was *A' Chananaich* 'the place of canons' or 'the chanonry' (Plate 21).

As the Gaelic settlement progressed, it began to establish itself in the

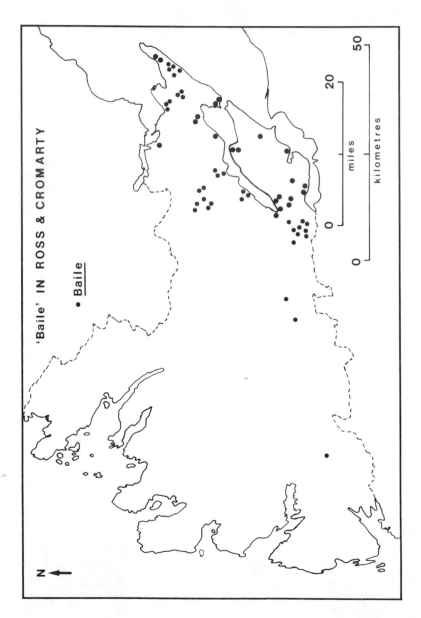

Figure 12 — "Baile" in Ross and Cromarty.

farmlands of the Moray Firth, where the Pictish traditions in naming were to some extent absorbed and adapted by the incomers. The old term *dubhach* 'vat', originally applied to a variable measure of land, is retained in names like *Docharty* in Fodderty (Dalcarty and Davachcarty 1541) 'the davach of the corn-enclosure' and *Lettoch* 'half-davach' in Killearnan, referred to as 'half the lands of Dawaucht' in 1530. The Gaelic custom of division of land into fifths is found in the current name *Coigeach,* 'place of fifths'.

Old Pictish fortified sites bearing the terms *rath* and *lios* are scarce in Ross, although *Ramore,* rath mòr, 'the great rath' in Edderton parish is one definite example. *Baile* (anglicised to *bal-*) is the standard Gaelic term for 'farmstead' and there are over eighty examples in the District, mostly in the east, for the obvious reasons of fertility and flat land. The term is scarce in the west, partly because of Norse influence, and partly because of the lack of large areas of cultivable land. Many of the *baile-* names are descriptive of the land and its qualities, such as *Ballone* 'bail' an lòin' 'wet meadow farm' in Avoch, *Balnacraig* 'baile na creige' 'rock-farm' in Alness, and *Balavullich* 'bail' a' mhullaich' 'summit-farm' in Urray. Others indicate ownership, like *Balnagown* 'smith's farm' in both Urray and Kilmuir Easter, *Balanrishallaich* 'Fraser's farm' in Rosskeen, or *Ballskllly* in Resolis which may be from *sgeulaiche* 'story-teller'.

In the west, the more common farm element is *achadh* 'field', with over forty examples. This element also occurs in the east, but to a much lesser extent. Again, there are topographic reasons for this, but *achadh* in settlement names is usually regarded as later than *baile* (Nicolaisen 1976, 141) and is applied to markedly smaller and less productive units. The normal anglicisations are *ach-* or *auch-,* but care must be taken when supplying derivations to distinguish *achadh* from *uachdar* 'top', 'upper part' which is usually anglicised as *auchter-. Achindrean* 'thorn-field' in Lochbroom and *Achnagart* 'corn-enclosure-field' in Glenshiel, are examples containing this element.

Tigh 'house' is a fairly common farm settlement element in the east, and limited largely in its extent, but occurring in some 20 instances, like *Teanafruich* 'heather-house' and *Teandalloch* 'house of the dale' in Urray, *Teanagairn* 'house of the cairn' in Urquhart, together with *Teandore* 'house of the thicket' in the same parish. This name also occurs twice in Knockbain parish where Watson gives the derivation as *tigh an todhair* 'bleaching house'. There is also the unusual *Teawig* in Knockbain, from *tigh a' bhuic'* 'house of the buck'. The old term *fàsadh* 'dwelling' is found in *Fasagrianach* 'sunny-dwelling', in Lochbroom.

Achadh, however, is not the only field-term which has been elevated to the status of true settlement names, although it is certainly the most prolific. Gaelic *dail* 'meadow', 'water-meadow', which is common throughout Gaelic Scotland, is also well represented in Ross, and may well have pre-Gaelic, i.e. Pictish forms. Old Welsh *dol* 'meadow' is found regularly in Scotland, and care should be taken to identify this element by examining early spelling forms. Most of the Ross-shire examples seem to be straightforward, descriptive names, like *Dalneich* 'horse-meadow' in Rosskeen, *Dalbreac* 'speckled meadow' in Contin and *Dalnacroich* 'gallows-meadow' in the same parish. *Dallas* in Edderton, however, which occurs in document as *Doles* in 1560, has as its Gaelic form 'Dalais'. This has in common with names like Alness (G. Alanais) and Farness in Cromarty (G. Fearnais) the terminal *-ais,* 'found only in Pictish ground' (Watson 1904, xlix) and meaning 'dwelling' or more likely 'place'. Watson suggests that Dallas has as its first element Pictish *dol* 'plateau', and the name hence means 'place of the plateau'.

In an area where transhumance was an important part of the economy, it is not surprising that many place-names reflect such shieling activity. The normal Gaelic word for shieling is *àirigh*, and while occasional examples remain in use, such as *Airigh nan Druineach,* which Watson thought could be 'shieling of the druids', in Applecross (Watson 1904, 215) most of them are anglicised to *Ari-* as in *Aridrishaig* 'thorny shieling' in Applecross, *Arinackaig* in Lochcarron, perhaps containing a personal name, and *Airiecheirie* in Contin 'waxen-shieling'. There is another group which have *àirigh,* or to be more precise, O.N. *erg* in a final position. These are common in the west, and many clearly have Norse initial elements, although some are obscure as regards their derivation. *Kernsary* and *Smiorasair* in Gairloch, and *Blughasary* in Lochbroom are in this category.

The term *ruighe* or *righe* 'hill-slope' is often confused with a similar word which is the general term for 'shieling' in Inverness-shire and Perthshire. In Ross it is extremely difficult to distinguish the origins of a large group of names which have emerged as settlements — usually hill farms in the east and central valleys, but with one or two examples in the west. These include *Rhidorroch* 'dark hill-slope' in Lochbroom, *Rhicullen* 'holly-slope' in Rosskeen, *Rhibreac* 'speckled slope' in Edderton and *Rheindown* 'slope of the *dùn*' in Urray. Some of these *may* at one time have been in shieling areas, however, so there could be a connection, although a close examination of the various sites in question would be needed for confirmation.

Gaelic topographic terms have been very important in the formation of settlement names. Most of these are of relatively recent coinage, but a few are clearly old, especially those which are at important locations, such as the mouths of major streams. Here, the term *inbhir,* 'confluence' is seen as a parallel to Pictish *aber,* itself borrowed into Gaelic as *obair.* *Inbhir* is normally found as *inver,* and appears as such in Ross as a simplex name — *Inver* near Tain. There are some 15 other examples, ranging from *Inverbreckie* in Rosskeen to *Inveralligin* in Applecross, and the recently-coined *Invergordon,* a product of the 18th century. In Gairloch parish, we find *Inverasdale,* a Norse-Gaelic hybrid. (Watson 1904, 229, 1v.)

Vegetational terms, such as *coille* 'wood', *preas* 'clump' and *doire* 'thicket' have found their way into settlement names in places like *Balnakyle* in Knockbain and *Coillymore* in Rosskeen, as well as *Tornapreas* in Applecross ('hill of the clump'). But the most prolific of these is undoubtedly *bad* 'clump' which in some parts of Western Gaeldom has the alternative derivation 'place', 'spot'. Most names in *bad-* occur in the West, such as *Badluachrach* 'clump of rushes' and *Badcall* 'hazel clump' in Lochbroom, *Badfearn* 'alder clump' *Badnasgalag* 'servant's clump' and *Badachro* 'cattle-fold clump' in Gairloch, although many are associated with woodland locations farther east, such as *Badenerb* 'roe-clump' in Urquhart, *Baddans* in Alness, and *Badrain* 'thorny copse' in Urquhart.

Stream- and loch-names have similarly provided material for settlement names, especially *allt* 'stream' with examples like *Aultguish* 'fir-burn' in Contin, *Aultanfearn* 'alder-streamlet' in Rosskeen and *Aultbea* (Plate 42) 'birch-burn' in Gairloch.

Certain coastal terms, especially on the west coast, have been absorbed as settlement names, in a region where there is a relatively small proportion of true habitative elements in the overall stock of settlement names. Typical of these, and among the most common, is *camas* 'bay', as found in *Camusterach* 'easter bay' and *Camusteel* 'linden-bay' in Applecross, *Camasaidh* 'little bay' and the evil-sounding Gaelic-Norse hybrid, *Camustrolvaig* 'goblin or troll-bay' in Gairloch. This last contains O.N. *vik* 'bay' as well as its Gaelic equivalent, and is a good example of the kind of tautology which evolved when Gaelic speakers no longer understood the original Norse.

If we now turn to purely topographic names, we find that in Ross, the large variety of terms used to describe the land has in most cases been adopted into place-name usage. In the west especially, there is a profusion of terminology available to fit such topographic situations. Mountain- and hill-names, for example, require terms which describe such features as height, position, shape, outline, surface, aspect, weather conditions, vegetation, wild-life, and so on. There are general terms like *bein, sgùrr, meall* and *carn* to describe the higher summits, and *cnoc, creag, druim, torr* and *tom* for the lower. Many of these occur in a

diminutive form, such as *meallan, creagan* and *torran*. Of the many prominent mountains in the district, there is space to mention only a few.
Slioch in Loch Maree (Plate 3) is *an Sleaghach*, possibly from *sleagh*
'spear'. *Liathach* (Plate 2) near Kinlochewe is from *liath* 'hoary' — 'the
hoary place', literally. *Stack Polly* (Plate 4) in *Coigeach* is *Stack Pollaidh*,
from the nearby river-name, meaning 'river of pools'. It is quite common
for a major stream to be the generator of names of adjacent topographic
features.

Stream-names, or course, are an important and frequently ancient
element in topographic names. Several Ross-shire river names are in this
early, possibly pre-Celtic, or Indo-European category. The *Carron*, for
instance, "can with confidence be derived from the Indo-European root
*kar- 'hard', 'stone', 'stony', with obvious reference to the quality of the
beds of these water sources" (Nicolaisen, 1976, 188). Other rivers which
undoubtedly come into this ancient category include Shiel, Conon and
Meig.

Most of the smaller streams have more recent Gaelic names, and
are, on the whole descriptive. *Abhainn* 'river' although the standard
Gaelic term, in reality rarely appears on maps, since most of the main
streams are marked as 'River . . .' in an anglicised form. Secondary
streams usually appear as *allt*, which is the equivalent of the Scots *burn*.
Farther down the scale, rivulets and brooks are named *caochan, feadan*
or *alltan*, the diminutive form of *allt*.

THE NORSE ELEMENT

Although the Scandinavians left a large number of place-names in
Ross-shire, few are names which, on first sight, at least, are indicative of
permanent settlement. This may sound a contradiction, but we find only
a handful of names which are habitative, and some of these are of doubtful derivation. Nevertheless, Norse influence must have been considerable, when we consider the presence of *Dingwall* (Plate 38), from
Old Norse (O.N.) *Thing-völlr* 'justice-field' or 'thing-field'. This occurs
in its earliest documented form in 1227 as *Dingwell*. The Norse term
bólstaðr, 'farmstead' is found in four instances in the east — *Arboll*
(Arkboll 1463, 1535) in Tarbat, from *ork-ból*, 'ark-stead'; *Cadboll*
(Cathabul 1529) in Fearn, from *kattar-ból* 'cat-farmstead'; *Culbol* (Eistir
and Wastir Culboll, 1560) in Resolis 'knob-farmstead'. The sole western
example is *Ullapool* (Ullabill, 1654; Plate 44), which is perhaps 'Ulli's
farmstead'.

The west coast, however, abounds with place-names which, if not
habitative names, at least provide concrete evidence of Norse activity and
influence. These almost all contain topographic elements, such as O.N.

dalr 'valley', *nes* 'point', 'promontory', *vík* 'bay', *ey* 'island', *gil* 'ravine' and various coastal features like *gjá* 'creek', *sker* 'sea-rock' and *rif* 'reef'.

Names in *dalr* are especially plentiful in the west, since they are often applied to small valleys off the main straths. *Mungasdale* 'monk's valley' in Lochbroom, *Erradale* 'gravel-beach-valley', *Inverasdale* (Inveraspidill 1566) 'aspen-valley', *Slattadale* 'even-valley' and *Talladale* 'ledge-dale' in Gairloch, and *Attadale* 'fight-dale' in Lochcarron, are all examples of these. Most of the names containing *vík* have Gaelicised forms in *-aig,* and are numerous in the west, usually on good, sheltered bays where boats could be anchored or drawn up on beaches. In this group are the two *Shieldaigs* 'herring-bay', one in Gairloch (Plate 46) and the other in Applecross, *Diabaig* 'deep bay' and *Melvaig* 'bent grass bay' in Gairloch, *Reraig* in Lochcarron 'reed-bay', and *Saraig* 'muddy bay' in Glenshiel. The term *gil* 'ravine' occurs in *Portigil* (Port Henderson) in Gairloch, 'gate-ravine', and *Udrigil* 'outer-ravine' in the same parish.

It is perhaps appropriate to mention here the term *skiki* 'cultivated strip'. This occurs in a Gaelicised form as *-scaig,* and one has to examine the locations of place-names containing this element in order to avoid confusion with those in *-vík/-aig.* Most, however, are on river-side locations, or beside lochs, such as *Calascaig* 'Kali's strip' in Lochbroom, *Ormiscaig* 'Orm's strip' near Aultbea in Gairloch parish, and *Toscaig* 'howe-strip' in Applecross.

Another 'field' element is O.N. *völlr* 'field', which occurs in *Mial* 'narrow-field' *(mjo-völlr)* in Gairloch, and in several instances farther east, such as *Braelangwell* in Resolis, and the intriguing *Scatwell* in Contin. This last appears as Litill Scathole, Sctholc Mekle in 1497, is in Gaelic *Scatail,* and may be from O.N. *scat-völlr,* common-grazing or 'scat' land.

MODERN NAMES

The introduction of non-Gaelic names came late to much of Ross, and their presence is largely seen in the more prosperous lands of Easter Ross and the Black Isle, where farms and estates came under Lowland Scots influence, at the expense of the Gaelic speech. In many instances, we can observe Scots replacing Gaelic names by direct translation, such as *Heathfield* in Kilmùir Easter, which occurs in 1479 as Kalruquhuy, and 1586 as Calrechy, *cala fhraochaidh* 'wet heather meadow', and *Cornhill* in Urray which was formerly Knochinarrow, *cnoc an airbh.*

It is obvious that Gaelic speakers in Easter Ross continued to use Gaelic forms of names which had been long established in a Scots form, in documents and on maps. *Castleton* in Avoch, spelt Castletoun in 1456 was nevertheless referred to as 'Bail' a' Chaisteil' until Gaelic died out in the area during this century, and there are scores of similar names in the east, including the various *Hiltons, Miltons,* and *Kirktons. Hilton* in Fearn, for example, appears as 'Balnaknok' in 1610. Most of the Scots names contain very simple topographic terms, often relating to the function of the settlement, to the main features of the landscape, or to its vegetation. Many also feature personal names, and several were 18th or 19th century coinages during the period when there was much agricultural and industrial development in the Moray Firth coasts. *Chapelton* and *Highfield* in Urray, *Crosshills* and *Millcraig* in Rosskeen, *Broomhill* in Kilmuir Easter, *Parkhill* in Logie Easter, *Rockfield* and *Wilkhaven* in tarbat, *Bayfield* in Nigg, and *Cotterton* and *Coldwells* in Knockbain are typical examples.

Charleston in Knockbain is named after Sir Charles Mackenzie of Kilcoy and dates from 1812. *Barbaraville* is in Kilmuir Easter; *Brucefield* in Tarbat is named after a former proprietor, as in *Hughstown* in Urray. A farm in Logie Easter, formerly called 'the Bog' was reclaimed in the first half of the last century by Hugh Ross of Culrossie, who named it *Arabella,* after his wife Arabella Phips. He took this a stage further by calling one of his neighbouring farms *Phipsfield.*

Names in this category in the west are relatively rare, but they are not completely absent, sometimes occurring near the centres of major estates, or where the fishing boom of the late 18th, and early 19th centuries demanded new buildings, or small, specialised industrial or agricultural communities. A good example is *Charlestown* in Gairloch, and Lochcarron village was formerly *Janetown.* In addition, a number of direct translations from the original Gaelic have appeared such as *Greenstone Point* (Rubha na Cloiche Uaine) in Gairloch parish, *Fisherfield* (Innis an Iasgaich) in Lochbroom, and *Courthill* (Cnoc a' mhòid) in Lochcarron.

CONCLUSION

Place-names are in a state of continual change and development. The situation in Ross and Cromarty is paralleled in many respects both in Sutherland to the north, and Inverness-shire to the south. This entire area has been subjected to Pictish, Gaelic, Norse and latterly Scots influences, and place-names have to be seen as part of the entire historical picture. It is always tempting to read too much into, for example, place-name distributions. For one thing, a distribution map showing names in *bal-* gives no indication of dating, nor does it tell us anything about the physical nature of the settlements involved.

Place-name data is by its very nature composed of small snippets of information, much of it, especially in Northern Scotland, lacking in documentary evidence. This is especially true in topographic names, for which our earliest written forms sometimes date only from the last century when the Ordnance Survey began to produce their first maps. It is only when the historical and archaeological record, coupled with place-name studies, is fully available that a clear picture emerges.

Having said that, Watson's work in Ross and Cromarty, despite the fact that it is now eighty years in print, is still a valuable reference work. It is fair to say that this chapter could not have been properly written without it. Modern place-name collections from Ross and Cromarty have concentrated on minor names at the level of parishes and individual farms, since the record of field-names and minor topographic names has gone largely unrecorded. It is this body of information that is most likely to disappear, since it is closely linked with oral tradition, something which is rapidly dying throughout Scotland, and which it is vital to record before it is too late.

It is hoped that this will complement what we already know about Ross-shire names, so that the onomastic record can be as complete as possible.

Chapter thirteen

FAMOUS PEOPLE

Jane Durham

Nowadays Ross-Shire does not have very many names that would be recognised as World Famous, so it seems reasonable to include people who, well known in their day, are now largely forgotten; but it must be remembered that, from earliest historical times the leaders of the great Clan groupings played major parts. These Chiefs and their collaterals were of an importance both locally and nationally that it is hard for us to comprehend today.

The traditional clan names still abound in Ross and Cromarty. The telephone directory has approximately 120 names in a column, and in 1984 there are 14 columns of McLeods, 13 for MacKenzies, 9½ for Rosses, 4½ for Munros and 9 for Frasers in the Highland area.

From earlier than the 10th century the Earls of Ross, who were also Lords of the Isles, were the leading family group, but the Earldom became forfeit to the Crown in 1493, and what was left of great power diminished with the line of Ross of Balnagown.

The Munros of Foulis are on record from the 11th century, and have maintained an almost unbroken line. It is not clear where they came from; it may have been Ireland, or they may have been in the Ross-Shire area long before that date.

A Royal Charter to Colin MacKenzie of Kintail was granted by Alexander III c. 1266 for Lands in Kintail. The Earldom of Seaforth was conferred in the early 17th century on Colin XIV. It died with the last male heir in 1815.

The Cromarty Earldom was granted to the other branch, descendants of the famous "Tutor of Kintail", Sir Ruraidh MacKenzie (1574-1626) in 1703. The present Earl lives in Castle Leod, Strathpeffer, and Captain Patrick Munro of Foulis resides in his Castle of that name near Evanton. David Ross of Ross, the Chief of the Clan, lives in Aberdeenshire, and the Frasers are just across the border in Inverness, whilst around the world are spread uncounted numbers bearing the familiar names, many of whom have achieved distinction away from Ross-Shire. It is with those who remained behind that this chapter is concerned.

In the 18th and 19th centuries, there was a group of lairds who altered the face of the countryside by removing townships, squaring fields, building big farm houses and steadings, and planting trees. There were men like Sir John Lockhart Ross of Balnagown, the Mackenzies of Gairloch, Sheriff Donald McLeod of Geanies, Hugh Ross of Calrossie, Cockburn Ross of Shandwick and many others. Known as 'Improvers', they were well documented in Mowat's *The Double Frontier Ross shire 1750-1850.*

If the notable literary figures slightly outweight the others, it is because the latter are largely unrecorded and there has always been a fine general tradition of writing and scholarship in Ross-shire. Beginning with two people who defy category, St. Duthac and the Brahan Seer, we are dealing with figures heavily cloaked with legend.

St. Duthac d. 1065

The tradition is that his birthplace was on the little hill below Tain, where the ivy-covered ruin of the chapel stands today. His death is recorded at the great religious centre of Armagh.

The Burgh Arms of Tain bear his figure, and in Gaelic Tain is called 'Baile Duthac' (Duthac's Town). The best known legend concerning his miraculous power is the one when he was sent to the smithy for fire and a bad-tempered Smith tipped live coals into his apron. He wasn't even burned and carried the coal safely to his master. His hair shirt later became a deeply venerated relic and was worn by the Earls of Ross when they rode into battle.

Tain became an important place of pilgrimage in the later Middle Ages, because of the veneration in which St. Duthac was held by the kings and nobles of Scotland.

The Brahan Seer, Kenneth Mackenzie

For a detailed analysis of the Brahan Seer, see chapter 14.

Sir George Mackenzie, 1st Earl of Cromartie — 1630-1725

A family which has had great influence on life in Ross-shire, particularly in the 17th and 18th centuries, is that of the Mackenzies. At one time in the 17th century, there were 25 landed families of that name in the area and shortly after 1600, five cadet families held a further sixteen properties or tacks. The chief of the clan was the Earl of Seaforth, a title created in 1623. The other main branch held substantial lands and acquired many titles; among the properties they owned were Tarbat, Lochslin, Ballone and Castlehaven, as well as lands in the west of the county.

A great statesman and man of the law, Sir George Mackenzie, was born at his grandfather's house 'Innertiel' in Fife, in 1630. In his long and active life, he did most for the Cromartie fortunes. To his first wife Anna, a Sinclair of Mey in Caithness, he was married for 44 years.

At Aberdeen University, he became an advocate and a passionate Loyalist. He was also a founder member of the Royal Society. (He is not to be confused with his wily cousin, Sir George Mackenzie of Rosehaugh).

From Edinburgh or Whitehall, he kept up a constant business correspondence with his factors. His boats sailed from the north of Scotland to Europe and Edinburgh. Among other things, they carried bere-barley for malting. Being very interested in agriculture and land reclamation, it is said that he brought over Dutchmen to reclaim the land below Meddat, in Easter Ross.

He was Lord Clerk Register and Secretary of State under Queen Anne, and was created Viscount Tarbat in 1685. Later he was made the Earl of Cromartie in 1703. He is reputed to have been one of the first to work for the Union of Parliaments for which he put forward a proposal in 1698. He lived through seven reigns and served five sovereigns.

Retiring to his great house at New Tarbat, he died in 1725.

SOLDIERS

MAJOR GENERAL SIR HECTOR MACDONALD, KCB, DSO, ADC, 1853-1903

Hector Macdonald was born a younger son of a small farming family in Rootfield, Muirblarie, Conon Bridge and joined the army in 1870 taking the Queen's Shilling from the recruiting sergeant in an Inverness pub, 'The Peahen'. He chose the 92nd Regiment, "The gay and gallant Gordon's", which was one of the 27 Scottish Regiments formed after the '45.

A brilliant soldier, he broke through the class-encrusted structure of the Victorian Army and rose to become a Major General (Plate 29). This must have been a very lonely position for him, particularly as his marriage had broken down and the existence of his wife and son were largely unknown.

His career is military history and his name became a household word. In the Afghanistan Campaigns in the '80's he earned the nickname 'Fighting Mac' which was to remain with him to the end. He had

44. Ullapool, superbly located on a delta in Loch Broom

(J. Campbell)

46. Shieldaig, set amid spectacular mountain scenery   (J. Smith)

47. Glenmorangie Distillery (registered in 1843) Tain   *(J. Campbell)*

48. Rig construction site of Highlands Fabricators, Nigg   *(J. Smith)*

immense courage, combined with a quiet and gentle dignity. Latterly, the pressures became too much for him and it is thought he took his own life in Paris in 1903 when returning to face charges relating to homosexuality.

His funeral in Edinburgh was hurried and aroused fierce controversies both as to the manner and reasons for the haste.

The Mitchell Tower on the hill above Dingwall (with the land given by Provost Mitchell) was erected to his memory with money collected by public subscription. It shows in what affection his memory was held, both at national and local levels.

GENERAL JOHN MACKENZIE 1st OF GAIRLOCH, 1764-1860

John Mackenzie, who joined the army in 1778, had a career of constant active service in Europe and was present at the capture of the Dutch fleet in Saldanha Bay near the Cape of Good Hope. For his personal daring and valour, he was known as 'Fighting John,' and for the quickness of his temper as 'Peppery Jack'.

At Tarragona, he was so incensed by the conduct of his superior officer, Sir William Henry Clinton, that he brought charges of incapacity and cowardice against him, for which the latter was tried, reprimanded and then had the sentence remitted. General Mackenzie was never employed again.

The 78th were in the relief of Lucknow. General Mackenzie was on a balcony to greet them during the civic welcome given to the regiment on its return to Inverness. Aged 96, he was the oldest officer in the British Army at that time.

GENERAL SIR HECTOR MUNRO OF NOVAR, 1727-1805

Hector Munro was the eldest son of Hugh Munro, 6th of Novar. There is a tradition that he owed his commission in the 34th Regiment to the Duchess of Gordon who was travelling, lightly attended, in Sutherland. She was having trouble with a drunken postilion and young Hector was able to rescue her from her predicament for which she reputedly procured him his commission.

There may be two distinct opinions on the value of his military career, in the aftermath of the '45 and later in India, where he rose to the rank of Major General, but there can be only one opinion about his capability to earn money — he excelled at it!

In 1792 Sir Hector 'was smitten with the mania for the introduction of sheep' and being a man of prompt action, he attempted to convert a portion of the estate in the northern part of the parish of Alness into a sheep walk.

The confrontation at Boath was one of the results. Sir Hector was well placed to play a large part in the dispersal of the flock gatherers as he was colonel of the Black Watch, who were conveniently stationed at Fort George.

He represented the Inverness district of Burghs in Parliament from 1786 till 1801 and from 1767 to 1776 he was Provost of Fortrose. In 1791 he gave Inverness the clock for its steeple. Both are still there today.

A local tradition has it, that in order to give work in a time of famine, he caused a copy of the Gates of Negapatam (at the sack of which he had been present) to be built on the top of the Hill of Fyrish.

Anyone who has ever stood beside those mighty pillars and looked out at the wonderful panorama of Ross-shire below must wonder what manner of man Sir Hector really was. The work involved, with the most rudimentary of carts, highland ponies and half-starved men, beggars the imagination. The giant stones remain today as an outstanding memorial.

MAJOR GENERAL DONALD MACINTYRE, VC, 1831-1903 — Bengall Staff Corps and 2nd Gurkha Rifles Indian Army.

He was born in Kincraig, Ross-shire in 1831 and died at Fortrose in 1903.

On 4th January 1872, during an expedition against the Losshai in North-East India their chief stockaded village was attacked. The small party of Gurkhas was led by Major Macintyre. The Stockade was burning, but, undaunted, he sprang up it, and with his party successfully stormed the place, while under heavy fire.

SERGEANT JOHN MACKENZIE, VC (later Major), 1870-1915 — 2nd Battalion Seaforth Highlanders (Ross-shire Buffs, Duke of Albanys).

He was born in Contin, Ross-shire in 1870 and died near Cuinchy, France in 1915.

On June 6th 1900, at Dompodssi, in Ashanti, Sergeant MacKenzie displayed courage under severe fire. He worked two Maxim guns with exemplary coolness and steadiness, and received a severe wound while so doing, but afterwards volunteered to clear the stockades, putting himself at the head of the men, and, by a daring charge driving the enemy headlong into the bush.

WRITERS

SIR THOMAS URQUHART OF CROMARTIE, 1611-1660

This splendid eccentric and scholar was sent to Aberdeen University when only eleven years of age. His tremendous gusto for the use of words shines through his writings. One biographer says that his true claim to fame rests almost entirely on his translations of the first three books of Rabelais which he ranks among the finest translations in the English language.

Sir Thomas was also a specialist in the art of pedigree faking. In one tract he showed how the Urquharts descended directly from Adam!

The family were staunch Loyalists and so he fought at the battle of Worcester where he was captured and later released. Not much is known of his later life, except that he was beset by creditors. There is a firmly held belief that he burst into a huge fit of laughter on hearing of the Restoration of Charles II — and then died happily one hopes.

SIR KENNETH MACKENZIE OF SCATWELL, 1659-1729

The astute Sir Kenneth Mackenzie was a landowner who acted as banker to his neighbours. He kept *Ane Memorandie Boke* which covers the years 1694 to 1720, into which he wrote, with care and precision, business dealings as well as family matters.

He lived at Findon in the Black Isle and was married three times. On 12th May 1720 he wrote 'The sed day I got a bond from young Cadboll and his curators for 3358: 6: 8 merks payable at Mart 1720. The sed bond was for the 5 yrs rent of Wladell and tua bills he oned me with oxin, horses and corne, he gott when I quit the laboureing of Wladell (Scotsburn)'.

His first wife, Lillias Mackenzie, 'died of a child' on the twenty first of October 1703 'regraited of al yt ever hade aquentance of hir.'

Later he took his 'dearest daughter Meggie' and his son George to the Parliament in Edinburgh on 3 June 1702. With him he took money, 18,000 merks, besides 'my expenses and hyring to Edr. qch amounted to 62 merks' — which seemed a modest sum.

Meggie married McLeod of Cadboll, whom she met in Edinburgh, though she may have known him in the north. He was then Town Clerk of Edinburgh, and called 'Clerk McLeod', in the family. The Rev Donald McLean of Dochgarroch, in whose possession the *Memorandie Boke* lies, has made a copy of the original, an interesting picture of life in Ross-shire in the late 17th and early 18th centuries.

SIR GEORGE STEUART MACKENZIE OF COUL, 1780-1848

Sir George was an agriculturalist and writer. Joseph Mitchell said of him 'he was an accomplished man of science'.

A Fellow of the Royal Society, he frequently contributed to its *Transactions* and to the other learned journals of the period. He wrote for the Board of Agriculture and Improvement (who were doing a National

Survey at that time) — *A General View of the Agriculture of the Counties of Ross & Cromarty, with observations on the means of their Improvement.*
He was a leading light in the Ross-shire Farmers' Society formed in 1811. He felt that 'the social intercourse between landlord and tenant was of the greatest benefit, and that the condescension of the landlords in associating freely with the class of farmers was considered by the latter as a pledge of friendship and protection, and it acted as a strong stimulus to exertion'.

It is over 170 years since these words were penned. Sir George may have been right, and the minutes suggest that the Society had some excellent dinners!

HUGH MILLER, 1802-1856

Hugh Miller, self-taught geologist and man of letters became Ross-shire's best-known author. His father, a ship's captain, was lost at sea when Hugh was five years old. Educated in Cromarty, he was a wild and intractable boy with a formidable intellect. Later, when he was apprenticed to his uncle, a stone mason in Lairg, he steadied and became a journeyman mason all over Scotland before engaging as bank clerk in Cromarty.

Through his flair for writing, and fervently held religious beliefs, he was well-suited to become the Edinburgh based editor of *The Witness,* a Free Church Newspaper. This gave him a platform from which to air his views and enabled him to play a considerable part in the politics of the Disruption, which dramatically split the Church of Scotland in 1843.

It is through his geological work that he made his considerable reputation, but he was also a fine essayist and had a needle sharp eye for detail. His work output was very large indeed. Two of his books *Scenes and Legends* and *My Schools and School-Masters* are the best sources available for a picture of life in Ross-shire at that date. His geological tome *The Old Red Sandstone* is a classic of its kind.

He had always been prone to nightmares and depression and under the stress of his work these worsened to the extent that he believed he was losing his sanity. On Christmas Eve 1856, he rose, wrote a letter to his wife and shot himself. It was a tragic end to a great Scottish geologist and writer, whose house (Plate 24) in Cromarty is under the care of the National Trust for Scotland.

ALEXANDER MACKENZIE, 1839-1899

Born in a croft near Gairloch, he had little schooling and earned his living as a ploughman and labourer. He joined the Scottish drapery trade in England and made his way as a business man. In 1869 he came to

Inverness, where he was appointed editor and publisher of the *Celtic Magazine* which ran from 1875 to 1888, and *The Scottish Highlander* (1885-1898). These Celtic Society magazines are now in an invaluable source of information. He published several Clan Histories, including those of the MacKenzies and Munros. He gained wider recognition with his book *The Highland Clearances*. He was also a founder member of The Inverness Gaelic Society.

PROFESSOR W. J. WATSON, 1865-1942

A Gaelic-speaking scholar, he was the second holder of the Chair of Celtic at Edinburgh University. He was born at the Tullich Smithy in Kilmuir Easter and sent to Strathrusdale School, where his uncle taught. At fifteen he went to Aberdeen Grammar School, then to Aberdeen University and Oxford, where he held a Half Blue for Throwing the Hammer.

He was rector of Inverness Academy and the Royal High School in Edinburgh before he took the Chair of Celtic in 1914. His reputation was that of a very stern disciplinarian and a somewhat ferocious teacher.

His first wife was Miss Ella Munro from Boath; he later married Miss Carmichael, who was a Gaelic scholar in her own right.

His valuable book *The Place Names of Ross-shire* was published in 1904, and recently reprinted by the Local Heritage Society; but possibly his most important one remains, *The History of the Celtic Place Names of Scotland* which derived from the Rhind Lectures given for the Society of Antiquaries of Scotland in 1916.

JOHN DIXON OF GAIRLOCH

The only Englishman in this list, John H. Dixon, did so much for the parish of Gairloch, he deserves inclusion.

A solicitor who retired early because of ill-health, he came to live at Inveran, at the west end of Loch Maree. Recovering completely, he took the greatest interest in the area and its history, his work culminating in the book *Gairloch & Guide to Loch Maree,* a totally comprehensive view of all aspects of life in the parish, and a minor classic of its kind. It was first published in 1886, and was reproduced by the Gairloch Parish Branch of the Heritage Society in 1974.

John Dixon was a very popular figure and when he retired, he was presented with an illustrated testimonial. In return, he gave each household a Gaelic Bible. Known as *Dixon's Bibles* they are still prized today.

W. M. McGILL, B.A., 1841-1928

In *Old Ross-shire and Scotland from Balnagown and Tain Documents* published by public subscription in 1909, McGill has left us a massive series of catalogued documents reaching as far back as the 15th century. It is unlike anything else in Scotland and well worthy of reprint. Another publication, the *Tain and Balnagown Documents,* followed in 1911.

He took up teaching, became a headmaster in Fraserburgh and eventually retired to Tain. He was a correspondent for the *Northern Chronicle,* but he must have spent most of his time burrowing in documents in Balnagown Castle and the Tolbooth in Tain. Vaguely remembered as a tall stooping figure with very thick pebble glasses, the tradition is that he wrote himself nearly blind.

An interesting snippet of his scholarship was a paper he read to the Glasgow Archaeological Society, April 15th 1920 — on the history of the manuscript *The Breve Chronicle of the Earls of Ross,* dated 1615, which is of local importance, as it contains the legend of the founding of Fearn Abbey in Easter Ross after its removal from Mid Fearn.

He appears to have received no thanks or public recognition of any sort.

ARCHAEOLOGISTS

ROBERT MUNRO, 1835-1920

Robert Munro, who was born in Evanton, was related on his mother's side to the nearby Munros of Foulis. He went to Kiltearn School and Tain Academy and then worked his way through Edinburgh University where he studied medicine. He thought of entering the ministry, but reading Darwin's *Origin of Species* removed that idea and ever afterwards his main interest was archaeology. For 32 years he was married to Anna Taylor who illustrated his books. After practising medicine in Kilmarnock for 16 years, he retired, as his wife had inherited business interests which allowed them to follow their inclinations and study the Lake Dwellings of Northern Europe. These, called crannogs in Scotland, are human habitations on top of man-made islands, mostly circular in shape. They are generally linked to the land by a submerged causeway or stepping stones (See chapter 6).

Robert Munro wrote many articles and twelve books. The two most important were *Ancient Scottish Lake Dwellings and Crannogs* published in 1882 and the *Lake Dwellings of Europe* consisting of the Rhind Lectures for the Society of Antiquaries of Scotland in 1880. In old age, he endowed a course of 10 lectures at Edinburgh University called the *Munro Lectures* to further the knowledge of anthropology and prehistory.

DR. W. MACKAY MACKENZIE, MA, D.Litt, 1871-1952

The eldest of a distinguished literary family from Cromarty, where there appears to be something in the air which breeds writers, he was a noted historian and archaeologist. He won a bursary from Cromarty School to Edinburgh and became a teacher at Glasgow Academy.

He was appointed secretary to the Ancient and Historic Monuments Board in 1913, where he supervised the production of many county Inventories. He was a Commissioner on the Board from 1943 to 1952. During this period he gave two separate series of Rhind Lectures to the Society of Antiquaries, *The Medieval Castle in Scotland* published in 1927 and *The Royal Burghs* published in 1949.

The Glasgow Herald obituary said that 'no scholar of his time was more concerned to winnow truth from legend' and this applied to his archaeological approach as well.

At the start of the Second World War he abandoned research to run the Department of History for Edinburgh University. Afterwards, he returned home to Cromarty, where he lived until he was eighty years of age.

JAMES SHAND — SCHOOLMASTER, TAIN

Among the lesser antiquarian figures from the District, mention should be made of James Shand, a schoolmaster at Tain Academy, who in 1815, produced noteworthy and accurate sets of measured drawings and analytical notes on Fearn Abbey, Tain Collegiate Church and Dornoch Cathedral. They were prepared for the benefit of General Hutton, as part of his intended but unpublished *Monasticon Scotiae,* the papers for which are now amongst the Advocates' Manuscripts in the National Library of Scotland.

DOCTORS

PROFESSOR SIR JOHN FRASER, KCVO, MC, MB, ChB, ChM, FRSE, FACS, FRACS, 1885-1947

One of Tain's most distinguished sons, he was made a Freeman of the Royal Burgh, where there is a stained glass window in the Parish Church, Tain, erected to his memory.

He specialised in surgery and children's ailments. His honours and appointments occupy a whole column in *Scottish Biographies*. During the '14-'18 war, he was a captain in the R.A.M.C. He was a Member of the Royal Bodyguard of Archers, and became Principal and Vice-Chancellor of the University of Edinburgh from 1944 until his death in 1947.

The story is told, that when he was a boy at Tain Academy, the Headmaster said to his mother, 'Your son is only fit for the plough'. What a celebrated misjudgement!

DR. ELIZABETH MCBEAN ROSS M.B., Ch.B., 1878-1915

At last a notable woman Dr. Elizabeth McBean Ross won the Dux medal at Tain Academy in 1901, studied medicine at Glasgow University, became parish doctor at Colonsay and then went to Persia in 1907.

She worked for years with the Bakhtiari tribe, miles from any other Europeans. In this remote environment she was frequently robbed. On one occasion brigands removed her corsets, extracted the whalebones and returned the remains to her! When she finally decided to return home, she signed on as a ship's doctor at 2/6 per day sailing from Madras. After studying at the School of Tropical Medicine, London, she sailed to Japan on the "Glenlogan" as the first woman doctor on any liner. She returned to Persia and on the outbreak of the '14-'18 war joined the Russian Red Cross, working as a military doctor in Serbia. The conditions were frightful and while working among the typhus-striken soldiers, she contracted the disease and died. She was buried in Serbia with full military honours in a coffin painted silver and gold.

Finally, a glimpse of one historical figure from the *Statistical Account of 1845.*

CHARLES MACKINTOSH

Charles Mackintosh, whose family came from Newmore, Invergordon, was a merchant in Glasgow. A Fellow of the Royal Society of London, he was the inventor of the process for waterproofing fabrics by the application of Indian rubber.

Chapter fourteen

TALES AND LEGENDS

Elizabeth Sutherland

If the Grey Magician of Coire Dhuinid were to bring to life the heroes and princesses, the witches and ghosts, the seal maidens, water horses and goblins which abound in Ross and Cromarty folklore, the District would be as populated as a city suburb.

The Celt from the dawn of history has enjoyed a mystic relationship with the earth. Every hill and glen, stone and spring had not only its guardian spirit but also its heroic or sinister inhabitant whose deeds long ago entered the oral tradition of the Gael. Humorous, haunting and historic, the stories are legion, only to be hinted at in this short chapter.

This is the land of the chivalrous Fiann, giant Celtic warriors who protected the small dark Picts from Viking raids and who hunted the deer forests from Mamratagan in the west to their fort in Knockfarril Hill above Strathpeffer. They lie sleeping in Craigiehowe Cave awaiting the third trumpet call to rouse them to fight for Scotland again.

Here the Five Sisters of Kintail, enchanted by the Grey Magician, raise dark heads above Loch Duich to watch for the ships of their dream bridegrooms who never come.

The little folk in red caps riding shaggy ponies were seen for the last time by a Cromarty lad at Ethic and the devil himself chained the Lady of Balconie in a dark cavern which she still haunts under the Black Rock Gorge at Evanton.

Ross-shire folklore is the product of four cultures: pre-Celtic, Celtic, Christian and Norse. Isle Maree, that green gem hidden behind the other islands on Loch Maree, perhaps best demonstrates the physical fusion of these creeds. Here may still be seen the healing well overhung by a dead oak studded with copper pence and nails, offerings of those seeking a cure for insanity. Here, too, surrounded by a Christian burial ground, are the remains of a hermit's cell, said to be the retreat of St Maelrubha who gave his name to the loch and island. Some believe, however, that Maree was Mourie, a Celtic god, and had nothing to do with the red-headed priest. Here too are the graves of a Viking and his princess who, like Romeo and Juliet, died untimely out of love. Dominating all, are the oak trees sacred to the Druids, self-seeded from that time, intertwined with holly, holy to the Christians. Mixed loyalties persisted as late as the 17th century when Dingwall Presbytery recorded the ritual slaughter of a bull by three sons to cure their mother of lunacy.

If the place of Isle Maree best demonstrates the fusion of three cults, the traditions, beliefs and myths are best summed up in the shadowy person of the Brahan Seer.

An da-shealladh, the second sight, is thought to have originated as part of ancestor worship practiced by the neolithic builders of the great burial mounds. Taken up by the waves of incoming Celts, it became an important part of their cult of the dead. Thought to be a gift of the sithean — fairies — who inhabited the burial mounds, it was bestowed upon certain mortals so that they might witness and communicate with these spirit beings. The sithean could take the shape of any person dead or alive, but second sight was generally associated with the ability to see their imitations of the living who enacted all that would one day happen to persons whose shape they had taken. Thus the vision of a neighbour seen in dripping clothes heralded his death. The phantom funeral — one of the commonest sightings — anticipated the true one.

The Druids perfected the cult of the "waking dream" which today has evolved to include three aspects of the paranormal: clairvoyance, pre and retrocognition and telepathy. It is interesting to note that the Gaelic language has a name for every type of spectre seen or heard where English has no way of distinguishing between the various haunts.

Whether the many stories relating to the life and prophecies of Coinneach Odhar Fiosaiche are factually true is of less interest and importance than the reasons why and the way in which folklore had turned him from a sinister figure in history into a folk hero, an anti-establishment people's man whose name has become synonymous with second sight.

The historical facts are scanty.

Coinneach Odhar is mentioned in a Commission of Justice issued in October 1577 and again the following January ordering the authorities in Ross-shire to arrest along with five other men and twenty-six women "Kenneth, alias Kennoch Owir, principal enchanter in the art of magic" for "using and exercising the diabolical, iniquitous and odious crimes of the art of magic, sorcery and incantation."

From this one fact we know that Coinneach was employed by Catherine Ross of Balnagown, Lady Foulis, to help her dispose of her stepsons so that her own son might inherit Clan Munro, and her sister-in-law so that her brother could be free to marry her step-daughter-in-law. When witchcraft failed, Catherine and her crew allegedly resorted to ratsbane.

We know from Pitcairn's report of Catherine's trial, which was postponed to 1590 after her husband's death, that some of the named witches were burned at Fortrose, or Chanonry as it was then called. We do not know for a fact that Coinneach was even arrested, but it is reasonable to suppose that he was caught. Tradition in Fortrose is strong that he was burned there in a spiked tar barrel, and through the centuries there have been a variety of stones to mark the site.

A futher clue to the identity of Coinneach is also given in Pitcairn's record of Catherine's trial when we are told that she went for advice to the "Egyptians". That blanket term included beggars, cairds, tinkers and other nomads all of whom were credited with sorcery. The description "odhar" which means brown or dun-coloured, could apply to someone who led an outdoor life. The title "fiosaiche" which means "one who knows" is applied to knowledge in the occult sense, sorcerer rather than seer.

From these few facts which involve an allegedly evil woman (Catherine was not convicted) sorcery, poison and death by burning in the 16th century, the following well-known legends have evolved.

Sometime in the first half of the 17th century, a young woman was herding cattle one night overlooking the graveyard of Baile-na-Cille by the sands of Uig on the Island of Lewis. Suddenly, as she watched, all the graves opened and the spirits flew away, young and old alike. She waited, and when, about an hour later all returned, the earth covered them as before, except for one. Curious, she entered the burial ground and placed her distaff, made of rowan, across the open mouth of the grave and waited. Soon, the last ghost returned, a beautiful maiden dressed in white with a gold band in her hair, who begged her to lift the rowan spell and let her return to her tomb.

"Not until you have told me why you are so late," the woman answered.

The spectre told her she was a Viking princess drowned long ago off the coast. Once a year all the spirits could return to their own homes but as hers was so much farther away than the rest, she was always late.

The woman lifted her distaff and as a reward for her bravery, the ghost took a stone from her breast.

"Give this to your son when he is seven. It will bring him the gift of prophecy."

The young woman's son was Coinneach Odhar. As soon as he received the stone he "saw" a whale stranded at the mouth of a distant cave, riches indeed for the crofter fishermen of Uig. From that moment his fame as a seer began.

This story incorporates a fine amalgam of Celtic and Norse mythology. The cult of the dead practised by the Druids led to the belief that once a year — at Samhain or Hallowe'en — the departed could return to their homes. The spectre in the story who was considered not to be the spirit of the dead person but rather its shape taken by one of the sithean who inhabited burial grounds, bestowed the gift of prophecy upon the chosen. The protective magic contained in rowan is Celtic while the prophetic stone bestowed in the story is Norse.

One of the early legends has Coinneach finding his stone in a raven's nest and describes how any may obtain the gift of second sight by removing, boiling and returning the raven's eggs. When she finds she cannot hatch them, she flies off to find the Victory Stone and places it in her nest to encourage the eggs. Anyone finding this stone will not only be victorious in battle but also gain the gift of prophecy.

The raven who flits in and out of Highland legendry, is featured in many of Coinneach's prophecies. In Norse mythology the "bird of Odin" was regarded with respect. To the Celt it was a bird of ill-omen and a harbinger of death. An old Gaelic curse "a raven's death to you" comes from the belief that the birds would kill their parents on Easter Day. It was from the captured King of the Ravens that the Gaels first learned the secret of "mouth music" played at their annual ball on the Raven's Rock at Achterneed above Strathpeffer.

The east Ross-shire version of how Coinneach acquired his prophetic stone is equally redolent of the old beliefs. While working for a farmer near Brahan Castle, he made himself so unpleasant to his employer's wife by his shrewd, sarcastic tongue that she decided to get rid of him. Mixing noxious herbs with his sowans, she took the pitcher out to the peat hag where he was working, and finding him asleep on a fairy mound, set down the food and hurried away.

Shortly after, Coinneach was wakened by the pressure of a stone against his temple. Round with a hole in it, he raised it to his eye and "saw" not only what the woman had done but other sights pertaining to the future.

Here again, the Celtic belief that second sight was within the bounty of the fairies who inhabited the ancient burial mounds or fairy hillocks, dominates this story. Note, too, the allusion to poison, but in this case, Coinneach is the victim not the culprit.

Hugh Miller writing in 1835 tells us that the seer "derived little advantage from his faculty for he led, it is said, till extreme old age, an unsettled, unhappy sort of life."

According to Alexander Mackenzie whose *Prophecies of the Brahan Seer* was the result of research into the oral tradition, his end was very different. His predictions soon caught the attention of Kenneth Mor of Kintail, third Earl of Seaforth and chief of the Mackenzies in the second half of the 17th century, whose lands included all Ross and who commuted between his castles in Lewis, Brahan and Chanonry.

Unfortunately, so the story goes, Coinneach made a bad impression on the Countess by announcing in her presence that he saw more of worth in the company of gillies than in the children of gentlefolk, a remark possibly calculated to irritate Isabella who had eight children of her own.

The Countess was generally unpopular with her peers and in the clan. The Rev. James Fraser, a contemporary chronicler, wrote in 1660 that Lord Seaforth had married "a kinsman of his own, a daughter of Lord Tarbet, after all men's hopes of him, debases himself mean-spirited to marry below himself getting neither beauty, parts, portion, relation." Isabella's portrait which may be seen beside that of Big Kenny and the other Seaforth earls in Fortrose Town Hall shows a lively, intelligent face dominated by a strong nose. She was probably too forceful to be endearing, yet she too, according to tradition, turned to Coinneach in her hour of need.

Kenneth Mor had been sent to Paris by Charles II on state affairs and when he stayed away too long, she called for the seer. At first he refused to predict, but finally, after pressure, told her in the presence of the assembled clan, "Your lord seems to have little thought of you, or of his children or of his Highland home. I see him in a gay gilded room, grandly decked out in velvets and on his knees before a fair lady, his arm round her waist, her hand pressed to his lips."

Isabella was outraged. She turned on the seer. "You have spoken evil of dignitaries, you have defamed a mighty chief in the midst of his vassals, you have abused my hospitality and sullied the good name of my lord in the halls of his ancestors — you shall suffer the death."

Strangely, his punishment was to be that of a witch, burning at the stake. Nowhere in the legend so far is there a hint that this Coinneach was involved with witchcraft, and second sight was never a burning affair.

Remembering the historical Coinneach and his association with Catherine Ross a century before, it is interesting to compare these two women. Both were strong-willed, dominating and unpopular in the clan. Both were responsible for the downfall of their Coinneach, yet there is a difference. Catherine's Coinneach was a witch, her initiator, whereas Isabella's Coinneach was the victim of an allegedly evil woman.

But Isabella's Coinneach took his revenge. Turning on her, he raised his stone to his eye and pronounced the Mackenzie Doom, a prediction which has dominated Ross-shire folklore for centuries.

"I see in the far future and I read the doom of my oppressor. The long-descended line of Seaforth will, ere many generations have passed, end in extinction and sorrow. I see a chief, the last of his house, both deaf and dumb. He will be the father of four fair sons, all of whom he will follow to the tomb. He will live careworn and die mourning, knowing that the honours of his line are to be extinguished forever, and that no future chief of the Mackenzies shall bear rule at Brahan or in Kintail. After lamenting over the last and most promising of his sons, he himself shall sink into the grave, and the remnant of his possessions shall be inherited by a white-coifed lassie from the east, and she is to kill her sister. And as a sign by which it may be known that these things are coming to pass, there shall be four great lairds in the days of the last deaf and dumb Seaforth — Gairloch, Chisholm, Grant and Raasay — of whom one shall be buck-toothed, another hare-lipped, another half-witted and the fourth a stammerer. Chiefs distinguished by these personal marks shall be the allies and neighbours of the last Seaforth; and when he looks around him and sees them, he may know that his sons are doomed, that his broad lands shall pass away to the stranger, that his race shall come to an end and his castle razed to the ground."

Having uttered the prophecy, he was siezed and taken to Chanonry for execution. On the way, he threw his stone into Loch Ussie and predicted it would be found by a child with two navels or four thumbs and six toes in the belly of a pike. Since then, many have claimed to have found the stone, and there is, currently, a man with two navels fishing the loch!

On his way to the flames, Isabella taunted him, "Today you will be with your unhallowed kin in the nether world."

"I will go to heaven," he answered her, "but you never shall, and this shall be the sign that I have spoken truly. A raven and a dove, circling my ashes, will alight. If the raven be first they you have spoken truly, but if it be the dove, then my hope is well founded." And so it turned out.

This prophecy is also ascribed to Michael Scot, the 13th century philospher and alchemist whose magical deeds were written down in cheap chapbooks and circulated throughout the Highlands by pedlars or chapmen. Many were to become incorporated into the local oral tradition.

Kenneth Mor arrived too late to save his favourite but Coinneach spoke to him from the flames, "For what your lady has done this day, your race will end, but mine will begin for after I am dead, a child of my seed will be born on Brahan land and will be called the Brahan Child and from his seed there will be a seer in every generation who will see as I have seen and let all beware who would do him harm for my spirit will be watching over him.''

Over a century passed before Francis Humberston Mackenzie inherited the clan in 1794. He was not born handicapped but became stone deaf after catching scarlet fever at Eton. Though practically inarticulate, he led a distinguished life as a soldier, politician and patron of the arts. Of his ten children four were sons so it seemed that the future of the clan was safe, yet one by one all died, the last just weeks before himself. His estates, largely impoverished by this time, were inherited by Mary, his eldest daughter and a widow of a few months. As the chieftainship was entailed through the male line she could not inherit the clan and the title was not awarded for another century and a half. While driving with her sister Caroline in a pony carriage, the horse bolted and both were thrown. Caroline died of her injuries thus bringing another clause in the prediction to fulfilment.

As for the four lairds, it is said that they were disfigured as in the prophecy, but as this tailpiece crops up with variations attached to other predictions concerning other clans, it looks as if it had been added later to give more weight to the main substance.

To be valid, a prediction should be written down before fulfilment. There is some evidence to show that part of it at least was known by Sir Walter Scott and other men of integrity before Francis Humberston's death.

One fact is clear, however, that the historical Coinneach could not have uttered it. The title "Seaforth" did not come into being until 1623, long after the sorcerer's death, nor was that style ever used in the Gaelic tradition. Caberfeidh or MacCoinneach were the clansmen's names for their chief. An old prophecy existed that when there was a deaf Caberfeidh, there would be an end of the line, and it is just conceivable that this could have been made by the historical sorcerer, but the rest belongs to a later generation.

There are some ancient predictions, that refer to bloody battles, which might also have been uttered by the sorcerer, but the majority are so diverse in style and period that they would seem to have come from not one, but a collection of different seers.

The Rev. William Matheson of the Department of Celtic Studies Edinburgh University reckons that "the name of Coinneach Odhar seems to have acted like a magnet drawing a host of prophetic utterances to itself." Canon Macleod of Macleod who edited the *Bannatyne Manuscript History of the Macleods* in 1927 called his predictions "nothing more than prophetic history". This would seem to be borne out by the fact that already predictions made by Swein Macdonald, the contemporary Ardgay Seer, have been ascribed to Coinneach Odhar.

Coinneach's predictions, at least 125 of which are known today, range over Ross and Cromarty north into Sutherland and Caithness and west to the Islands. As recently as 1977 three facts — a wedding in the Chanonry Cathedral ruins, the opening of a new cemetery in Fortrose and a temporary rise in the death rate for that year — produced yet another prediction that "when a marriage was celebrated in the ruins of Chanonry kirk, Fortrose would be a town of widows with the graveyard overflowing."

Certainly there is no written evidence to show that the prediction predated the event.

The Kishorn oil rig construction industry produced another: "the one-legged monster will leave Loch Kishorn and will go twice below the water breathing fire and the third time will spell disaster in the German Ocean."

Perhaps the best-known of Coinneach's predictions today is the one that tells us that the day will come "when the Highlands will be devastated by horrid black rains". Speculation ranges from nuclear fall-out to acid rain.

It would seem, then, that Coinneach Odhar is as alive and well in the 20th century as ever he was in the past. Why?

Myths, legends, folklore fulfil a need. The clutch of devastating prophecies recorded not only against the Seaforth Mackenzies but other contemporary lairds was one way, possibly the only way, of hitting back at landlords who had the power to put up rents or evict their tenants at will. To those whose tongues were tied in public, the ceilidh hearth offered a means of revenge that was sweet. It is clear to see why Coinneach evolved from sinister sorcerer to seer, from perpetrator to victim, from humble labourer to anti-establishment folk hero. He became what the cottar and crofter wanted him to be, scapegoat and martyr, certainly, but ultimately "fiosaiche" the one who knows-not only what will happen but how to make it happen.

Myth conveys a truth more than facts and dates. Every great event in Highland history has been pre- or anteceded — does it matter which? — by a prophecy. Culloden, the Clearances, the changes in clan property, in religion, communication and industry, wars and disasters. Each reflects not just the event but the Highlanders' attitude to that event.

Lesser happenings, trivial on the surface, have their own importance, such as the prediction that a cow would calve in Fairburn Tower. Behind the simple image lay not only the decline of the Mackenzies of Fairburn, a powerful and wealthy branch of the clan, but the attitude —

unconscious no doubt — of the tenants which could perhaps be summed up as humorous contempt.

The prediction "Duncan Macrae will die by the sword" which anticipates the death of an old man past sword-bearing age, only becomes significant when placed in historical context. In 1654 when Cromwell's men were swarming all over the Highlands, Duncan "was all the blood that General Monck or his soldiers, amounting to 1500 men, had drawn and all the opposition he met with."

For Highlanders of Ross, then, it would seem that second sight is one way of making sense of the world. The story of Coinneach Odhar tells us more about Ross-shire, its history, traditions and culture than any text book.

Folklore and myth, too, tell more of the deep-rooted fears and prejudices of a people than any handbook on psychology. Remembering Coinneach's original profession, belief in witchcraft also dominated Ross and Cromarty folklore. Like second sight, witchcraft owes its origins to Celtic sources. A hangover from Celtic ritual, it was practised by the Druids who were not only bards, lawyers, historians, but also doctors, diviners and magicians to their people. In the beginning there was no such thing as black and white witchcraft. The coming of Christianity with its emphasis on dualism separated the two, the white witch being the healer, the black the harmer.

There is no history of naked midnight revels or broomstick rides or sexual orgies in the Ross-shire tradition. The power of witches lay in "eolas" — knowledge of charms — and a strong personality which gave them the courage to use that knowledge.

From the practical point of view the profession of "buidseach" or "bao" offered the crofter or his wife with the right talents, a useful livelihood for not only could he or she sell charms in exchange for cash, but also protection, for regular bribes of meal, tobacco or butter.

Powers ascribed to the witches were legion. They could take milk, cause fish to swarm, raise storms, sink ships, fly, cross water in sieves or eggshells, cause sickness, prevent childbirth and assume shapes of birds and animals. They could also create and destroy the "corp creadha" or clay image of their enemies until they died of a wasting disease.

The Black Isle was a favourite haunt for witches. There was Ipach who lived on Ord Hill and terrorized her neighbours by scudding across Munlochy Bay in a lippie measure. The stone on the golf course at Fortrose said to be the site of the burning of the last witch is thought to be hers.

There were four Ferintosh witches who in 1662 were taken to Kirkhill to be pricked by a certain Paterson who had worked his way north growing rich by testing witches "with a large brass pin and they felt it not, but he left in into the flesh deep to the head". Although Paterson was discovered to be a fraud — a woman acting as a man — there is no record that the witches were released.

Hairy Alice lived at Alness Ferry. In the form of a hare she ravished the crops of the laird of Braelangwell until he wounded the beast with a silver bullet, followed its blood trails back to the Ferry and discovered the witch in a towering rage nursing a broken leg.

Osgood Mackenzie tells of the Tarradale game-keeper, a well-educated man who told him that his "own cow's milk had been stopped by a witch. One morning at dawn I went to the byre and on opening the door, a hare sprang out and ran between my legs and away to John Maclean's house which she entered, that being her home."

A Rosemarkie witch took her "corp creadha" up the Fairy Glen every day to hold under the waterfall. Meanwhile her victim, a local bodach, died of a wasting disease.

One of the powers ascribed not only to witches but also to strangers, tinkers or anyone who looked odd or acted suspiciously, was that of an Droch Shuil, the Evil Eye.

First documented in a 15th century manuscript relating to the Fiann where a young prince was attacked by a "sore lung-disease" by the "evil eyes of the multitude", belief in the Evil Eye dominated the life and folklore of the Highlander.

Children were particularly vulnerable and it was the custom for a mother to make sure her pretty child looked less than perfect — for example, by wearing a stocking inside out — as a means of protection. Not long ago in Munlochy it was thought by a few that a child who had been killed by a car had been "overlooked" by a neighbour.

Cattle and other farm animals were also targets and a woman from Strathconon at the turn of the century refused to let anyone near her when she was churning.

Envy was said to be the main cause. In Applecross a man bought a horse which a neighbour was equally anxious to buy. When the horse died soon after, the local people declared it had been blighted by the eye of the man who had wanted it.

Charms abounded for prevention and cure. These were often made of strands of coloured yarn intertwined, knotted and placed round the necks of children or threaded into the tails of animals. Water which had been "silvered" by coins and blessed in the name of the Trinity was effective. Water from particular springs such as the two Clootie Wells by Munlochy was also useful.

Sprigs of juniper and rowan placed over lintels or bound into tails were good protections. To this day there are few houses in the Highlands that don't grow a rowan in the garden to ward off evil. Horse shoes still hang in most steadings.

The best prevention of all was a generous spirit as is evidenced in the following tale which dates from bardic times. A poor bodach stopped by a farm and asked the woman of the house for a drink. She left off churning to fetch him some water. After he had gone, she returned to her work but try as she might, the butter would not come. The milk frothed up, and the same happened with the next and successive churnings. Then one day, the old man came back and again asked for refreshment. The farmer himself was there and being a good-hearted fellow fetched milk and food in plenty. As the bodach ate, he looked up at the farmer and said knowingly, "If a man asks for a drink, never give him water".

The farmer recognised that he was a man of eolas and asked what should he do to bring back butter to the churn. In exchange for a reward, the bodach told the woman to put some money in the churn and try again. Thereafter the butter came, and every scrap that had been lost recovered in one churning.

The story tells us just as much about the Highlander's attitude to hospitality as it does about the power of the Evil Eye.

Ghosts abound in Ross-shire legendry. It was probably the vision of a spectre that first induced the neolithic farmers to reverence the dead. Sometimes they appeared in strange disguises such as in the story of Fiddler's Well, recounted by Hugh Miller in his *Scenes and Legends of the North of Scotland.*

Two young men who were great friends were seized with consumption at the same time. One died quickly while the other whose name was Willie Fiddler, survived to attend the funeral. That night he felt deeply ill and unhappy. His dreams were all of coffins, decaying flesh and unquiet graves.

Towards morning, however, they vanished and he had a strong vision of himself on a beautiful summer day walking along the shore towards the South Sutor. A familiar voice whispered in his ear, "Go on, Willie. I'll meet you at Stormy".

This was the name of a rock so called for it took the force of an easterly gale.

On he went but when he reached the rock there was no sign of his friend so he broke down and wept. Just then a bee began to hum round his head. The more he tried to brush it aside, the more it persisted. The humming grew louder until it began to sound like words that repeated over and over again, "Dig Willie, dig and drink".

Obediently Willie pulled up a clod of earth and a spring of clear water gushed out of the bank. The bee, still humming, flew happily away. When the vision faded, Willie was back in his bed with the sun shining through his window. Weak as he was, he rose, reached Stormy and searched till he found the spot, dug as the bee had advised, and when the water gushed out, drank deeply. Thereafter he was cured and it is said to this day that the spring has healing properties.

It is generally thought that ghosts, witches, seers and the stories connected with them belong to the age of superstition and the remote past. This is, however, not the case. Just as many people today experience ghosts and visions that they cannot explain. There are supposed to be at least two witches covens in Easter Ross, and Swein Macdonald is reckoned by many to have inherited the mantle of Coinneach Odhar. Travelling people are still credited with the power to blight.

The passing of the oral tradition has not, as folklorists like Alexander Mackenzie feared — put an end to the old tales. While lecturing on the Brahan Seer in Ness on the Island of Lewis in 1982, I asked a group of teenagers how they had first come to hear of Coinneach Odhar. Shyly, they told me they had read about him in a girl's comic book.

The means of communication may change, but it would seem that folklore, that densely patterned mystery, is as important as ever it was in satisfying the deeper needs, the hopes and dreads of Highlanders.

Chapter Fifteen

SETTLEMENT GAZETTEER

Donald Omand

This gazeteer of towns and the more populous villages gives estimates of the number of people living in each settlement.

ACHILTIBUIE: a scattered settlement on the coast north of Loch Broom.
Population 500

ALNESS: (Plate 37), a town on the R. Averon, E. Ross.
Population 6200
Close to the town is Obsdale monument where communion was dispensed to the Covenanters. There are two distilleries, Dalmore and Teaninich. Alness is a dormitory town for nearby industries, such as the rig fabrication yard at Nigg (Plate 48).

APPLECROSS: a S.W. Ross coastal settlement.
Population 210
Maelrubha founded his church here in 673 A.D. The road across the hills reaches a height of 626m (2054 ft) and passes through the spectacular Bealach nam Bo, the pass of the cattle.

AULTBEA: (Plate 42), a W. Ross village.
Population 520
During the 2nd World War the sea inlet of Loch Ewe was an assembly point for convoys to Russia. There is an old NATO base. Occupations include crofting, fishing and fish farming.

AVOCH: (Plate 34), on the Black Isle peninsula.
Population 1800
Fishing is still of importance but the boats use other ports as their main base.

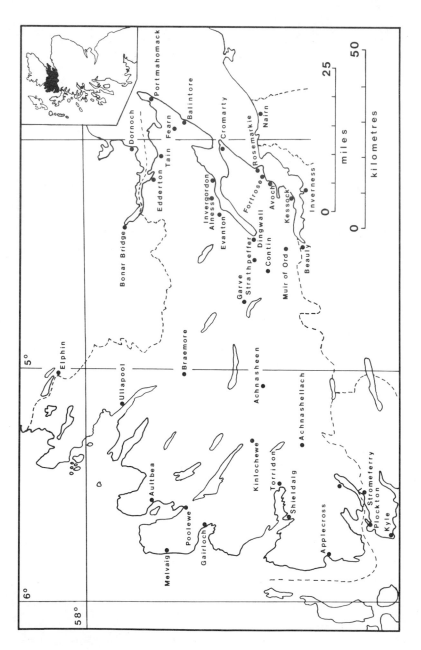

Figure 14 — Settlements.

BALINTORE: an E. Ross coastal village.
Population 850
Balintore is a 19th century fishing port, with salmon fishery. It is the largest of the three closely located seaboard settlements, the others being Hilton (page 214) and Shandwick where there is an outstanding symbol stone.

CONON BRIDGE: an E. Ross village on the lowest bridging point of the river.
Population 1250
Nearby is 17th century Kinkell castle. The village has a variety of small industries. Commuters travel to Dingwall and Inverness.

CROMARTY: (Plate 24), on the Black Isle peninsula.
Population 750
It is a long established settlement, which was a fishing port and major trading centre in the late middle ages with flax, linen and rope industries. Many interesting old buildings survive. It now has oil-related employment. Hugh Miller, geologist and writer lived here.

CULBOKIE: on the Black Isle peninsula.
Population 450
It is a former centre for agricultural trade with farming and forestry. Commuters go to Inverness and platform fabrication sites at Nigg (Plate 48) and Ardersier.

DINGWALL: (Plate 38), a town at the head of the 30km (19 mile) long Cromarty Firth.
Population 5000
It was made a royal burgh in 1226. It has a Museum, a Pictish symbol stone and the prominent Memorial to General Sir Hector Macdonald (Plate 29).
With good rail and road connections it became the county town. Its role of District H.Q. provides considerable employment. It is a market town and service centre with soft drinks industry. From the summit of Ben Wyvis is one of the most stunning panoramas in Scotland.

EDDERTON: an E. Ross village.
Population 330
North of the village is a Pictish symbol stone. In the old kirkyard (the church dates to 1794) is the Crusader's stone. Nearby is Balblair distillery. There is farming, forestry and oil related employment.

EVANTON: an E. Ross village.
Population 1000
The village, with its Seceder's chapel, is of early 19th century foundation. Evanton is a dormitory settlement for oil-related industry and farming.

Close to the village is the spectacular Black Rock gorge. On Fyrish Hill (Plate 37) is a curious monument, the replica of an Indian gateway erected by General Sir Hector Munro in 1782.

FORTROSE: (Plate 21), on the Black Isle peninsula.
Population 1300 (including Rosemarkie)
Fortrose succeeded Rosemarkie as the centre of the early church. It is a cathedral town and royal burgh with a long established academy. Fortrose is a focal point of the Black Isle and former terminus of the Black Isle railway. The Brahan Seer, Coinneach Odhar, was reputedly put to death in Fortrose (see Chapter 14).

GAIRLOCH: (Plate 40), a W. Ross village.
Population 800
It has a Museum, with a Pictish symbol stone. There is quarrying; white fish, and salmon are caught. A well-established shellfish factory employs over 40 people. Tourism is significant.

HILTON OF CADBOLL: an E. Ross coastal village.
Population 350
The Hilton of Cadboll symbol stone (in the National Museum of Antiquities) is an excellent example of Pictish art.

INVER: an E. Ross coastal village.
Population 250
It is a former fishing village. An earlier village was sited farther east. The new village was established because of a cholera outbreak. The present settlement was evacuated in the 2nd World War and used as a practice area for the Normandy landings.

INVERGORDON: an E. Ross town.
Population 4800
An early castle site was replaced in 1872. Although the foundation of the settlement may be centuries old, the town is modern. It was a sheltered harbourage from which considerable quantities of grain and cattle were exported. Invergordon became the ferry terminal for the short crossing to Balblair in the Black Isle. Because of its excellent deep

water facilities it was made a naval base (with coal and oil services) in both World Wars (Plate 32). In the early 1960s a grain distillery, the largest in Europe, was established. In 1968 British Aluminium's smelter was located in the town. Regrettably the smelter has now closed. In 1974 the Cromarty Firth Port Authority was established. There is a pipe-coating yard for North Sea oil installations.

KISHORN: a W. Ross coastal settlement.
   Population: Some 50 full time residents and around 800 that are employed at the oil platform site of Howard Doris, established there in 1974. Places of historical interest include the Courthill and Gallow's hill. A font allegedly associated with St. Donan lies in the old graveyard.

MARYBURGH: a village close to Dingwall.
   Population 1500
   Workers commute mainly to Dingwall and Inverness.

MUIR OF ORD: an E. Ross village.
   Population 900
   The village was an important focal point in the days of the cattle drovers. It is a former junction of the Black Isle railway to Fortrose. A distillery is located close to the village.

MUNLOCHY: (Plate 9), on the Black Isle peninsula.
   Population 580
   This is an important farming area.

NORTH KESSOCK: on the Black Isle peninsula at the entrance to the Beauly Firth.
   Population 1000
   The village grew around the ferry terminal for Inverness. Many workers commute to Inverness and Dingwall across the bridge opened in 1982.

PORTMAHOMACK: (Plate 31) an E. Ross village.
   Population 350
   There is an interesting old church. Nearby is the ruinous Z plan 16th century castle of Ballone. The old harbour buildings indicate the former importance of grain storage and fishing. Two old meal girnels, one dating to the 17th century, still stand.

ROSEMARKIE: on the Black Isle peninsula.
Population 1300 (including Fortrose)
It is the site of an early Christian foundation. The Museum has a fine Pictish symbol stone. Nearby is the tall mast bearing the BBC TV transmitter.

STRATHPEFFER: (Plate 39), the village lies in the shadow of Ben Wyvis.
Population 1000
There is a Pictish symbol stone nearby and a vitrified fort on Knock Farril.
Strathpeffer was a renowned Victorian spa whose springs were known for their curative properties as far back as the 18th century. Tourism is important. There is a youth hostel. The village was the terminus of the rail route from Dingwall. Many workers now commute to Dingwall and Inverness.

TAIN: (Plate 47), a town on the south shore of the Dornoch Firth.
Population 3600
A historic town with St. Duthac's chapel, the Collegiate Church and Tolbooth. There is also a Museum. Tain claims to be the oldest royal burgh in Scotland with a charter dating to 1066. Industries include: Glenmorangie distillery, cheese processing and seafoods. The town has retail services and oil-related employment, and is the focus of a rich agricultural hinterland.

ULLAPOOL: (Plates 43 and 44) a W. Ross village on Loch Broom.
Population 1350
The British Fisheries Society established a planned village here in 1788 on a pre-existing settlement and the herring fisheries expanded rapidly. Ullapool is an important tourist centre with 14 hotels. It is the ferry terminal for Stornoway. Nowadays it has prawn fishing, fish farming and mackerel fishing, attracting many "klondykers". There is splendid mountain scenery in the neighbourhood. The Falls of Measach in Corrieshalloch gorge (Plate 7) have been described as the finest in Scotland.

Bibliography

SECTION I
Selected Bibliography (The Physical Background)

Anderton, R. et al.	A Dynamic Stratigraphy of the British Isles.	Allen and Unwin.	1979
Armstrong, M. in Gill, G. (Ed.)	The Old Red Sandstone of Easter Ross and the Black Isle. The Moray Firth Area Geological Studies.	Inverness Field Club.	1977
Barber, A. J. et al.	The Lewisian and Torridonian Rocks of North-West Scotland. Geologists' Association Guide No. 21.	The Geologists' Association.	1978
Birse, E. L. & Dry, F. T.	Soil Survey of Scotland. Assessment of Climatic Conditions in Scotland. Part I — Accumulated Temperature and Potential Water Deficit.	The Macaulay Institute for Soil Research.	1970
Birse, E. L. & Robertson, L.	Soil Survey of Scotland. Assessment of Climatic Conditions in Scotland. Part 2 — Exposure and Accumulated Frost.	The Macaulay Institute for Soil Research.	1970
Bibby, J. S., Hudson, G. & Henderson, D. J.	Soil Survey of Scotland. Soil and Land Capability for Agriculture. Western Scotland (1:250 000 Sheet 4).	The Macaulay Institute for Soil Research.	1982
Brown, P. E. in Craig, G. Y. (Ed.)	Caledonian and earlier magmatism. Geology of Scotland.	Scottish Academic Press.	1983
Chesher, J. A. & Lawson, D.	The Geology of the Moray Firth. Rep. Inst. Geol. Sci. No. 83/5.	HMSO.	1983
Chesher, J. A., Smythe, D. K. & Bishop, P.	The Geology of the Minches, Inner Sound and Sound of Raasay. Rep. Inst. Geol. Sci. No83/6.	HMSO.	1983
Donovan, R. N. et al.	Devonian palaeogeography of the Orcadian Basin and the Great Glen Fault.	Nature, vol. 259, pp. 550-551.	1976
Duff, P. McL. D. in Craig, G. Y. (Ed.)	Economic Geology. Geology of Scotland.	Scottish Academic Press.	1983
Futty, D. W. & Towers, W.	Soil Survey of Scotland. Soil and Land Capability for Agriculture. Northern Scotland. (1:250 000 Sheet 3).	The Macaulay Institute for Soil Research.	1982
Hallam, A. in Craig, G. Y. (Ed.)	Jurassic, Cretaceous and Tertiary Sediments. Geology of Scotland.	Scottish Academic Press.	1983
Harris, A. L. in Craig, G. Y. (Ed.)	The Growth and Structure of Scotland. Geology of Scotland.	Scottish Academic Press.	1983
Horne, J., Peach, B. N. Hinxman, L. W. et al.	Geology of the lower Findhorn and lower Strath Nairn, including part of the Black Isle near Fortrose (explanation of Sheet 84 and part of 94). Mem. Geol. Surv. Scot.	HMSO.	1923

Horne, J. & Hinxman, L. W.	The geology of the country around Beauly and Inverness, including a part of the Black Isle (explanation of Sheet 83). Mem. Geol. Surv. Scot.	HMSO.	1914
Johnson, M. R. W. & Parsons, I.	Macgregor and Phemister's Geological Excursion Guide to the Assynt District of Sutherland.	Edinburgh Geological Society.	1979
McClay, K. R. & Coward, M. P. in McClay, K. R. and Price, N. J. (Eds.)	The Moine Thrust Zone. An Overview. Thrust and Nappe Tectonics.	Geological Society of London and Blackwells.	1981
Mendum, J. R. in Harris, A. L. Holland, C. H. & Leake, B. E.	Caledonian thrusting in NW Scotland. The Caledonides of the British Isles — reviewed.	Geological Society of London and Scottish Academic Press.	1979
Miller, H.	The Old Red Sandstone.	Edinburgh	1841
Mykura, W.	The Old Red Sandstone east of Loch Ness, Inverness-shire. Rep. Inst. Geol. Sci. No. 82/13.	HMSO.	1982
Mykura, W. in Craig, G. Y. (Ed.)	Old Red Sandstone. Geology of Scotland.	Scottish Academic Press.	1983
Ogilvie, A. G.	The physiography of the Moray Firth coast.	*Trans. roy. soc. Edin.*, vol. 53, pp 377-404.	1923
Peach, B. N., Horne, J., Hinxman, L. W. et al.	The geological structure of the North-west Highlands of Scotland. Mem. Geol. Surv. Great Britain.	HMSO.	1907
Peach, B. N. et al.	The geology of Ben Wyvis, Carn Chuinneag and Inchbae (explanation of Sheet 93). Mem. Geol. Surv. Scot.	HMSO.	1912
Peach, B. N. et al.	The geology of the Fannich Mountains and the country around upper Loch Maree and Strath Broom (explanation of Sheet 92). Mem. Geol. Surv. Scot.	HMSO.	1913
Peach, B. N. et al.	The geology of central Ross-shire (explanation of Sheet 82). Mem. Geol. Surv. Scot. 1913.	HMSO.	1913
Phemister, J.	Scotland: the Northern Highlands. British Regional Geology.	HMSO.	1960
Read, H. H., Phemister, J. et al.	The geology of Strath Oykell and lower Loch Shin (explanation of Sheet 102). Mem. Geol. Surv. Scot.	HMSO.	1926
Smith, D. I. in Gill, G. (Ed.)	The Great Glen Fault. The Moray Firth Area Geological Studies.	Inverness Field Club.	1977
Smith, J. S. in Gill, G. (Ed.)	The last glacial epoch around the Moray Firth. The Moray Firth Area Geological Studies.	Inverness Field Club.	1977
Sissons, J. B.	The Evolution of Scotland's Scenery.	Oliver & Boyd.	1967
Sissons, J. B.	Scotland: The Geomorphology of the British Isles.	University Paperback.	1976
Synge, F. M.	Land and sea level changes during the	Inverness	1977

in Gill, G. (Ed.)	waning of the last regional ice sheet in the vicinity of Inverness. Moray Firth Area Geological Studies.	Field Club.	
Watson, J. in Craig, G. Y. (Ed.)	Lewisian. Geology of Scotland.	Scottish Academic Press.	1983
Whittow, J. D.	Geology and Scenery in Scotland.	Penguin.	1977
Wood, R. M.	On the Rocks — a Geology of Britain.	BBC.	1978

Selected Bibliography (Plant Life)

Aitken, T.	On the disappearance of certain plants.	*Transactions Inverness Sci. Soc. and Field Club* (vol. III) P. 316-20	1888
Burnett, J. M (Ed.)	The vegetation of Scotland.	Oliver & Boyd.	1964
Druce, G. C.	The Flora of Wester Ross.	Buncle & Co.	1929
Duncan, U. K.	Flora of East Ross-shire.	Bot. Soc. Edin.	1980
Grigson, G.	The Englishman's Flora.	Paladin.	1975
McVean, D. N. & Ratcliffe, D. A.	Plant Communities of the Scottish Highlands.	HMSO.	1962
Perring, F. H. & Walters, S. M. (Eds.)	Atlas of the British Flora.	B.S.B.I.	1976
Ratcliffe, D. A.	Highland Flora.	H.I.D.B.	1977
Raven, J. & Walters, M.	Mountain Flowers.	Collins.	1956
Steven, H. M. & Carlisle, A.	The Native Pinewoods of Scotland.	Cunningham & Sons.	1959

Selected Bibliography (Woodlands)

Anderson, M. L.	A History of Scottish Forestry.	Nelson.	1967
MacDonald, D. & Polson, A.	The Book of Ross.	Menzies, Glasgow.	1938
Mitchell, A.	Personal Communication. Forestry Commission. Census of Woodlands. Forestry Commission Annual Reports (Various).		1983 1947-49 1965-67
O'dell, A. C. & Walton, K.	The Highlands and Islands of Scotland.	London and Edinburgh.	1962
Sinclair, Sir John	The Statistical Account of Scotland.	Edinburgh.	1793
Slich, W.	Working Plan for Ardross Woods.	Agnew & Co.,	1907
Slich, W.	Novar Woodlands.	London.	1907
Steven, H. M. & Carlisle, A.	The Native Pinewoods of Scotland.	Robert Cunningham & Sons.	1959

SECTION II
Selected Bibliography (Archaeology)

GENERAL:

Bradley, R.	The Prehistoric Settlement of Britain.	London: Routledge & Kegan Paul.	1978
Feachem, R.	Guide to Prehistoric Scotland.	London: Batsford, 2nd Edn.	1977
Fowler, P. J. (Ed.)	Recent Work in Rural Archaeology.	Bradford-on-Avon.	1975
MacKie, E. W.	Scotland: an archaeological guide.	London: Faber.	1975
Megaw, J. V. S. & Simpson, D. D. A. (Eds.)	Introduction to British Prehistory	Leicester: University Press.	1979
Renfrew, C. (Ed.)	British Prehistory: A New Outline.	London: Duckworth.	1974

INTRODUCTION:

Evans, J. G.	The Environment of Early Man in the British Isles.	London: Elek.	1975
Pennington, W.	The History of British Vegetation.	London: 2nd Edn.	1974

MESOLITHIC:

Campbell, J. B.	The Upper Palaeolithic of Britain: a study of man and nature in the late ice age.	London: 2 vols.	1977
Lacaille, A. D.	The Stone Age in Scotland.	Oxford: University Press/Wellcome	1954
Mellars, P. (Ed.)	The Early Postglacial Settlement of Northern Europe.	London: Duckworth.	1978

NEOLITHIC:

Henshall, A. S.	The Chambered Tombs of Scotland, Vols. 1 and 2.	Edinburgh: University Press.	1963/ 1972
Piggott, S.	The Neolithic Cultures of the British Isles.	Cambridge: University Press.	1954
Simpson, D. D. A.	Economy and Settlement in Neolithic and Early Bronze Age Britain and Europe.	Leicester: University Press.	1971

BRONZE AGE:

Anderson, J.	Scotland in Pagan Times: The Bronze and Stone Ages.	Edinburgh: David Douglas.	1886
Burgess, C. B.	The Age of Stonehenge.	London: Dent.	1980
Burl, H. A. W.	The Stone Circles of the British Isles.	New Haven: Yale University Press.	1976
MacKie, E. W.	The Megalith Builders.	London: Phaidon.	1977

| Thom, A. | Megalithic Sites in Britain. | Oxford: University Press. | 1967 |
| Thom, A. | Megalithic Lunar Observatories. | Oxford: University Press. | 1971 |

IRON AGE:

Cunliffe, B. W.	Iron Age Communities in Britain.	London: Routledge & Kegan Paul, 2nd Edn.	1978
Harding, D. W. (Ed.)	Hillforts: Later prehistoric earthworks in Britain and Ireland.	London: Academic Press.	1976
Hogg, A. H. A.	The Hillforts of Britain.	London: Hart-Davis MacGibbon.	1975
MacKie, E. W.	'The vitrified forts of Scotland' in Harding D.W., 1976.		1976
MacKie, E. W.	'The Brochs of Scotland' in Fowler, P.J., 1975.		1975
Munro, R.	Ancient Scottish Lake-Dwellings or Crannogs.	Edinburgh.	1882
Rivet, A. L. F. (Ed.)	The Iron Age in Northern Britain.	Edinburgh: University Press.	1966
Ross, A.	Pagan Celtic Britain.	London: Routledge & Kegan Paul.	1967

PICTS, VIKINGS AND THE EARLY CHURCH:

Allen, J. R. and Anderson, J.	The Early Christian Monuments of Scotland.	Edinburgh: Neill/Society of Antiquaries of Scotland.	1903
Bronsted, O.	The Vikings.	Harmonds-worth: Penguin.	1965
Chadwick, N. K.	The Celts.	Harmonds-worth: Penguin.	1970
Graham-Campbell, J.	The Viking World.	London: Frances Lincoln.	1981
Henderson, I.	The Picts.	London: Thames & Hudson.	1967
Laing, L.	The Archaeology of Late Celtic Britain and Ireland.	London: Methuen.	1975
Meldrum, E. (Ed.)	The Dark Ages in the Highlands.	Inverness: Field Club.	1971
Thomas, C.	The Early Christian Archaeology of North Britain.	Oxford: University Press.	1971
Wainwright, F. T. (Ed.)	The Problems of the Picts.	Reprint Edition: Perth: Melven Press, 1980.	1955

In addition to the publications listed, most of which contain extensive bibliographies, more detailed descriptions and excavation reports on some of the sites can be found in the *Proceedings of the Society of Antiquaries of Scotland*. An invaluabe guide to the eastern portion of the District is contained in two *lists* in the Archaeological Sites and Monuments series, No. 6 Easter Ross and No. 9, The Black Isle, published by the Royal Commission on the Ancient and Historical Monuments of Scotland. They are available from the Royal Commission (RCAHMS), 54 Melville Street, Edinburgh. The *National Monuments Record* is held in the same building and is open to the public during normal office hours.

Selected Bibliography (History)

Anson, P.	The Catholic Church in Modern Scotland.	Burns Oates.	1937
Bain, R.	History of Ross.	Dingwall.	1899
Bumsted, J. M.	The People's Clearance.	Edinburgh.	1982
Donaldson, G.	The Scottish Reformation.	Cambridge.	1960
Donaldson, G.	Scotland, Church and Nation through 16 centuries.	S.C.M.	1960
Dunlop, J.	The Clan Mackenzie.	Edinburgh.	1953
Forbes, R.	Journals of Episcopal Visitations.	Skeffington.	1886
Fraser of Reelig, C.I.	The Clan Munro.	Edinburgh.	1954
Goldie, F.	Short History of the Episcopal Church in Scotland.	S.S.P.C.K.	1951
Graham, C.	Portrait of the Moray Firth.	Hale.	1977
Grant, I. F.	The Macleods. The History of a Clan.	London.	1959
Hay, G.	The Architecture of Scottish Post-Reformation Churches.	Oxford.	1957
Hunter, J.	The Making of the Crofting Community.	John Donald	1976
Kennedy, J.	The Days of the Fathers of Ross-shire.	Maclaren.	1867
Macdonald, D. & Polson, A.	The Book of Ross, etc.	Glasgow.	1938
Macdowall, C. G.	The Chanonry of Ross.	Inverness.	1963
MacGill, W.	Old Ross-shire and Scotland (2 vols.).	Inverness.	1909 — 1911
MacInnes, J.	The Evangelical Movement in the Highlands.	Aberdeen University Press.	1951
Mackay, J.	The Church in the Highlands.	Hodder & Stoughton.	1914
Mackay, W. (Ed.)	Inverness and Dingwall Presbytery Records.	Scottish History Society.	1896
Mackenzie, Sir G. S.	A General View of the Agriculture of the Counties of Ross and Cromarty.	London.	1813
Mackenzie, O.	A Hundred Years in the Highlands.	London.	1921
Mackinnon, D.	The Clan Ross.	Edinburgh.	1957

MacLean of Dochgarroch, L. (Ed.)	The Middle Ages in the Highlands.	Inverness.	1981
MacNaughton, C. (Ed.)	Church Life in Ross and Sutherland.	Inverness.	1915
Macrae, N.	The Romance of a Royal Burgh. Dingwall's Story of 1000 Years.	Dingwall.	1923
Marshall, E.	The Black Isle: A Portrait of the past.	Fortrose.	1973
McNeill, P. & Nicholson, R.	An Historical Atlas of Scotland, c. 400-c. 1600.	Conference of Scottish Medievalists.	1975
Meldrum, E.	The Black Isle: Local History and Archaeology guidebook No. 3.	Inverness.	1979
Meldrum, H. M.	Kilmuir Easter.	Inverness.	1935
Miller, H.	Scenes and Legends of the North of Scotland.	Nimmo.	1834
Mowat, I. R. M.	Easter Ross 1750-1850. The Double Frontier.	John Donald.	1981
Munro, J.	'The Earldom of Ross and the Lordship of the Isles' in the Firthlands in History (Forthcoming).		
Munro, R. W. & J.	Tain through the centuries.	Tain.	1966
New Statistical Account (N.S.A.)			1841
Noble, J.	Religious Life in Ross.	James Thin.	1909
Polson, A.	Easter Ross.	Tain.	1914
Richards, E.	A History of the Highland Clearances.	London.	1982
Richards, E.	The Last Scottish Food Riots.	London.	1982
Ross, A.	Ross-shire Past and Present.	Invergordon Times.	
Scott, H. (Ed.)	Fasti Eccles. Scot. Vols. 7 & 8.	Oliver & Boyd	1928 and 1950
Sinclair, Sir John	The Statistical Account of Scotland (O.S.A.).		1791-9
Symon, J. A.	Scottish Farming, Past and Present.	Edinburgh.	1959
Watson, W. J.	Ross and Cromarty (Cambridge County Geographies).	Cambridge.	1924
Watt, D. E. R.	Fasti Eccles. Scot. Medii Aevi.	S.R.S.	1969

SECTION III
Selected Bibliography

Allen, N. G.	Walling materials in the eighteenth century Highlands — *Vernacular Building*, 5.	SVBWG Dundee & Edinburgh.	1979
Bain, R.	History of Ross.	Dingwall.	1899
Beaton, E.	'Late Seventeen and Eighteenth Century Estate Girnals in Easter Ross and SE Sutherland' in Bladwin, J. R. (Ed.) The Firthlands in History (forthcoming).		

Blaeu, J.	Theatrum Orbis Terrarum sive Atlas Nova.	Amsterdam.	1654
Boston, R.	The Admirable Urquhart.	Gordon Fraser.	1975
Campbell, J. F.	Popular Tales of the West Highlands. (4 vols.)		1890/92
Campbell, J. G.	Witchcraft and Second Sight in the Highlands and Islands of Scotland.	Maclehose & E. P.	1902/74
Chambers, R.	Domestic Annals of Scotland, Vol. 1.		1858
Chambers, W.	Exploits and Anecdotes of the Scottish Gypsies.		1886
Clough, M.	Making the most of one's resources: Lord Tarbat's development of Cromarty Firth.	*Country Life.*	1977
Dixon, J. H.	Gairloch and Loch Maree.	Edinburgh.	1886
Dunlop, J.	The British Fisheries Society 1786-1893.	Edinburgh.	1978
Earl of Cromartie	A Highland History.	Gavin Press.	1979
Earl of Cromartie.	Short Account of the Long History of Clan MacKenzie.	Privately printed.	
Fairrie, A.	Queens Own Highlanders, Seaforths and Camerons.		1983
Fenton, A. & Walker, B.	The Rural Architecture of Scotland.	Edinburgh.	1981
Fraser, J.	Chronicles of the Frasers known as Wardlaw MS.	Scottish History Society.	1905
Fraser, W.	The Earls of Cromartie, Kindred Country and Correspondence (2 vols.)	Edinburgh.	1876
McCourt, D.	Two cruck-framed buidings in Wester Ross, Scotland.	*Ulster Folklife.*	1967
MacGill, W.	Old Ross-shire and Scotland.	Inverness.	1909-1911
Mackenzie, A.	Prophecies of the Braham Seer.	Constable.	1877, 1977
Mackenzie, A.	History of the Mackenzies.	Inverness.	1879
Mackenzie, A.	History of the Munros.	Inverness.	1898
Mackenzie, Sir G. S.	A General View of the Agriculture of the Counties of Ross and Cromarty.	London.	1813
Mackenzie, O.	A Hundred Years in the Highlands.	Bles.	1921, 1972
Mackenzie,. W. M.	Some stray inscriptions (1) . . . (5) Two carved stones of the Urquharts of Cromarty.	*PSAS.*	1926-7
Macleod of Macleod, Revd. Canon R. C.	The Macleods of Dunvegan.		1922
Maclagan, R. C.	Evil Eye in the Western Highlands.	London & EP.	1902, 1972
Macrae, Rev. J.	Genealogy of the Macraes, printed in Highland Paper I.	Scottish History Society.	1914 c.1700
Marshall, E.	The Black Isle, Portrait of the Past.	Protheroe.	1972
Matheson, Rev. W.	The Historical Coinneach Odhar and some Prophecies attributed to him.	Tesi Xlvi.	1971
Miller, H.	Scenes and Legends of the North of Scotland.	Nimmo.	1834
Morrison,	Highland Second Sight.	Dingwall.	1908

Rev. W. & Macrae, N. Mowat, I. R. M.	Easter Ross 1750-1850, The Double Frontier.	Edinburgh.	1981
Nicolaisen,	In an Historical Atlas of Scotland, c.400-c.1600, ed. P. McNeill and R. Nicholson.	St. Andrews.	1974
Nicolaisen, W. F. H.	Scottish Place Names. c.400-c.1600, ed. P. McNeill and R.	London.	1976
O'Malley, R.	One Horse Farm: Crofting in the West Highlands.	London.	1948
Pitcairn, R.	Criminal Trials in Scotland (Vol. 1)	Bannatyne Club.	1833
RCAHMS	Archaeological Sites and Monuments Series, No. 6 Easter Ross and No. 9 The Black Isle.		1979 1979
Ross, J. C.	The Great Clan Ross.	Canada.	1972
Royle, T.	Death before Dishonour.	Mainstream Publishing.	1982
Scottish Development Department	List of Buildings of Architectural or Historic Interest (District of Ross and Cromarty).		1982-3
McInnes, C. T. (Ed.)	Calendar of Writs of Munros of Foulis 1299-1823.	Scottish Record Society.	1940
Sinclair, C.	The Thatched Houses of the Old Highlands.	Edinburgh.	1953
Squire, C.	Celtic Myths and Legends.	Newcastle.	1975
Stell, G.	'Architecture and Society in Easter Ross' before 1707 in The Firthlands in History (forthcoming).		
Swire, O.	The Highlands and their Legends.	Oliver & Boyd.	1963
Thomas, F. W. L.	On the primitive dwellings and hypogea of the Outer Hebrides.	*PSAS.*	1866-8
Thompson, F.	The Supernatural Highlands.	Hale.	1976
Walker, B.	Report on 2 New Street, Shandwick *Vernacular Building*, 4.	SVBWG Dundee & Edinburgh.	1978
Walker, B.	Report on cottages with cross passages in Inver, Tain, Ross-shire.	*Ibid.*	
Watson, W. J.	The Place Names of Ross & Cromarty.	Inverness.	1904
Watson, W. J.	The History of the Celtic Place Names of Scotland.	Edinburgh.	1926
Wilkins, P. A.	The History of the Victoria Cross.		1904

Index